'Simon's passion for helping yo[...]This
book is packed with great advic[...]ur
relationship with alcohol – have [...].'

Laura Willoughby MBE, Founder of Club Soda

'Simon's enthusiasm, drive and passion for singing the praises of an alcohol-free life is contagious. It is a gift to a world that is drowning in messages that promise that alcohol is what they need to hold everything together when really it is the very thing that may be tearing their lives apart. *How to Quit Alcohol in 50 Days* is part inspirational manifesto, part practical tips and tools. An effective and useful guide for anyone who is curious about the benefits of an alcohol-free life.'

Annie Grace, Author of *This Naked Mind*

'You don't have to admit powerlessness over a disease and turn your will over to a higher power to quit drinking. Chapple's message is hopeful and inspiring; plus, many of his strategies are based on evidence-based practices, including CBT and mindfulness.'

Cassie Jewell, M.Ed., LPC, LSATP (on *The Sober Survival Guide*)

'A powerful book where the author skilfully supports the reader on the often-difficult journey to a place where they can comfortably choose to be free from drinking alcohol. Simon has a superb way of holding the reader's hand to move them forward which I have not seen in any other quit drinking books.'

Neil M., Reader

'In Simon Chapple's own words, "Alcohol made me lose my smile". From designing your own sober toolbox to thinking like a liquid vegan, Simon cleverly shows you how to change your mindset leading to an alcohol-free life. He will take you on a step-by-step journey of exploration to sobriety, showing you the path to set yourself up for success... for freedom from alcohol.'

Judy C., Reader

'I am over ten days sober for the first time in over 25 years! I can't wait for every new day so I can enjoy being sober. Thank you! Your book has saved me.'

Russ F., Reader

How to Quit Alcohol in 50 Days

Stop drinking & find freedom

Simon Chapple

sheldon PRESS

This book is dedicated to my mum, Pauline Chapple, and my dad,
Michael Chapple.

First published by Sheldon Press in 2020
An imprint of John Murray Press
A division of Hodder & Stoughton Ltd,
An Hachette UK company

3

This book is for information or educational purposes only and is not intended to act as a substitute for medical advice or treatment. Any person with a condition requiring medical attention should consult a qualified medical practitioner or suitable therapist.

A CIP catalogue record for this title is available from the British Library

Trade Paperback ISBN 9781529357585

eBook ISBN 9781529357592

Typeset by KnowledgeWorks Global Ltd.

Printed and bound in the United States of America by LSC Communications

John Murray Press policy is to use papers that are natural, renewable and recyclable products and made from wood grown in sustainable forests. The logging and manufacturing processes are expected to conform to the environmental regulations of the country of origin.

John Murray Press
Carmelite House
50 Victoria Embankment
London EC4Y 0DZ

www.sheldonpress.co.uk

Contents

Acknowledgements

Thanks to my wife, Michelle, and my daughter, Robin, for being the most awesome people in my world, you are both incredible, beautiful, patient and kind, and without your support I doubt I would have found the strength to become true, honest and free – don't ever change; my friends in the sober community, including Annie Grace, William Porter, Alex Walker, Lisa Elsworth, Scott Pinyard, Rob Wolman and David Wilson (aka Sober Dave); a special mention to Jackie McCarron, Kelly Wooderson, the 'Wednesday Men', and to Matt, for making me see the light.

About the author

For over two decades Simon Chapple was the classic example of a heavy daily 'at home' drinker, enduring daily hangovers, engaging in regretful behaviour, and suffering from severe anxiety and a complete lack of energy and motivation as a result of his inability to stop drinking.

Despite all of this, he was somehow able to function, and built a successful business, ran marathons and tried his best to be a father and a husband. But something was lacking in his life. He knew he wasn't the best version of himself, and felt like his life was hollow and slowly falling apart around him.

He chased happiness, and no matter where he looked, or how much more he achieved, it seemed to elude him. All the while his anxiety became worse and his mood became lower, so he drank more in an attempt to deal with discomfort.

It took time, but he eventually realized that his love affair with red wine had become toxic. It was destroying his life and no longer serving him in a way that was positive. He knew that something needed to change, but didn't know what to do for the best.

Eventually, Simon managed to quit alcohol and went on to discover a life of peace and happiness. Joy flowed back into his life for the first time since he was a child, all as a result of ending his unhealthy relationship with booze.

What Simon experienced after he quit drinking was so profound that it became his mission to raise awareness about the dangers of alcohol and to spread the word about the huge benefits that an alcohol-free life can bring.

Simon is a Certified Sobriety Coach and also the founder of Be Sober, one of the largest quit drinking communities in the world. He has appeared on television and radio and spoken at live events in the US and the UK about his very personal jouney from heavy daily drinking to becoming passionately sober.

He has worked with thousands of people from all over the world in coaching programmes and helped them make a powerful and lasting change to the way that alcohol features in their lives. His entire approach to quitting drinking is that it should be a positive experience and a life choice that we feel empowered in making for ourselves. He does not ascribe to the outdated methods of 'recovery' and 'alcoholic' that keep many people stuck for the rest of their lives, but instead works with his clients to help them find true freedom and peace in sobriety by making choices that they feel passionate and empowered about.

Simon has written this book to help anyone who is worried about their own relationship with alcohol and wants to make a change. He draws on his considerable life experience and of those he has helped in order to provide a structured path to freedom from alcohol over a period of 50 days.

Join the alcohol free movement at: <www.besober.co.uk>

Join the quit drinking programme at: <www.joinbesober.com>

Reach out: <info@besober.co.uk>

Follow Simon on Instagram: @besoberandquit

Foreword

I first 'met' Simon Chapple during the COVID-19 pandemic in 2020. I had been asked to join a live panel for a sober event in London which Simon was also due to be a guest on. This was early spring 2020, and sadly the event was cancelled due to the country being restricted by the lockdown, but instead of cancelling the event we used the opportunity to create an online weekly feature which went on to become known as The Sober Sessions.

What struck me most about Simon was his approach to sobriety; it was unlike anything I'd ever come across before, and that is saying something bearing in mind the sober movement is fast growing momentum and there is no end of inspiring and enthusiastic proponents of the cause. He's genuinely passionate about the topic, enthusiastic and articulate. But so are many others. What I found most impressive about Simon was the manner in which he attacked the topic; he is like a determined entrepreneur who rises to every problem and finds a solution to it.

The main challenge with trying to quit alcohol is that it's such a wonderful substance. It tastes incredible, it's healthy, it makes you feel great and it's not addictive for most people. It has very few downsides – it helps you sleep, you need it to have a good time, to socialize, to celebrate, to commiserate, to bond, to enjoy life to the full. That's why it's so hard to quit.

Imagine how much easier it would be to stop drinking if it was, instead, an absolutely horrible substance; if it tasted vile, if it made you feel heavy, lethargic and tired, if it made you feel anxious, if it ruined your sleep and left you feeling drained all of the next day, if it made you feel irritated and argumentative, if it ruined friendships and broke down marriages, if it caused violence and cancer and ruined lives. Imagine if there was very little real pleasure in drinking at all, that the true joy in it was actually in the situations we tended to drink in; when we are relaxing at the end of the day or out with our friends and not in the act of drinking itself.

In fact, the reality is that alcohol is the vile substance, not the wonderful one we believe it to be. This is, in essence, what the 'quit lit' writer's job is. It's to show you the truth about alcohol and sobriety and to strip away the nonsense and the hype which leads us to believe that alcohol is something it isn't, which in turn makes quitting not only easy, but enjoyable.

When you take that all-inclusive holiday, and you see all the so-called normal drinkers sitting around 'relaxing' early in the day, having their fill of alcohol from sunset until sunrise, and you look at them with a feeling of pity and sheer relief that you are no longer being conned into pouring a sticky, cancerous poison down your throat for the dubious pleasure of feeling heavy and lethargic for a few minutes, before feeling a corresponding increase in anxiety, then suffering a ruined night's sleep and a following day of tiredness and exhaustion, that is when you know you've really made it. There is no resisting temptation because there is no temptation.

In reality, the sober life is so far superior to the drinking life that there is no contest. But the problem lies in taking the individual from the 'sweetness and light' view of alcohol to the harsh reality, and that part isn't so easy. Even though we proponents of sobriety have the truth on our side, most drinkers have been drinking for umpteen years or even decades and find long-standing habits hard to change.

They've dealt with every problem, every upset, every life event, with a drink. Their personal relationships, their careers, their social life, their hobbies, all revolve around alcohol and drinking. Although their lives will improve dramatically when they stop drinking, it can be scary for them. They are like prisoners who have been institutionalized, who hate their prison but fear release even more.

So the job of the sober coach or 'quit drinking' writer is to take the hand of the reader and show them the beautiful truth: that alcohol is, in reality, a pathetic and unpleasant little drug. That it gives so little and takes so much. That even the so-called normal drinker is being robbed of their energy, health, sleep and peace of mind by chemical poisoning. And, above all, that a sober life is a far better and far more enjoyable life in every way.

This is where Simon comes into his own. He's gone from heavy daily drinker to totally embracing the sober life. He has gone from one to the other, thinking, analysing and solving problems along the way.

Each and every challenge he's come across he's attacked with his usual determination and enthusiasm, and he's come up with techniques and methods that work. In stopping drinking he's uncovered and got to grips with his own mental health issues. I've never known him to be at a loss for an answer.

The old way of quitting drinking was to grit your teeth and just do it. It's hard work, and many people fail. If they do stick with it, then over time they will find their sleep improves, that social occasions aren't the horror they feared they would be, and that sober life in general isn't actually the misery they thought it would be. It takes time, and it takes effort, but given enough of both they eventually prove to themselves that life doesn't end when the drinking stops.

But there's a far easier way to quit, and that's to do the groundwork either before you quit or directly after. If you can get some way down the line to at least begin to entertain the possibility that quitting drinking will open up a far, far more enjoyable life, then the time and work required to reach your goal are correspondingly reduced. This is where the quit lit author and the sober coach come in; they can take your hand and show you a far better world for you to inhabit. To do this they need enthusiasm, imagination and determination.

This is where Simon truly comes into his own. Think of being lost in a strange and unpleasant land, a land that you don't like but you're half afraid to leave in case the country you end up in is even worse than the one you're currently existing in. What you really need is a guide, someone who has been exactly where you are now and has found a way to a far better land, someone who can take you by the hand and lead you somewhere far, far better.

This is where you are now. You've had enough of feeling tired and drained, of living a half-life. You've found your guide. All you need to do now is hold tight and enjoy the ride!

William Porter, author of *Alcohol Explained* and *Alcohol Explained 2*

July 2020

Introduction

'Dad, can we go to the bowling alley?'

'Dad, can we go to the cinema?'

'Dad, will you come and listen to me playing the piano?'

These are all things that my daughter asked me to do, and I firmly said no. These are the fun activities that I avoided because I wanted to drink instead. For years I chose to put alcohol ahead of the most important things in my life, ahead of my daughter, ahead of my wife, ahead of my career and even my own health. I often ask myself what kind of person would do that, and then I realize it was me. I did that.

Thankfully, it was the old version of me who did those things. Once I finally found freedom from alcohol I reconnected with my daughter, my wife, my family and my friends, and since then I have experienced a true change in my relationships. Without alcohol around I have found myself far more present and engaged and, most importantly, excited to be involved in any activities or outings. In fact, these days it is often me who organizes the activities as I am so keen to enjoy them.

After more than 20 years of daily heavy drinking, I now realize that alcohol completely sucked the joy out of everything in my life. Normal pastimes seemed so boring and a huge drain on my time, I just didn't want to be there. I was far too busy obsessing about wine and wondering how much I should buy at the shop, what time I could start drinking and how much I would have when I finally got to pour my beloved booze. There was always a justification to drink: was it the weekend yet? No, it's Thursday today. Well, that's practically Friday, so two bottles will be fine tonight.

I clearly recall going to a firework and bonfire evening at my daughter's school. She was so excited and proud to be there with her mum and dad. But Dad wasn't really there. Dad was there in body, but not in mind. He wanted to drink and this wretched bonfire night was clashing with wine-o'clock. I made my frustration glaringly obvious, and my wife quickly spotted that I was in a childish mood because I couldn't drink. I hated the fact that I was stuck there, and I ruined the evening. We argued, and as soon as I returned home, I drank as much wine as I could in a futile attempt to escape the emptiness I felt inside.

Two years later we returned to the same event. This time I had been sober for around six months. What a difference! There was no preoccupation with alcohol, my mind was only focused on one thing – I was fully present, and guess what? I was enjoying myself. I felt joy. It was a wonderful night, and when my little family and I finally returned home with our ears ringing from the noise of the children and the bangs from the fireworks and our clothes smelling from the smoke of the bonfire, we all had huge smiles on our faces.

I started exploring alcohol in my teenage years. I was around 14 years old when I had my first sip of wine. It tasted revolting, but I stuck with it and pestered my parents to allow me to have a regular drink with my evening meals. My dad drank red wine almost every evening, and I thought it was grown-up and sophisticated. I looked up to my dad and wanted to be just like him when I was older. My parents were quite permissive in terms of allowing me to do pretty much what I wanted. I imagine this came from a place of wanting me to grow into an adult with broad horizons, but I quickly realized I could take full advantage.

I didn't really pay attention to the effects of alcohol until I started taking the remains of my dad's wine to my bedroom without him knowing. It was at this point that I was starting to drink more regularly. I began to look forward to the sense of euphoria and relaxation that washed over me from the first glass. Little did I know this was the start of a very slippery slope that would see me heading downhill for over 20 years.

Around the same time, my friends and I started to do all we could to get our hands on our own alcohol. I can remember many occasions where we would huddle in a group outside the local off-licence and send the oldest-looking member of our little gang inside to buy the booze. We would then hole up at one of our houses while their parents were out at work and spend the entire day getting drunk, listening to music, dancing and talking nonsense.

This became a school holiday routine, and I can remember multiple occasions where I ended up being sick after sinking numerous cans of beer during the afternoon. It still surprises me that my parents never said anything about my drinking when I returned home from one of these all-day benders. Maybe they didn't notice or maybe they weren't that bothered because everybody drinks – it is what we all do, right?

My friends and I were also visiting local pubs underage. It was easy to get served, and before long we were drinking in them several times a week. I was often staggering home from the pub after multiple pints of beer and strong chasers and crashing out in my bed. The room would spin as I closed my eyes, but it never felt like a problem. It was my idea of fun times and growing up.

When I was 15 I went on a school trip to Paris. My friends and I had been discussing long in advance how drunk we planned to get when we finally arrived. We weren't interested in museums and art galleries – we were on a mission to get smashed. This is exactly what we did. We had parties in our hotel every night and would sneak into the bars at every opportunity. We thought we were so grown up and clever. Our plan worked perfectly until we had an early-morning excursion which involved a long coach trip on windy roads. I felt really rough from the late-night drinking and before long I knew I was going to be sick. The coach was packed full of my classmates and I was always very self-conscious – vomiting in front of them all was my idea of the ultimate shame, but there was no way that this French wine and beer was staying down.

As the journey continued, my efforts to fight the Parisian puke were failing and eventually it reached the point of no return. I had prepared well by holding on to a carrier bag I had found nearby with my sweating hands and knew that I had no option but to let it go. The bag filled with what looked like two litres of beer, and my friends, who were falling about with laughter, took great delight in pointing out that it even had a foam head on the top. This was the point that I realized the carrier bag I had vomited into was totally transparent and I now had to somehow dispose of it in front of the entire coach full of laughing teenagers.

Eventually I took the warm, see-through bag to the teacher at the front of the coach and explained that I had travel sickness. Unbelievably, he bought my story even though I was holding on to what looked like a plastic pouch of France's strongest ale. Thankfully, the driver pulled over so I could dispose of the disgusting bag, and I shuffled back to my seat knowing that the rest of my school life would involve constant reminders of this embarrassing episode.

Even this shameful situation wasn't enough to stop me. Far from it – I was just getting started. The following evening I helped organize a big party in my hotel room. We had stocked up on as much alcohol as we could lay our hands on, and planned to drink into the early hours. Before long the room was packed and the drinks were flowing. In an attempt to look cool I decided to shake up a bottle of cheap sparkling wine before popping the cork. As I released the cork it shot out of the bottle with an almighty pop and struck the ceiling of the room, the bubbling cascade of low-cost booze sprayed all over the place.

Unbeknown to me the room above was occupied by our head of year. He was a pretty nasty character at the best of times and seemed to enjoy punishing pupils for even the most minor of offences. A few minutes later there was a loud bang on the door and he was standing at the entrance to the room looking extremely angry. He told everyone who had been stupid enough to attend our illegal event how disappointed he was and took delight in grounding us all in the hotel for the next 24 hours, which meant we would all miss a trip to the theatre to see *The Rocky Horror Picture Show* the next evening. Once again, my friends were less than impressed with me.

After they had left, I saw the cork on the floor, I picked it up and kept it. I still have it to this day – it serves as a poignant reminder of the damage that alcohol caused to my life.

There were a couple of incidents in my teenage years and my twenties that I believe contributed to the anxiety that I would battle over the next two decades. The first involved a much older boy who I considered a friend. He lived close by and I looked up to him – he was popular, good-looking and incredibly cool. I was around 13 and he was six years older. He took it upon himself to gain my trust, groom, coerce and sexually abuse me.

I have only recently found the strength to speak openly about this episode because I felt shame and a sense of needing to take responsibility for my own actions. But now, with a clear mind and peace in my life, I feel strong enough to share what happened, and it has helped me feel as though I have claimed back the power in this episode. It is my story now, nobody else's. I realize I did nothing wrong and was taken advantage of, and I can also find forgiveness as the older boy who did it probably had issues of his own that led to his behaviour. Not that this makes what he did OK, but I have no desire to see him punished; for now, I have peace.

When this incident happened, I didn't really give it much thought. I was a carefree teenager and didn't dwell on it too much. This meant that I never took the time to search for any closure on it. I just shut the entire thing away deep in the back of my mind to fester like an untreated wound. It clearly scarred me, and I now know that it contributed to the state of my mental health as the years passed.

The second incident was when my parents got divorced. My 'dad' is actually my stepdad and had been my 'father' since the age of two after my birth father walked out on my mother and me. I have since been informed on good authority that this departure left me with childhood PTSD alongside rejection and abandonment issues, so please don't stop reading this book until the end or you will add to my trauma! I will talk more about this later in the book as you may find that issues from your own childhood have played a part in your own addictive behaviour and you didn't even realize it.

My stepdad brought me up as a true father and I think the absolute world of him. My mum was overprotective of me when she was around, but allowed me to do what I wanted when she wasn't. Sadly, she was not always there for me emotionally when I needed support or acknowledgement. I didn't give this any thought at the time. I thought having so much freedom was wonderful, and I felt fairly safe and secure in my home. However, I now recognize that the emotional neglect I suffered caused issues that would mean I would struggle to form true emotional bonds with people in my later life.

Unbeknown to me, my parents had realized early on in their marriage that they didn't love each other and had made an agreement when I was just eight years old that they would stay together until they felt it was safe to separate without it having an impact on me. This probably worked for them on a financial and practical level, too, and they no doubt assumed it would be beneficial for me after having one dad walk out on me already.

They effectively lived their own lives from then onwards. They saw other partners but played pretend happy families when I was in the vicinity until I was in my mid-twenties. They did a pretty good job because I didn't ever realize this was going on, but subconsciously I must have been affected by the complete lack of love within the family unit. It took until I was 25 years old before they finally informed me that they were getting divorced. It rocked my world. My stepdad moved to the Greek island of Corfu to start a new life, and my mum stayed in the same home where she still lives to this day.

Looking back, the warning signs had actually been there for years. I had overheard arguments between my mum and dad, and I knew they had their fair share of problems. My dad had been living out of the spare bedroom for as long as I could remember. I had been told it was because he worked unusual hours and he slept in there so as not to wake my mum up early in the morning. Of course, none of this was true.

Their separation was like a hammer blow for me. I couldn't believe they were breaking up. I was being abandoned again. It was my worst fear coming true. They had stayed together for my sake and only announced they were separating after I had told them I was planning to move into a new home with my girlfriend. This should be a time for celebration, not tears and pain.

While their 'sacrifice' seemed like an act of kindness, it tore me apart inside. They had pretended everything was fine to avoid further disruption in my life. Why had they not been honest and authentic? Had this done more harm than good? I must have subconsciously picked up on the signals and noticed the coldness and distance between them both. No wonder we rarely had family days out or holidays together. But at least their decision was based around my needs regardless of whether it was the right thing to do or not. I don't hold any resentment – they were doing the best they could with what they had to work with at the time.

I didn't do anything to get closure on their break-up. I just accepted it for what it was and parked it away in the back of my mind along with the sexual abuse. My parents' separation left me heartbroken, but I knew there was nothing I could do to change the situation and just tried to let it be and get on with building my own life. I developed an attitude of looking forward and avoiding the past as it all seemed to hurt too much when I looked backwards.

I can see with complete clarity now how these episodes in my early life played a part in shaping me into the anxiety-ridden adult who self-medicated with booze that I went on to become. I was constantly afraid of people leaving me, I couldn't face conflict and I could never say no. I became a huge people-pleaser, and it was all from a fear of abandonment and a lack of emotional connection that was instilled in me from an early age.

I often think about what I would say to my younger self if I had the chance to go back in time and talk face to face with him. I am pretty sure I would tell myself not to be afraid to do what I love instead of doing things to please people, and I would also give a stern warning that I was starting to head down a very slippery slope. But I don't think the teenage version of me would bother listening to this advice, even if it came from a time-travelling bald guy in his mid-forties.

As the years went by, my anxiety became worse and worse. I would worry about things that never happened and would get myself worked up over the slightest thing. I have had panic attacks and anxiety to the point where I have made a decision not to do something fun in favour of letting the anxiety win the internal battle. I even remember bursting into tears a few years ago because I couldn't face going out for a run. Anxiety had taken over my life.

I also suffered from intense embarrassment issues and an extreme phobia of blood (I am cringing now just from typing the word out). Any situation that drew attention in my direction or made me feel ashamed would result in a fight-or-flight reaction, much to the amusement of my schoolmates. The slightest mention of a nosebleed or blood would cause me to either pass out or end up in a recovery position having almost fainted. This phobia related to an incident where I broke my nose after falling from my new skateboard age seven. I was left alone in the street outside my house with blood pouring from my nose. Nobody came to my aid, and when they eventually did I felt embarassed, not comforted.

To add to the trauma, neither my mum nor dad realized I had actually broken my nose. It wasn't until years later during an examination that a medical specialist informed me that my nose had previously been broken. I always wondered why it was crooked – now I knew.

By the time I reached my late teens I had found that drinking seemed to help in so many different ways. When I drank, my worries and the anxious feelings seemed to fade away. It was like a magic medicine that made everything seem fun. After a couple of glasses of wine I would become carefree and would feel as though I was full of laughter and joy in a world that was otherwise starting to feel rather dark.

At the same time as my parents announced they were divorcing, I moved into my first home with my then girlfriend (and now wife) Michelle. We had scraped together enough of a deposit to buy our own small house, and we were so happy to have a home of our own. It was nothing fancy, but we didn't care. We felt free – it was our home and we were proud of what we had achieved.

Unfortunately, this new-found freedom also gave me the perfect excuse to drink more. Before long I was finding that I couldn't spend a single evening without drinking wine, often two bottles and sometimes more. On top of this, Michelle and I would regularly visit the pub and return home worse for wear before I would start on the red wine until either the room started to spin or I made myself sick.

In 2006 we got married. It was a brilliant day from what I can remember, and it was so lovely to spend it with friends and family. I was so happy – I hadn't felt joy like this in my life before. When I look back at the wedding photographs it is clear how drunk everyone was. There is one photo of me that sums up the day – I am dancing on a table, much to the disgust of the venue staff who were trying to get me down. There is also a video of our first dance as a married couple; in the background someone can be heard saying, 'They're so drunk they're holding each other up,' as we drunkenly shuffled around the dance floor to 'You Do Something to Me' by Paul Weller. At the time I thought this was hilarious; looking back now it makes me cringe.

Michelle rarely mentioned my drinking. To her it wasn't really a problem. I was always conscious that she might work out I had a problem and would try my best not to act too drunk and normalize my behaviour around her. I would also often encourage her to drink with me to take the spotlight off of myself.

It astounds me that I managed to function and hang on to a half-decent career. At the time I was working for an insurance company and I was in the office ready for work every morning by 7:30am. Over the years I progressed my way up through the firm and ended up landing a management role. As the money improved so did my ability to buy more expensive wine in even greater volumes. I believed that if the wine was more expensive it was somehow more sophisticated and therefore less harmful. Clearly, all the marketing messages had worked on me – a connoisseur is surely the complete opposite of an alcoholic, so of course I didn't have a problem!

So the daily wine intake continued and the amounts I was drinking each day rose to ever greater levels. When I hit 30 my wife fell pregnant and we had our first (and only) child, Robin. She changed my world in so many ways. Of course, our lives were turned upside down during those early baby years, and we were both tired from the midnight feeds and the early-morning routines, but it was all so worthwhile. It felt magical having our own daughter to bring up, and I clearly remember thinking that I was going to do all I could to be a great dad.

We had recently sold our first business, and this enabled me to take 18 months away from work and spend it with Michelle and Robin. This period of my life was one of the happiest times I had ever experienced, and I look back on those long and lazy daytime walks as I pushed my daughter and walked hand in hand with Michelle through the countryside with a real sense of happiness and contentment.

But I didn't stop drinking – all this change was just an excuse to carry on. If I had a stressful day, I needed wine; if I had a good day, I needed wine. No matter what kind of day I had, I needed wine. There was always a reason and there was always a bottle (or three) ready and waiting in the kitchen cupboard, I made sure of that.

We moved home twice in the years that followed, until we finally settled in our current family home. We have been here in Surrey in the UK for over 15 years and have made some great memories. I used to enjoy throwing wild parties that wouldn't end until the early hours. These involved some seriously regrettable drunken behaviour that left me with memories of cleaning up the next morning with the hangover from hell. Not only would I have to clean up the mess from the spilt drinks and discarded food, I also had to deal with the mess I had caused by saying or doing something awful. Yet I would still drink the next day even with a pounding head. Nothing could stop me and I had never even considered not drinking. Why would I do that?

For years it went on, the cycle of daily drinking. I would head to the shop during the day and pick up a couple of bottles of wine (or a wine box) and then every single night I would drink. There were only a handful of occasions over the entire period (which spans beyond two decades) where I didn't have wine and these were when I was in hospital after an operation or laid up in bed with an illness and I physically couldn't get my hands on alcohol.

In all those years Michelle and I never slept together once without me drinking. The booze also caused numerous arguments and disagreements when my mouth got out of control or I did something stupid. But I always believed I had a special love affair with red wine and it was truly helping me get through each and every day by injecting happiness into my life that was otherwise lacking. Plus, if I said or did something wrong, it wasn't my fault – I was drunk so I could blame the wine.

In the five years before I quit drinking I had started to have worries about how much alcohol I was putting into my body. I had begun to google things like 'Am I an alcoholic' and 'How much alcohol is safe' and then skim past any search results that would scare me until I found something that would put my mind at ease. I used to do this all the time and have since learned that this behaviour is called 'confirmation bias'. This causes us to choose to look at only what we want to see in order to reinforce our beliefs, even if those beliefs are actually wrong (we will explore this in more depth later in the book).

These days my wife and I run our own business, a marketing company which we had started together back in 2004. We have a team of staff based in an office in Hampshire, and it can be a challenge managing the team at the same time as ensuring our clients get the very best levels of service. In 2016, it all started to get too much for me. My anxiety had reached new levels and I was finding it a struggle going into the office. The slightest hint of a complaint or an issue with a staff member or client would trigger my abandonment and rejection issues and set me off into a childish meltdown. I was worrying all the time about things that usually didn't even happen, and I realized that I wasn't enjoying life. I just wasn't happy – there was no joy and I felt stuck in a huge rut.

So I decided to take some time out to try to find some much needed headspace. We hired a brilliant manager to run the business alongside Michelle and agreed that I would be much less involved in the day-to-day running of the company. My plan was to venture forward on a journey towards beating anxiety, understanding why I felt so empty and ultimately finding happiness. The only problem was that I had no clue where to start.

In this book I will share with you everything I learned on that journey, and I am certain that as you turn the pages you will find yourself relating to some of the experiences I describe that also feature in your own life. My goal is to help you find the answers you need to become free, happy and at peace.

On my quest to deal with my anxiety I visited doctors, counsellors and even a hypnotherapist. None of them were much help and – incredibly – none of them dug into my drinking. One doctor did ask how much I drank, and obviously I lied. I have heard that doctors usually double the amount patients tell them to get to the true figure. Have you ever done that?

After I stepped away from the business, my days had become a routine of lying in bed until whenever I wanted, checking my emails and then heading out for a coffee (via the shop to buy wine), and then off to the gym before my wife returned home from work. It was a pretty lonely existence, but to me it beat all the stress and drama of being in a work environment. I was still drinking two or three bottles of wine every day, even though my life should have been way less stressful. I was also worrying more about my drinking. I had more time on my hands and was looking much closer at every area of my life. It was starting to bother me, but I kept pushing the thoughts to the back of my mind.

Then one morning I was at my computer and noticed my hands were shaking and I couldn't stop them. It was awful and I wondered what the hell was going on. This had never happened before and it really worried me. It happened several times over the next month and before long (and after a few searches on the internet) I realized it was probably my drinking that was causing it. This was the moment where I knew something had to change. I didn't want to end up in an early grave, but I also didn't know how or even what to do for the best.

I also recall watching a feature on the television news where an expert was talking about the dangers of alcohol. They went into detail about how damaging drinking was to physical and mental health and I couldn't stop watching. Usually, I would have changed the channel because I didn't want to hear what they were saying, but I listened and paid attention. In the following days I felt like a seed had been planted in my mind, and I could sense an internal conflict starting to brew as my conscious mind began to give me messages about reducing or quitting drinking; at the same time, my subconscious wanted me to continue believing that I didn't have a problem and that carrying on with my drinking habit wasn't an issue.

I couldn't stop thinking about it, but the thought of not having alcohol in my life filled me with a sense of complete and utter dread, so I started to look for ways to cut down or change my drinking habits without feeling like I was being deprived or missing out. I tried only drinking on certain days of the week. This lasted for a few days before I was back drinking at my usual levels again. I also tried watering my wine down with some success, but again after a short period of time I was back to my old habits.

The shaking hands and the news feature had given me a real wake-up call and I continued to search for some kind of solution. Eventually, I stumbled across a book called *This Naked Mind* by author Annie Grace. I felt like I had nothing to lose so I got myself a copy and started reading.

As I worked through the chapters of the book I felt like all my beliefs about alcohol were being examined and challenged and I could feel some of them unravelling. I learned things that I could never unlearn, and I knew that after reading that book I would always have a different view about alcohol.

After reading Annie's book, I started to get quite excited about what a sober life might look like for me. I had read so many articles and blog posts about the positive effects of not drinking that were making me become more and more motivated to explore the alcohol-free world. I wouldn't say I was ready to quit drinking at this point, but I had certainly become very 'sober-curious'. In particular, I had been astounded to read that alcohol can make anxiety much worse and given how much I was drinking it was no wonder mine was starting to head off the scale.

I kept reading books about quitting drinking, signing up to online programmes and joining Facebook sober groups. The more I read, the more my knowledge expanded and the closer I came to feeling strong enough to make a commitment to walking away from alcohol for good. I had considered committing to taking a break from drinking, but I am an 'all or nothing' type of person and felt that I needed to make one firm decision to end the toxic relationship with Ms Shiraz and never look back.

It felt much easier to say it than it did to actually do it though, and once I had decided I wanted to experience what a life without drinking felt like I began making attempts at getting through one or two days without wine. I ended up failing every time and found myself right back at the start with a glass in my hand. There were plenty of tears and I would beat myself up with negative self-talk, telling myself I could never quit and that I was an alcoholic and should just accept it, this was who I was and change was impossible for me.

But it wasn't 'who I was' as a person – that wasn't me. It was 'where I was' at that point in my life, and I needed to move forward to grow stronger so I could become the authentic version of myself. So I kept picking myself up, dusting myself down and learning from the setbacks just like the books had told me to do. I also continued to put the work in. I was journaling my experiences and learning from all the resources I could find to expand my understanding about how to successfully quit drinking.

Eventually, I made it through the first couple of days booze free. I was feeling really positive about myself and wanted to keep building on my success. Those couple of days turned into weeks, and before I knew it the weeks became months and then the months became years. Eventually, after numerous setbacks, I was finally able to make it through the first couple of days. Since then, I have not had one alcoholic drink and I have also never looked back. It was the best decision I have ever made. If I can do this after drinking heavily daily for such a long time, I firmly believe anyone can break free if they really want to.

Not long after I managed to quit drinking, I decided to start my own website www.besober.co.uk. I used it as an online version of my journal and also wrote articles about the techniques and tactics that had worked for me. After a couple of months of updating the site, I started to get comments from visitors who were finding the information helpful on their own sober journeys. I found this a huge motivator and decided I would also set up a private Facebook group and start an online community for people who wanted to help each other become free from alcohol.

The Facebook group is called Be Sober and it quickly became one of the fastest-growing sober communities in the world. I couldn't believe that so many people were in the exact same trap that I had been stuck in. I wanted to help everyone in the group and connect personally with all the members, but with the group growing so fast it was impossible, so I enlisted the help of a couple of other members to assist in running the group and ensuring everyone felt supported and looked after.

If you aren't already a member of the Be Sober Facebook group, you can join using the link on my website – it is free to join and you will be welcomed with open arms. It will allow you to discover a whole community full of support, advice and encouragement.

As the months went by I thought it would be a great idea to ask Annie Grace (the author of *This Naked Mind*) to do an interview for my newly created Youtube channel. She kindly agreed, and after the interview Annie invited me to America to train as an alcohol coach so I could join her team. What an opportunity – I couldn't believe it! She clearly saw something in me that made her believe I could help and inspire other people in sobriety.

Since then I have gone on to help thousands of people change their relationship with drinking. I regularly coach in online groups and have spoken on stage at This Naked Mind Live in Denver, Colorado, and at the Club Soda Mindful Drinking Festival in London. Bear in mind this was the guy with awful anxiety who used to have a meltdown at the thought of standing up in a small staff meeting at work. Hopefully, this shows you what can happen when you discover the best version of yourself by cutting alcohol out of your life.

The anxiety is now a thing of the past. I will talk more about anxiety and depression later in the book, but I am free from it now and find myself in a place of peace, calm and happiness, all from making a firm and final decision to quit drinking.

Stepping away from my business has enabled me to do what I love and discover what I am truly passionate about. My life mission has become all about sharing the benefits of an alcohol-free life and helping anyone who wants to make a positive change.

In 2019 I released my first book, *The Sober Survival Guide*, and Annie Grace wrote the foreword. There are plenty of books that provide tactics and techniques that help people quit drinking (including this one), but there was very little to help set people up for the months and years ahead. So I wrote the book as a guide to provide tools that readers can dip in and out of as and when they need them. The book was a huge success, and I have had amazing feedback from readers all over the world telling me how much it has helped them on their path to freedom from alcohol. (I actually think that this book should have come first and *The Sober Survival Guide* should have been the second one. If you haven't read it yet, it is the perfect follow-up to this one and I recommend getting yourself a copy.)

What I am trying to say in all of this is that I know where you probably are right now in your life and I understand exactly how it feels, because I have been there. I was stuck in an alcohol trap and I didn't know what to do to get out of it. But I did it. I found complete freedom and turned my life around – I have never been happier. The great news is that you can quit alcohol, even though it might feel really hard right now. You need to know that it really isn't as difficult as you might think and I am going to show you how. In the next section I will explain how to use this book before we get started on our 50-day journey to freedom together.

Part 1

First steps to stopping drinking

How to use this book

I wrote this book to provide you with a structured way to find complete freedom from alcohol, if that is what you decide you want by the time you reach the final page. My approach uses proven techniques that have helped thousands of people change the way that alcohol features in their lives. My strategy is different to others you may have experienced, I want this to be an experience that you enjoy and a choice that you feel empowered in making, above all I want it to feel like an enjoyable and fun journey towards changing your life for the better.

If you have already stopped drinking, well done. My hope is that everything contained in this book will serve to make you stronger and help you build on what you have already achieved.

If you are still drinking, there is no need for you to stop at this point unless you wish to do so. However, if you wanted to make a commitment to stop right now as you start to work your way through the book, it would be fantastic. But I also don't want you to feel under any pressure to stop drinking until you feel completely ready. You might choose to make a commitment not to drink for the period that you are reading this book and then look at what has changed and improved in your life before making a choice as to whether you want to continue being alcohol-free or not, but the decision is entirely yours. I want you to feel empowered in your choice, not pressured.

If you want to carry on drinking as you read through the book, that's fine, but I would like you to start to be much more mindful about it. Start to take note of when you are drinking, how much, how often and how it feels for you. If you have a journal, start writing in it and exploring the feelings you experience before, during and after drinking. Get really curious and inquisitive about your drinking habits so you can begin digging into them in more depth.

This book is split into two parts. In Part 1 we will look at the reasons why you want to quit, the impact alcohol has on your life and most importantly the best strategy for quitting drinking successfully.

As you move into Part 2, I will ask you to consider making a commitment to taking a break from alcohol. But for now I just want you to commit to reading one chapter a day and answering the questions that will come up each day.

If you don't have a journal, I recommend getting one and using it to track how you feel. Write down your mood, your emotions and what feelings you experienced during the day. Start to notice as much as possible and log all the data you can. You can also use it to write about any changes you experience along with new achievements and learning points. Keeping a journal will allow you to look back at your entries and learn from them. You can also reflect back on anything you write to see how far you have progressed.

An excellent structure for journaling is to write down your intentions for the day ahead each morning. This might include any tasks you need to complete, work-related commitments and leisure activities. I also recommend writing down your intention to read a chapter of this book each day to ensure you make a firm commitment to your personal development every morning for the next 50 days.

A journal can be one of your best friends on this journey. It doesn't need to be anything fancy; a simple notepad will do.

There are exercises for you to complete after most of the chapters in the book, so you will need to keep a pen handy. If you don't want to write your answers in the book or if you are reading on an electronic device or listening on audio, you can download the accompanying PDF workbook to use as you move through the daily chapters. Simply visit <www.library.johnmurraylearning.com>. It also includes space for you to make journal entries over the coming 50 days.

Ensure you commit to reading one chapter a day and stick with the book until the end. If you find yourself skipping days, simply recognise that this has happened, reset and dive back in with a new sense of momentum. Each day will address different topics that will help expand your knowledge, change your mindset and allow you to learn how to look within to discover the answers to questions about how you want your relationship with alcohol to change.

If you wanted to move through more than one chapter a day during Part 1, it's not a problem, but do make sure you are not rushing. I would like you to allow the information to sink in and also take the time to consider and reflect on the responses you provide where you are asked to do so. In Part 2 please stick to one chapter a day. The book has been carefully structured to help you, and it is important you follow the process to ensure you achieve the best outcome.

By the time you reach the end of the book, my hope is that you will be in a place where you can make a firm decision as to how alcohol will feature in your life going forward. If you decide you no longer want to drink alcohol, this book will provide you with all the tools and tactics you need to remain alcohol-free, thrive and enjoy life long term.

If you like to share, I would love you to upload a picture of yourself with your copy of this book on Instagram. Follow and tag @besoberandquit in your picture so I can be part of the amazing journey you are embarking on. You can also:

- **join the alcohol free movement at: <www.besober.co.uk>**
- **reach out: <info@besober.co.uk>**
- **find Be Sober on Instagram and Facebook: <@besoberandquit>.**

Before we move on to Day 1, it's important to be clear that this book isn't a replacement for professional medical advice. If you're physically addicted to alcohol, or experiencing severe withdrawal symptoms such as shaking, tremors, hallucinations or any other side-effects that cause you concern, please visit your doctor and seek medical advice.

However, if you're either ready to start thinking about what a life without alcohol might look like for you. Or if you have already quit drinking and are looking for further support, inspiration and tactics as you move forward on your alcohol-free journey, this book is for you.

Let's get started...

Day 1 | Why are you reading this book?

You picked up this book for a reason, and I would like you to think about exactly what that reason was. Maybe you were curious? Maybe you have been worrying about your drinking and the cover of the book caught your attention? Or maybe you know you need to change the way alcohol features in your life and searched online for a book that might help?

When I brought my first 'quit alcohol' book it was because I had become sick and tired of the hangovers, the regretful behaviour and the whole routine associated with drinking every day. I was also being torn apart by my anxiety and constant worrying, as well as feeling guilty for putting alcohol ahead of the most important things in my life. On top of this, my hands had started to shake and I was worrying about my health and the impact booze was having on me. I was looking for guidance and advice to help me make a change.

At the end of this chapter there is space for you to write down the reasons why you are exploring your relationship with alcohol. Give it some real thought. Is it because there is something you want in your life that alcohol is preventing you from having? Or is it because you are worrying about, or suffering from, the effects of drinking? Or maybe it is a combination of both? There are no right or wrong answers, but it is important for you to look closer at why you are questioning your relationship with alcohol.

As well as exploring the reasons why you are examining your relationship with alcohol, I would also like you to think about the reasons why you believe you like to drink. Maybe it is the taste or the sense of relaxation you feel? Or maybe you think you can't have fun or be happy without it? Again, have a really good think about why you believe you like to drink.

Be open and honest with yourself. Nobody is judging you. This is simply a process of self-examination and beginning to explore exactly how alcohol features in your life.

Below I have shared my answers to these questions from my own journal, which I wrote around the time I quit drinking. I would like you to do the same in the space at the end of this chapter.

These are the reasons I believed I liked to drink:

- **Wine stops me feeling stressed out and anxious. It helps me forget my problems.**
- **Wine makes me relax.**

- Wine is something I can look forward to at the end of each day. It feels like a reward.
- I have drunk wine every night for so long that it is a daily habit. It is just what I do.
- Wine is a sophisticated drink. I enjoy buying an expensive bottle and giving myself a daily treat.
- I enjoy trying and tasting different wines, the fuller bodied the better.

And these are the reasons I gave as to why I was wanting to examine how alcohol was featuring in my life:

- I am sick of having hangovers and headaches that I can't seem to shake off.
- My hands have been shaking and I am certain alcohol is causing this.
- I worry about being over the drink drive limit, especially on the morning school run.
- I often can't remember what happened the evening before as I have been too drunk.
- I often get out of control and do things I regret when I drink too much.
- I am often grumpy, irritable and moody. It feels like the more I drink the less happy I become.
- My anxiety is becoming out of control and I am wondering if alcohol is playing a part in this.
- I often put alcohol ahead of the most important things in my life like my daughter, my wife, my health and my career.
- I don't like a substance having control and power over me. I would like to claim this back, but it feels like my drinking is out of control and I am addicted.

Write down the reasons why you have started to look at your relationship with alcohol in the space provided.

_____

_____

_____

_____

_____

_____

_____

Use the space provided to write down the reasons why you believe you like to drink alcohol. Consider what you believe alcohol gives you and the positive benefits you receive from drinking in your answers.

_____

_____

_____

_____

_____

_____

_____

When you write down your answers to the questions you will be asked throughout the book, it is important that you take some time to reflect on them and start to think about how the issues they raise impact your life. Do your answers represent the person you truly are? You don't need to act on anything yet, just start digesting the material and get curious about the answers you provide.

So what are the real reasons we drink alcohol?

The decision to drink is largely formed by the value that we place on it. The value we give alcohol can be strongly determined by how we believe it impacts on things like mood, anxiety, relaxation, stress or confidence (to name just a few). Once we have formed beliefs that we will get positive outcomes from alcohol, it then becomes our expectation that this is what will happen when we drink.

We can subconsciously treat alcohol like a medicine for achieving these outcomes, and over time we start to believe that drinking is the route to achieving these changes in how we feel. We form neural pathways that train our brains to believe that drinking is the only way to achieve the desired state, and once these pathways are formed it can take time to create new ones and allow the old pathways to fade away. When we use alcohol this way we can also neglect how we might feel without drinking and whether we can achieve the same changes and feelings naturally.

The value we place on drinking is often elevated by our past experiences. We tend to remember the good times with fondness and laugh about the drinking stories and memories, continually reinforcing our belief that alcohol equates to fun times. We often choose to forget the arguments, the fights, the hangovers and the regretful behaviour. But when we do recall the bad experiences or experience something traumatic as a result of drinking it can impact negatively on the value we place on alcohol and cause us to consider stopping. If we have formed beliefs that drinking alcohol brings with it positive and enjoyable experiences, we are likely to feel more motivated to drink more in the future.

I found that my impulsive personality was another reason I drank alcohol. I wanted to feel good fast and wanted to get rid of any internal pain right then and there, and alcohol promised to solve this problem quickly. I didn't think about the long-term consequences, I just wanted the rewards and instant gratification. Heavy drinkers are usually more impulsive than moderate drinkers.

Our society and culture also play a huge part in the reason we drink. It has become the social norm that we drink alcohol. We are bombarded by messages on every form of media that alcohol is just 'what we do' and is the route to fun and happiness in our lives. Alcohol is the only drug you have to justify not taking, and people who don't drink are often viewed as the odd ones out. Although culture is shifting (I will talk more about this later in the book), our current culture has set an expectation that drinking alcohol is how we behave and this contributes to the value we place on drinking. A great example of this is the tradition of after-work drinks on Friday nights. This ritual makes us feel connected and part of our tribe, and making the choice not to drink on a work outing to the pub might make us feel like an outcast and experience a sense of missing out.

Alcohol is addictive, and research has shown that addiction to booze stems from the effect that alcohol has on the reward centre of the brain. When we drink alcohol it causes a release of endorphins, the naturally occurring feel-good opioids that lead to a short-term sense of happiness, euphoria and a loss of inhibition. Recent studies have shown that heavy drinkers release more endorphins than light drinkers after drinking the same amount of alcohol, and this amounts to a higher sense of pleasure. The bad news is that after the unnaturally high rush of endorphins the brain and body will attempt to return to homeostasis, the natural state of equilibrium between being too happy and too sad. Because the overload of endorphins creates an unnaturally high response in the pleasure centre of the brain, we then release a chemical called dynorphin, which is essentially a downer that is designed to block the pleasure responses and bring the unnatural feelings back down to normal levels.

When we take another drink more endorphins are released, but not as much as the first drink, followed by yet more dynorphin. This cycle of artificially stimulated highs followed by the release of dynorphin to block the pleasure response and bring us back down explains why, when we are drinking, we can feel happy one moment, and then anxious, emotional and even angry the next. This cycle can also lead to a slippery slope of continually seeking the pleasure reward (or outcome) and placing a very high value on achieving it.

So the simple reasons we drink alcohol are twofold. The first is the value we place on it, and the second is the expected outcome we get from drinking it. But when you look in more detail at the reality of the outcomes you get from drinking you will likely find that you have given too much value to the part that booze actually played and will begin questioning how you allowed it to happen. I gave alcohol so much value – to me it was one of the most important things in my life. By exploring the truth around the value I placed on it and the reality of the outcomes it was giving me, I was able to start understanding more about how it should feature in my life.

Day 2 | What are your hopes and expectations?

Yesterday we talked about the reasons why you decided to read this book and looked at why you believe you like to drink alcohol. Today I want to explore your hopes and expectations for the future in a bit more depth.

As you start to explore what life without alcohol might look like, you may find that you have conflicting feelings. You might have questions and worries at the same time as feeling positive, excited and motivated about making a big life change. This is perfectly normal, so don't worry. But I do want to make sure you answer any questions and address any concerns to ensure you feel confident as you move forward.

If you can gain clarity on the areas where you have concerns or questions, you can take steps to address the specific issues. Bringing your worries out into the light is an excellent process. Equally, by writing down the positive hopes and expectations you have it will serve to reinforce those beliefs and shape the whole experience in the best possible way as you begin your journey.

It is important to understand that you may have given yourself unrealistic expectations in the past. Quitting alcohol is a bit like learning a new skill – it takes time and there are almost always setbacks along the way. If your expectations are unrealistic or possibly unachievable (for example: 'I want to never drink again as of now'), I hope that as you work through the book you will become aware of this and realign them accordingly. In other words, be gentle with yourself and take it one step at a time.

This is not to say that it is not possible to quit drinking right now; spontaneous sobriety can happen, although I know of only a handful of people who have made that decision and never touched alcohol again. I would prefer you to have hopes and expectations that you are confident will be met.

We tend to get what we expect, so if you explore an alcohol-free life with a negative approach and feeling like you are having your best friend taken away from you, then you will probably have a pretty negative experience. Whereas, if you approach this process with an open mind, a positive outlook and a sense that you are not losing anything but gaining back control and happiness in your life, then you will likely find the journey much more enjoyable.

I honestly don't feel as though I have lost anything by choosing not to drink. In fact, I feel as though I have joined a very exclusive community. The sober world feels like a hidden secret to me – it is as though I have now been given access to a new and wonderful world and become part of an incredible club. This is something I am very proud of, and I would love for you to experience it and join me.

Use the space provided to write down your hopes and expectations as you approach this process, along with any worries, fears and questions you have.

_____

_____

_____

_____

_____

_____

Start to become mindful about trusting yourself. Are you willing to believe that you can achieve what you want? Do you feel your hopes and expectations are realistic?

Think about whether you are prepared to work for what you want, and consider if you are willing to be patient at the same time as accepting that setbacks are likely to happen. Make sure that you understand that setbacks serve only to help you learn and grow stronger, and that it takes time to get to a place where you are truly free from the grip of alcohol.

You also need to ensure you can invest time in learning your new skill. Nobody becomes an expert overnight. The more time you put into learning and expanding your knowledge about quitting drinking, the more you will get out of it. Try to allow at least 30 minutes each day to read a chapter of this book and write in your journal.

We will address your worries, fears and questions as we go forward. Make sure you keep a note of them as I want to ensure that you feel really confident and have no doubt about the choices you make. In the unlikely event any of them are not covered in the contents of the book, you can search for answers in the Be Sober Facebook group or look on my website <www.besober.co.uk>.

Day 3 | Just because you believe it

Until I started exploring my relationship with alcohol, I didn't realize that what I believed about drinking might actually be wrong. It wasn't just my beliefs about alcohol either; it was the same with many areas of my life. I always thought that, if I believed it, it must be right and had to be true. These days I have a much more open mind and have learned that, just because I hold a belief about something, it might not be true and I try to keep myself open to new ways of thinking and my beliefs being challenged so I can allow them to adapt accordingly.

I used to believe that I couldn't have fun without drinking, that I couldn't relax or be happy without booze, and I strongly believed that alcohol was calming my anxiety rather than making it worse. I now know that all these beliefs and a whole lot of others were totally wrong, and I am so happy that I took the time to explore them, challenge them and ultimately change them.

On Day 1 you wrote down some of your beliefs about why you think you like to drink alcohol. Take another look over your list. If you need to add or change anything, you can go ahead and do it right now.

My mind was full of beliefs that were serving me in a negative way, and the more I carried on drinking, the more I created a false reality that supported these beliefs being true. This resulted in me being stuck in the alcohol trap for years.

Our beliefs are formed from our past experiences and influences throughout our lives. Everything from the society we live in through to our parents, friends and peers can have a huge influence over what we believe. Once we have formed a belief, it can become firmly ingrained and we take it as an absolute fact and usually for granted. We rarely stop to consider whether it might be true or not. What we believe gives us our view of the world, and we use our beliefs to decide if we think something is right or wrong, good or bad, safe or dangerous or possible or unachievable.

Most of the beliefs we hold serve us well; they allow us to assess risk and danger and avoid potentially uncomfortable situations. But other beliefs can be limiting and hold us back from reaching our true potential. The following is an example of a belief that limits someone from reaching their full potential:

Limiting belief: 'I will always be overweight, my body is just fat and I can never lose weight no matter what I do.'

And here is a belief that allows someone in the same situation to reach their full potential:

Full potential belief: 'I can lose weight and become slim and healthy if I change my diet and exercise regularly. This is in my control.'

My first big step to becoming unstuck from the alcohol trap was searching for the real truth in what I believed about how drinking was benefiting me. The way I did this was by writing down all of my limiting beliefs and replacing them with new and empowering belief statements that were still totally factual and true.

I want to invite you to undo any limiting beliefs you have and replace them with new ones that will empower you. Your limiting beliefs have very likely become ingrained and reinforced over the years, so this task can require some effort and repetition. I would urge you to keep coming back to this chapter and looking at your beliefs on a regular basis. You may even want to put your new belief statements somewhere prominent so you are regularly reminded of them as new 'belief affirmations'.

As you encounter new experiences and find your beliefs changing, make sure you write them down and take steps to reinforce only the beliefs that empower you. Try to avoid feeding the beliefs that are not serving you in a positive way, and become mindful about what you are choosing to believe as you go forward. Paying attention to your beliefs is an incredible exercise in personal growth and will allow you to begin a journey to opening your mind as well as your heart.

Once I had carried out the exercise that follows, I started to become really mindful about the limiting beliefs I held, and whenever I considered acting on one of them I would make a conscious choice to act against it. For example, my belief may have been 'I can't have fun at a party unless I drink alcohol', so I would consciously act against it by saying 'I can have fun at a party without drinking and I am going to prove it to myself'. Then I would go and do it. Once I had been to the party and experienced fun without drinking, my original belief was no longer looking so solid and a new belief had started to form based on the fresh evidence and the new experience I had had.

I would like you to complete the following exercise in the space provided. You can do it with as many beliefs as you wish, although you may need a separate piece of paper if you run out of space.

Pick a belief that you believe is holding you back, for example 'I can't relax without drinking alcohol'.

Write down how this belief has worked against you in the past. In this example, it could be 'I use alcohol to try to relax but it causes me to say and do things I regret'.

Then find some evidence that proves this belief is actually untrue. It is important to ensure your answers are completely factual. In this example it could be 'Alcohol may relax me for an hour or two, but I never feel relaxed in the morning when my anxiety is raging and I have a hangover and fuzzy head'.

Finally, write down a new and empowering belief to replace the original one. Again, it needs to be completely true for you, so have a good think about what would be right. In this example it could be 'I believe I would probably be more relaxed if I didn't drink alcohol and I would like to experience how that feels for me'.

_____

_____

_____

_____

_____

_____

_____

It is important to regularly remind yourself of your new beliefs, rather than just writing them down and forgetting about them. I know some people who have stuck a list of them on the door of their fridge and others who have put them on their smartphone lock screen so they see them each time they pick up their phone.

Think about how you can keep on reminding yourself of your new, empowering beliefs every day and write it down in the space provided.

_____

_____

_____

_____

_____

_____

_____

What we believe is incredibly powerful and it impacts the way we think and act. If you can make the effort to get really curious about your beliefs and examine them closely you can single out the ones that are holding you back and take steps to change them. You can then move towards living the life you deserve and finding freedom from alcohol for ever.

Become mindful of what you believe, start paying close attention and begin questioning whether specific beliefs serve you, whether they are boosting your self-esteem and if they are allowing you to be the very best version of yourself.

If you find a limiting belief, take the time to explore it and form new and healthy belief statements so you can begin to change your belief and prevent it from holding you back. So much freedom awaits in unlocking your unhelpful beliefs. I want you to become really curious about what you notice as you move through this book.

Day 4 | Why alcohol may not be the problem

This might sound like a rather strange statement! Why would I write a book about alcohol addiction and then tell readers that alcohol is not the actual problem? The reason is because addiction is usually the result of us attempting to suppress, avoid or deny something that runs much deeper. We often become addicted in order to comfort ourselves from past pain, hurt, neglect or trauma.

This book will help you understand everything you need to know in order that you can quit drinking successfully, but it is also essential to build your sobriety on firm foundations. If you don't address the root causes of why you turned to alcohol in the first place, it is the equivalent of building a beautiful new house on sand instead of concrete foundations. The last thing I want is for your new home to collapse on you right after you have moved in.

So what is the problem?

I have worked with thousands of people who have become addicted to alcohol from all over the world, and almost without exception I find one common theme. They have usually experienced some kind of hurt, pain, emotional neglect or trauma as a child and this has shaped them and their subsequent behaviours as they moved into adulthood.

My father walked out on my mother and me when I was just two years old. I didn't know it until I was much older, but that episode of my life (along with a few others) left me with issues around abandonment and rejection. In later life this was diagnosed as complex post-traumatic stress disorder (CPTSD). It turned me into someone who overcompensated by trying to please other people. I would be overly nice, go the extra mile for approval and avoid conflict at all costs. I found it extremely hard to say 'no' even if it made me uncomfortable or went against my values.

For decades I felt as though there was something missing in my life, as though I was somehow different from everyone else. They all seemed to be so happy, but I had what I can only describe as a huge void in my soul.

Through my entire life, I have reacted irrationally to anything that made me feel even a mild sense of rejection or abandonment, but I didn't understand why. I now know that my inner child was taking over in those situations. But for years, I couldn't understand why other people didn't get upset like I did. Why didn't they sulk and feel sadness like I did or fly off the handle when faced with similar situations?

I need to share this with you in order that you can move into your alcohol-free life and then heal. I often see people who quit drinking and then discover that there remains an underlying sense of sadness, pain or frustration when they had expected pink clouds, rainbows and happiness for ever. I haven't yet read a quit drinking book that draws readers' attention to the fact that the underlying problems very often relate to issues in childhood, and I feel as though I wouldn't be doing my job properly if I didn't make you aware of this.

That is not to say we don't feel happier when we quit drinking; we absolutely do. This is just one of the many things that improves alongside mental health, self-awareness, mental resilience and all-around wellbeing. We need to approach sobriety as a journey of personal growth. Addressing any issues or traumas from the past is the second phase that should be healed from a place of sobriety. This book will set you up for sober success. My job is to make you aware that when you remove the mask of alcohol you will connect with the true version of yourself, and there may be some further work to do in order to find complete peace in your life. Treat it as part of the incredible journey; it is not something to fear.

We all have an inner child. Children who grow up in a loving home, where their voice is heard and they are never criticized, stressed, ignored, rejected, abandoned, traumatized or abused, will usually turn out to be confident, smart and well-rounded adults. But such people are few and far between, because parents tend to project their stress, pain and suffering onto their children, often without even realizing it.

In almost every case where addictive behaviours have developed, parents have shaped the child through their own projected stress, pain and traumas, and it leaves wounds that mould the adult that the child goes on to become. Often, the parents will have had the same type of experiences in their own childhood. Mine certainly did.

Now you might be thinking that you had the perfect childhood and there were no episodes of trauma, yet you still find yourself reacting irrationally in certain situations. So let's work through it. I want you to have a clear understanding of what your inner child looks like so you can begin your journey of growth.

Let me be really clear here: it doesn't have to be 'trauma' in the sense that you might think, for example sexual or physical abuse. As developing children we constantly soak up what is going on around us. Our brains are like powerful computers on a data gathering and learning exercise. We seek out information and notice cues and stressors. We need to feel a sense of safety and when that feels compromised it creates a reaction, but young children don't think like adults and simply assume that because something is bad that they are to blame, they must be a bad person and they aren't good enough. Without reassurance or understanding, the child will likely form the conclusion that they must be a bad person and that they aren't good enough.

This isn't an exercise in blaming 'bad' parents. Very often this is about what our parents didn't do, as opposed to what they did do, and it is rare for a parent not to love their children. With busy and stressful lives, it can be all too easy for parents to project anxieties and discomfort onto their children.

As I explored my own childhood in more depth, it started to become really clear that my issues hadn't just been caused by my absent father – my mother had a part to play, too. As I started to join up the dots, gather information and build an understanding it became apparent that she had caused me to suffer CEN (childhood emotional neglect) as my primary caregiver. This wasn't through intention – it wasn't something she set out to do to me. In fact, it was what she didn't do that had caused most of my problems.

As an example, if a child has a parent who is incredibly stressed with their commitments and busy career and it feels like they never have time to listen, that can create a feeling within the child of their voice never being heard, and over time this will usually reinforce the belief that nobody ever listens to them. This can lead to irrational reactions in later life when they are triggered in situations where they feel they are not being listened to or ignored.

Consider this scenario. Sophie is four and her mum and dad have taken her to the park for the afternoon. Both parents have good jobs, the family lives in a nice house and they meet all of Sophie's needs, or so they think. To an outsider looking in they appear to be the perfect family unit. As Sophie plays on the swings her mum and dad look on from a nearby bench. Before long her dad joins in. He pushes her higher and higher as she squeals with delight and excitement. Before long her mum, who has been reading a magazine while sitting and relaxing, looks up and says, 'Sophie, enough playtime now. Today is your father's day off work and he should be relaxing.' The play abruptly ends, and Sophie's father returns to the bench beside his wife.

This might seem like a minor exchange that is a common occurrence in many families, but it is a prime example of the subtle nature of emotional neglect. Over time, this type of behaviour reinforces a message in Sophie that her parents aren't interested in her, that they don't have time for her, and that even when there are fun times she should expect disappointment.

In a situation without emotional neglect, Sophie's mother would have joined the fun on the swings, laughing and playing along while making her daughter the centre of the wonderful game. Or, when her mother called an abrupt end to the play, Sophie's father would have explained that playing with his daughter is exactly how he liked to relax and that he wanted the fun to continue.

As a child like Sophie moves into adulthood, the likelihood is that they will find themselves reacting irrationally in situations where they feel disappointment or rejection or where they feel unwanted or unheard. This is the unhealed inner child reacting, not the adult. Most of the time we have no idea why we react in unhelpful ways or where these overwhelming emotions have come from; we just assume that it is the way we are and live our lives suffering in silence and accepting that sometimes we simply have a childish tantrum.

These irrational reactions come in many different shapes and sizes, as does childhood emotional neglect. But if you can join up the dots and trace them back to childhood, it is remarkably easy to work out how they were formed. Awareness of the behaviour is a huge step on the path to healing.

Can you think of a few occasions where you have reacted in an irrational or childish way in your adult life? If so, write it down in the space provided.

_____

_____

_____

_____

_____

_____

_____

Now take a moment to look for a common theme in your answers. Understand that this is most likely your inner child talking, not the adult version of you. Can you see where the link might be?

As you read your statements, ask yourself this one question: 'What is it I really needed in those situations?'

For example, if you had answered that 'I last reacted irrationally when someone shamed me and made me feel embarrassed with a hurtful comment on Facebook', then what you probably needed instead was to feel appreciated or acknowledged.

Or, if you had written 'I reacted badly at work when a brilliant idea I had was totally ignored', then what you may have needed was for your voice to be heard and not to have been ignored. Did your parents hear your voice when you were younger or were they always too busy to listen? Maybe you had siblings who always seemed to get your parents' attention over you?

The first step on the path to healing is for you to become aware when your inner child is speaking instead of the adult. I like to call mine Little Simon, and these days I notice straight away when he starts to throw his toys across the room.

You also need to understand why your inner child reacts to certain triggers. Now you have worked out what your reactions look like, can you identify past events, behaviours of others or traumas that you believe may have shaped this? In most cases our inner child is shaped by our parents, but there may be wider influencers such as siblings or episodes at school. It is unlikely to be one specific incident; it could be a certain type of behaviour over a period of time or the same behaviour from multiple different people.

Remember, it may not be a specific traumatic event. When repeated over time, signs of negativity like a sigh or rolling of eyes from a parent when you were trying to speak can be enough to create an inner child that reacts to similar situations in adulthood. This process can feel uncomfortable and may stir up some painful memories, but if you don't look into the darkness you will never find the light, so trust yourself and trust the process.

If you don't feel ready to look closer at your past right now, come back to this chapter when you feel ready. Know that it is here for you when the time feels right.

Use the space provided to identify what may have shaped your inner child to react to the situations you described.

_____

_____

_____

_____

_____

_____

_____

When I raise the subject of childhood emotional neglect and trauma, people will either quickly identify with issues from their past or look confused because they hold a belief that their parents were perfect. It is therefore important to pay attention to the different types of parenting styles that can cause the problems that many people experience in later life.

As you read on, please hold a space of compassion in your heart for your parents. In most cases their behaviour stems from their own childhood, not a decision to make life hard for their children. Please let go of any urge to point the finger of blame – it won't serve you in a positive way.

Some of the common behaviours of parents who emotionally neglect their children or cause trauma are:

- emotionally distancing themselves from their children
- limited interaction with their children because they are either too busy, too overwhelmed with their own problems or struggling with addiction
- displaying little by way of compassion, warmth, affection or love towards their children
- failure to acknowledge their child's achievements – often physically absent from important events, especially at school such as sports days, parent evenings or award ceremonies

- overreacting to minor problems or issues – sometimes these reactions can be displayed as aggression or even violence
- failure to provide suitable supervision or set appropriate boundaries for their children.

Some of the most common symptoms of emotional neglect and trauma that emerge as a child moves into adulthood are:

- anxiety, depression and increased stress
- a feeling that something is missing from deep within the soul, often described as feeling emotionally numb or empty
- mood swings or a generally flat mood most of the time
- emotional withdrawal from others
- difficulty feeling, identifying, managing or expressing emotions and feelings
- appearing to have a lack of empathy or being uncaring towards others
- a belief that you are fundamentally flawed and that something is wrong with you, even though you can't explain what it is
- becoming easily overwhelmed and giving up on things quickly
- low self-esteem
- self-directed guilt, shame, anger and blame
- anger and aggression towards others
- inability to achieve and thrive
- hyperactivity and inattention, often diagnosed as attention deficit hyperactivity disorder (ADHD)
- risk of becoming dependent on other people
- inability to connect with others on an intimate level
- irrational fears based around the specific style of parenting the child was exposed to – for example fear of abandonment, rejection or conflict
- sexual acting-out and sexual problems
- addictive behaviour – this could be alcohol, drugs, gambling, shopping, eating, work, sex, porn, exercise, gaming or any other compulsive behaviour.

Can you identify with any of the following styles of parenting? Bear in mind that there is no one size fits all and many parents crossover and have elements of a number of different styles:

The narcissistic parent

Narcissistic parents are usually interested only in themselves. They don't have the best interests of their child at heart and tend to use their children to make themselves feel good or special. They may live out their own dreams or desires through their children, basking in the glory when they make the football team or land a prestigious new job and reacting badly as though personally offended if they don't.

These types of parents can be particularly abusive, often ruling the house with firm authority in their quest for power and control and in some cases displaying sociopathic traits.

The permissive parent

Permissive parents are often seen as the 'cool parents' in the eyes of their children's friends. But this parenting style is anything but cool. They often fail to set boundaries and limits or deliver consequences to help their children learn from their actions and behavioural mistakes. Instead they let things slide, they might tell their child that achieving a C grade in their maths exam is fine because they did their best and that's all they can do. This can cause a child to grow up believing that their best is mediocre and that pushing themselves harder in life is both pointless and impossible.

Permissive parents can also expose their children to danger by allowing them to engage in inappropriate activities or behaviours, such as underage drinking, hanging out with unsuitable friends, or not even knowing or worrying where their children are or what they are doing while they are away from the family home.

The workaholic parent

Workaholic parents are generally emotionally and physically absent in their children's lives. They tend to spend so much time away from home immersed in their career that they have no time to engage in true emotional connection. Even when they are around their children, they are often so wrapped up in thoughts and talk about their work life that they leave little room for a child to be heard.

Workaholic parents are also prone to giving love through material wealth and possessions as a way of compensating for their emotional absence. Children of workaholic parents are pushed out as they receive a message that their parents career is more important than they are, these children often grow up believing that love is conditional on their own future career success, wealth, possessions and superficial achievements.

The perfectionist parent

The perfectionist parent thrives on the accomplishments of their children. They will often push them hard to achieve more and excel in a particular area – often at the expense of their child's happiness. An example might be a father who pushes his son to play hockey, driving him to practice sessions and matches while enjoying the feeling of witnessing his own flesh and blood excelling and becoming the best player in the local league.

Unfortunately, perfectionist parents tend to offer love and emotional support only when their targets are hit. Failure to achieve their desired goals or do things their way can result in cold treatment and leave a child feeling that they need to achieve in order to get their needs met. This style of parenting can lead to resentment and conflict in later life, especially when the child forms their own opinions about the activities they want to engage in.

The addicted parent

I work with many people who have parents who have become addicted to alcohol or drugs. While these parents may not be selfish or uncaring at heart, their addiction causes them to become emotionally unavailable for their children. Their priority is to feed their addiction; it is what drives them and sadly this usually comes before anything else.

Addicted parents can make their children fearful. The child doesn't know which version of their parent they will be engaging with. Sometimes they can be attentive and loving, while at other times they can be angry, aggressive or irrational.

Children of addicted parents often grow up anxious with very little emotional support and often form stronger bonds with grandparents or family friends who have the time and caring nature to take an interest and truly connect with them.

The struggling parent

Struggling parents neglect the emotional needs of their child because they are too busy coping with challenges which leaves them with little time or energy. They may be dealing with illness (in themselves or another family member), a disability, depression or a bereavement. They would be much better parents if only they had more hours in the day.

In some cases this can result in the child taking on the role as the parent themselves, which can cause the child to grow up being incredibly self-sufficient but blaming themselves for their struggles in adulthood. Often, the child is left starved of the comfort and emotional support they need. They don't get the attention they so desperately crave, feelings go unnoticed and the child can end up feeling unimportant.

Soothing the pain

When we have experienced trauma, neglect, rejection, shame, abuse, blame, hurt or pain as a child, we have an inbuilt need to soothe our pain: we don't want to feel this way and we try to do something about it.

I often see people who overcompensate in life to try to find the soothing feelings we crave so much. In my case, I became an overconfident, egocentric, people-pleaser, I would go out of my way to be extra nice to other people and would often do things that did not reflect the true version of myself just to make others happy so they would like me and wouldn't reject or abandon me.

Another tendency is to overcompensate by becoming a high achiever with work, sports or other activities in adult life. It is common to see people with addictions who have climbed to the top of their career ladder at the same time as feeling a sense of sadness that they aren't truly fulfilled or happy. Our logic is that if we do well we will receive the acknowledgement and praise that we so sorely lacked as a child.

Overachieving is another way that our inner child drives us to seek the sacred feeling that comes from soothing our pain, which in my case is to be wanted and feel appreciated. I built a successful business, ran marathons, strived for bigger houses and better cars, and felt like I had achieved so much in my life. But it was all superficial and didn't come close to filling the void of rejection and abandonment. Did I ever get the praise I desired so badly? No.

In my mid-teenage years I discovered a way to soothe the pain with alcohol. I also dabbled with drugs for around a year, but drinking became my true friend. After all, alcohol would never reject or abandon me. It felt safe and gave me what I needed. It allowed me to numb out my inner child and feel disconnected for an hour or two. It became a crutch, I needed it daily to manage the discomfort that was stemming from my experiences in childhood.

The renowned addiction expert Dr Gabor Maté speaks extensively about how in almost every case of addiction – whether it is to alcohol, drugs, porn, gambling, sex, work, shopping, eating or exercise – there is an underlying issue from childhood that the addict needs to heal. I urge you to look closely at this element of your own life when you feel ready. Ensure this is done in a gentle and caring manner, and start paying close attention to what you notice.

If you have found yourself nodding your head and saying 'That's me' as you have read this chapter, then I would urge you to watch some of Dr Maté's videos on YouTube or read his book *In the Realm of Hungry Ghosts* so you can start to explore the healing of your inner child in more depth. But don't dive into that yet – for now, simply notice any behaviours and make a note of them in your journal. Treat it like a data-gathering exercise as you work through this book.

Don't feel down about what you see or recognize in yourself signs of neglect or trauma. Imagine if you had continued through your entire life having irrational reactions, feeling unfulfilled and never knowing why, all the while fighting the desire to drink to suppress the feelings or numb it all out. That sounds like a pretty painful existence to me. Celebrate the fact that you may have had a breakthrough and started to unearth the root of the problem. This is a gift.

You won't ever unlearn this, but from this moment on you will start to notice when it is your inner child speaking and not the adult. In these moments try to pause and ask yourself: 'Who is this speaking now?' If you know it is the childhood version of you, try to show them love and give them what they need in that moment. Welcome the child and let them know that you (the adult) have got the situation under control. This will often snap you out of the child mode and back into the rational adult that you really are. Now you are aware of how your inner child reacts in certain situations, you can start taking steps to heal and find peace.

But you need to seek out the meaning, too; you have to understand where the reactions are coming from and what caused them. The moments of childish responses are your key to discovery. This is where you will learn exactly what your inner child needs and how this behaviour is driven by wounds from deep inside of you. It can be hard to unravel exactly where the wounds have come from, especially if you believe you had a perfect childhood. Explore with an open mind.

By bringing this into the light, you can move towards peace and healing and this will create the perfect solid foundation for success in sobriety. If I was only to give you a strategy for quitting drinking, along with support, tactics and tools, I would feel as though we were cutting off a few branches of the 'habit tree' instead of ripping it up at the roots; your inner child is the roots, and it is time to start thinking about when might be the right time to begin digging.

Put some time into working on this. It takes practice and can feel uncomfortable, but it is also incredibly rewarding and it is an essential part of personal growth and development. Try to understand what it is your inner child wants to feel in that moment. Avoid leaving any situation feeling sad, embarrassed, unheard, shamed, hurt or unloved.

My daughter has always been a loving child, and I enjoy nothing more than a big hug from her. After all, it makes me feel wanted instead of rejected, so it is obvious that a huge cuddle would light me up. But since she has entered her mid-teens the hugs have become much less frequent. I expected this – I know teenagers need space and hugs are no longer top of their priority list. But I still crave them; it triggers those feelings of abandonment and rejection when they are withheld. Often, I will ask her for a hug only to be met with a firm 'no!' Or 'Leave me alone'. This stings, it stirs up my inner child, and I have had to learn how to heal and handle the triggers.

I have found the best solution in these moments is to know exactly what my inner child desires at that point in time and to ensure I can get it somewhere else. In this case the need is to feel wanted, not rejected, and thankfully my wife is usually on hand to give me a big hug if I ask nicely. This allows me to leave a situation with my inner child getting what they needed alongside a feeling of positivity and empowerment that I overcame what could have turned into a tantrum from Little Simon.

Take these moments as your chance to learn and to practise compassion with both the adult version of you and your inner child. If you can identify with what I have written about in this chapter, make sure you take steps to heal and move forward. Don't leave it suppressed or it will never change. Instead of dealing with the effects, start addressing the cause.

It can also be incredibly beneficial to seek professional help through psychotherapy or therapy sessions with a like-minded group. However, I would not consider doing this until you have successfully cut alcohol out of your life and moved to a place where you feel more grounded and mentally resilient. Alcohol destabilizes the emotions, and attempting to deal with something challenging from the past is best done from a place of inner strength. If you feel you may need professional help with healing, try to view it as the second phase of your self-growth and development plan after addressing how alcohol features in your life.

If you are a people-pleaser, start learning to say 'no' to others when you believe it is the right decision, and find the joy in being the authentic version of yourself. Reconnect with the true version of you – discover the light within and you will soon find yourself on a wonderful path to freedom and happiness.

Notice when you judge or criticize other people. When we do this we are almost always projecting a dislike of ourselves onto someone else in order that we don't have to face up to it and deal with it. Take the time to start examining your own judgements.

A powerful tactic is to keep a note of how many times a day you are able to say 'no', and keep a tally of how often you judge others. By bringing a mindful awareness to these traits you will be able to catch yourself in the moment and your behaviour will start to change.

It can also help to work on being more grounded. There are some excellent meditation exercises you can find online to work on this. When we feel grounded we lower our centre of gravity and are less easy to knock over in times of discomfort. We also feel connected and stable, and these calming practices can help us get into a much stronger state of mind.

Take the time to practise gratitude, as it will help you stay present and appreciate the good things in your life. An excellent tactic you can use when a negative thought comes to mind is to do a countdown from ten and in that moment list out ten things you are grateful for.

You can also use your journal to practise gratitude. Try to take the time to think about your life from a different perspective. Instead of feeling down because you believe your life should be better, start to consider how it could be worse. This perspective can improve your overall outlook on life and provide you with a sense of satisfaction.

A good exercise is to answer the following two questions:

1 I wish I was a…
2 I am glad I am not a…

You will find that the answer to the first question might make you feel a sense of envy or some other negative emotion, whereas the answer to the second question will make you feel grateful for what you have. If so, ask yourself the second question whenever you feel you need to.

All of the negative feelings from my childhood left me feeling empty inside, as though something was missing in my life. I struggled to make true emotional connections with people and put myself first in almost every situation as a default defence mechanism to protect myself from my own insecurities. I didn't want to hear what other people had to say. I was too interested in talking about myself so I could compensate for the emotional void that existed inside.

Over time I realized that I needed to change my intention. In every situation we have 'intent' and we can make a choice about what that intent will be. As far as I am concerned, there are only two kinds of intent:

- **Intent 1:** To learn to do everything in life with a sense of love for yourself and others, even if that means facing up to pain.
- **Intent 2:** To protect yourself and hide from facing up to the pain, often with controlling, narcissistic or addictive behaviour. Failing to take responsibility for your own feelings and actions.

My biggest breakthrough to date was the day that the pain became unbearable. The depression, the anxiety and self-loathing had built inside me to a point that I couldn't handle it any longer.

My absent father let me down (he passed away several years ago). But now I realized my mother had damaged me through her own emotional neglect, and I needed to do something to begin the process of healing. I could see that I had lived in a state of 'ignorant bliss' since I was a child. In fact, it was just ignorance as there had never been any bliss; I just never understood why I felt the way I did.

I had been undergoing therapy for a few months, and it had been a roller-coaster journey of revelations and emotions. In one of the sessions I asked how I could let go of my trauma, and the therapist said that one method is to give it back to the parent who caused it. He stressed that, when confronted, parents often react with defensiveness or complete denial, and I should seriously consider any decision to confront my mother. He also made it clear that it didn't matter how my mother might react; this was about me stepping up, speaking my truth and letting her know how I feel.

This was the day everything began to change. I told my mother that I needed to talk, and she agreed to meet in a local park. As we sat on the grass, the sun was shining and young children were playing football nearby as they laughed and played with their parents. The irony of their happiness was that I was about to unload the broken, sad little boy who lived inside me and who had ruined my life onto my mum.

And that is exactly what I did. I told her everything. I explained how I believed I had been emotionally neglected by her, that I understood she had been neglected herself by her controlling and violent father, and that it had been passed on to me unintentionally. I told her how I felt we had never bonded or connected emotionally, leaving me with a black hole in my soul as a result.

There were a lot of tears. I felt sad for her, but I knew I also had to give her back the trauma – this sad little boy shouldn't be living in me any longer. I had expected her to play the victim and become defensive, and I was more than ready for that. What I wasn't prepared for was for her to admit that she had been a poor mum, to open up about how hard it was for her and tell me how I was put in an incubator because I had jaundice straight after I was born, which meant she didn't have any physical contact with me for my first three weeks of life.

She went on to tell me how her marriage had broken down not long after I was born, and how she struggled for money before being evicted from her home. Then she married my stepfather (a wonderful man who I idolize) but she did so for the wrong reasons – she needed security and certainty and that was what he offered – there was no love. She shared so much; we had never spoken like this before. It was wonderful, yet heart-breaking at the same time.

On that day, we began to bond, and I was able to set healthy boundaries. With time and more therapy, the trauma started to heal, and I felt that I could finally start to move forward. She had taken ownership of her mistakes, and I experienced a weight beginning to lift off of my shoulders that I had carried for over 40 years. I have learned that it is incredibly rare for parents to admit their shortcomings, and I am blessed to have a mother who was able to acknowledge that she had let me down. I know that she loves me – she just wasn't prepared for the job of parenting at that time in her life. This process wasn't about her admitting what she had or hadn't done. It was simply a process of me letting her know. Even if I hadn't had contact with her, I would have written a letter or had a virtual conversation that represented me telling her and offloading the trauma. There is no way I could ever have had the strength to deal with something as emotionally challenging as this when I was drinking.

In addition, I have learned that being open and honest by sharing my feelings and emotions with people who I consider safe has allowed me to grow in confidence and let go of the feelings of fear and shame that I have held on to for most of my lifetime. An excellent way to do this is in a therapy group with other people facing similar challenges.

It was a huge part of the process of healing. If you have experienced any of the challenges I have described, I recommend that after you have cut alcohol out of your life you begin exploring CEN and start your own journey of healing. It is an emotional experience and you need to be mentally tough enough to get through it. Quitting alcohol will set you up for success by making you more resilient. I could never have dealt with this when I was still drinking. For some people, the fear of facing what lives in the shadows is what prevents them walking out into the light. Don't stay in the darkness, it is painful.

If anything in this chapter is resonating with you, I don't recommend taking action right now. Let's work on removing alcohol from your life so you can focus on this from a much better place when you are stronger. This chapter is all about bringing awareness to any childhood issues so you can start to understand what might be going on. It also means you can let go of any sense of blame or shame by knowing that none of this is your own fault.

When you feel ready and strong enough in your sobriety, I would encourage you to read the book *Running on Empty: Overcome Your Childhood Neglect* by Jonice Webb as the first step into addressing emotional neglect.

There is no need to dwell on this, simply become aware and start to notice your behaviour. Take comfort in the knowledge that this is an area of your life that you will address after you have moved through the first phase, which is to become alcohol-free and grow stronger and more self-aware.

Now let's move on to the first day of your journey to quitting drinking. As you digest the information in this book I want you to open your heart, relax, stop trying to force things and avoid focusing on your feelings too much with your brain. Learn to pay attention and actually feel your feelings instead of thinking about them. Start listening to your gut and trusting your intuition – they are almost always right.

Day 5 | You have nothing to lose...

... and everything to gain.

Hopefully now you have looked at your beliefs and written out new and empowering statements that will no longer hold you back. Maybe you have already started to realize that by cutting alcohol out of your life you really aren't going to be losing anything and have started to think about how much you are going to gain from an alcohol-free lifestyle.

It can be very easy to feel as though you are being deprived of something when you cut alcohol out of your life. I know that I felt like I was losing a dear friend who had helped me through so many difficult times. But when I started looking at my beliefs more closely, I realized that it was that same dear friend who had caused most of the difficult times in the first place. Did I really still want that so-called 'friend' around? No, thanks.

Stay mindful about any feelings that come up as you go on this journey. Try to avoid reacting emotionally if anything uncomfortable comes to mind. Instead, stay curious and inquisitive and use your journal to explore what you are feeling in more depth. Ask yourself, 'Where is this feeling coming from?'

Later in the book we will talk more about the negative effects of drinking on your mind, your body and your life as a whole, as well as exploring the wonderful benefits of not drinking. But for now I would like you to write down in the space provided anything that comes to mind in answer to this question: What do you think you will be losing if you cut alcohol out of your life?

You might think that quitting drinking will make you lose friends because they will think you are no longer fun, or you might fear that, without alcohol, you won't be able to relax in the evenings. There is no judgement and no right or wrong answers; simply write down whatever comes to mind.

_____

_____

_____

_____

_____

_____

I am confident that whatever you think you might be losing will be covered in later chapters and your beliefs will slowly begin to change. Check the contents of this book to ensure it has been included. In the unlikely event that it's not you can search the Be Sober Facebook group or look on my website <www.besober. co.uk> for more in-depth answers.

What I would like you to know right away is that, whatever you think you might be losing, you are probably wrong, and as you keep moving through the book my hope is that you realize that you have absolutely nothing to lose and everything to gain.

Try to dig into your statements a little deeper as you did with the exercise on Day 3 on beliefs. Maybe you could change them to become something more empowering or find new truths in the comments you have written?

You may have already read about the many changes and positive benefits that happen when you quit drinking. If not, you have all of this to look forward to in the later chapters. For now I would also like you to write down what you think you will gain by cutting alcohol out of your life.

You might find that you gain more quality time with the most important people in your life by being fully present, and having more time with them because you are no longer putting drinking ahead of them. Or you might believe you will experience health benefits, more productivity at work, or a sense of peace and calm in your life.

Use the space provided to write down what you think you would gain from an alcohol-free life.

_____

_____

_____

_____

_____

Take some time to reflect on your answers. I am confident that most of what you have written down is exactly what will happen if you cut alcohol out of your life. Think about how much you desire these things. How motivated are you to have these 'gains' in your life? What is more important to you at the moment: is it alcohol, or is it bringing about a true and lasting change to make what you have written down a reality?

Day 6 | Who you are versus where you are

I used to believe that heavy daily drinking was just what I did. When I found myself in a rut, which was often, I would say things to myself like 'I am just an alcoholic. It is who I am and this is the way I am always going to be'.

Over time I realized that I was wrong. I was stuck in an addictive pattern of behaviour, and it felt like a challenge to know what to do for the best. But it didn't define 'who I was'; it was a problem that I was facing at that particular point in time. This was 'where I was' on my journey, not 'who I was' as a person, and when I became clear about this it helped me gain so much more understanding. I grew to understand that I could move to another place and find complete freedom.

We are all in different situations: some of us have drunk regularly for years and never tried to quit alcohol, while others have attempted to stop and returned to the booze over and over again. Some of us are daily drinkers while others have days off the booze and then binge drink until blackouts occur. No matter what your situation or patterns of behaviour, this loop of destruction can make you start to believe that this is who you are, that it is the way you are meant to be and that you have to remain stuck like it for ever. You might say to yourself 'I am just a drunk' or 'I can never change, what's the point in trying', or you might feel that alcohol in some way defines who you are as a person.

So is it really true? Is that who you are? Some people hope that it is true because it can feel easier than facing up to the problem. But the fact you are reading this page makes me believe that you probably know better than this. Maybe you have had an episode of drinking or a regretful incident fuelled by alcohol that has made you feel that this really is not the person you want to be any longer? Or perhaps the long-term cycle of pain from being caught in this trap has left you exhausted from fighting and wishing you could change?

Telling yourself that 'this is just who I am' when it comes to justifying your drinking habits is an easy option; some might even describe it as a cop-out. It allows you to silence any concerns or thoughts that come to mind about your behaviour by shutting them down with 'this is just who I am' along with a belief that because that is 'who you are' nothing is going to change.

It can also be easy to blame external sources, such as people and places, for our behaviour instead of taking responsibility for our own actions. Part of the process of successfully quitting drinking involves taking complete ownership and becoming responsible for the choices we make.

There is a huge difference between 'who you are' and 'where you are'. Right now you are travelling through a particular point in your life. Maybe you feel trapped and you are wondering what to do for the best. But that is 'where you are'; it is not 'who you are'. In fact, your use of alcohol may actually contradict who you really are as a person and go against your values. When you start to think about it, you might feel that the behaviour is opposing who you want to be and that the true version of you is actually much better than this.

When I realized that my daily use of alcohol did not actually represent who I was or who I wanted to be, I felt a huge sense of relief. This realization allowed me to work towards finding a true and better version of myself and an understanding that in order to find freedom I needed to move forward from 'where I was' to become 'who I really am'.

When you feel stuck, your mind can spew out negative self-talk that doesn't serve you in a positive way. Try to be very aware when this happens. Catch yourself when you do it, then pause and reach for your journal. Keep reminding yourself that this is simply 'where you are', not 'who you are', and that you are on a journey towards the best version of you.

Try to understand that you are not the cause of this struggle. We live in a society that has set us up for failure when it comes to drinking, so don't beat yourself up for being weak or think that you are unable to quit alcohol. Instead, take the time to keep working on expanding your knowledge and becoming more and more aware about how external influences can mess with your mind and the decisions you make.

No matter how stuck you feel or how long you have struggled, I can tell you that this is not who you are. You are way more than this and you are most definitely better than this. Do you believe that your struggle is where you are or who you are?

Take some time to think about who you really are. What excites you? What motivates you? What do you enjoy? What are your dreams and aspirations? What do you want to do more of? Where do you want to be in the future? What are your core values and the qualities you admire about yourself?

Write your answers down in the space provided and start putting together a picture of who you really are. What does the authentic version of you look like aside from the use of alcohol?

_____

_____

_____

_____

_____

Take some time to reflect on your answers, and ask yourself whether you want to start moving forward to become the person you know you really are and start creating change to shift away from where you are at this point in time.

Day 7 | How to handle uncomfortable feelings

I had drunk alcohol almost every day for over 20 years, so when I realized I needed to make a change I felt pretty sure that I would experience some uncomfortable feelings at some point. After all, this was a huge adjustment to my life and I was trying to learn a new habit at the same time as quitting an addictive substance. I didn't think it was going to be easy, but I also wanted to stop drinking so badly I felt like I was willing to go through anything to get where I wanted to be.

The pain of carrying on stuck in the daily cycle of addiction had become worse than the pain of living with the discomfort I believed I would experience when I quit. I had to make this change if I was ever going to break free from the tight grip of alcohol.

The first couple of weeks were the most challenging in terms of experiencing uncomfortable feelings. I found that my mood was up and down, I felt irritable and quite emotional much of the time. I also had trouble sleeping during this time and was thinking about alcohol a lot. Cravings would come and go, and there were points where I believed taking a drink would be the easiest route to feeling better, but I knew this was a cruel illusion and that alcohol was trying to lure me back by playing games with my mind.

The good news is that it all settled down over time. My sleeping improved, and I found myself in a much better mood than ever before. More importantly, the cravings for drink and the thoughts about alcohol became less and less frequent. After a few months of not drinking I was in a place where I hardly ever had cravings for alcohol any longer.

It is important to know that these feelings always pass and it all gets much easier once you have got the first few weeks without drinking out of the way. I put a sticky note on my fridge to remind myself that nothing is permanent. It said: 'This too shall pass.'

When we quit alcohol we can experience psychological and physical symptoms of withdrawal. Usually, these are mild to moderate, but if anything causes you concern please seek medical help straight away. I have listed some of the common symptoms that can occur. These usually appear in the first week or two after quitting drinking, and I want you to feel prepared for whatever might arise.

Psychological symptoms:

- Heightened anxiety
- Feelings of depression
- Feeling irritable
- Feeling on edge or nervous

- Rapid changes of emotion
- Fatigue or feelings of tiredness

- Difficulty thinking clearly
- Problems with sleeping

Physical symptoms:

- Cravings for drink
- Headaches or migraines
- Sweating and clammy skin
- Heart palpitations

- Heightened blood pressure
- Shaking (often in the hands)
- Loss of appetite

It is essential that you are prepared and know that some difficult feelings will probably come up. I want you to ensure you have the right strategies to handle them effectively and take the time to know what works best for you whenever discomfort arises.

I started to feel significantly better after the first week without alcohol, but there were other areas of discomfort that took longer to settle down. You have to remember that your brain and body are rebalancing and undergoing a big change; it can take weeks or even months for everything to stabilize and for you to start feeling great again. But believe me, it really is worth it. Make sure you use the tactics I share in today's chapter to handle any uncomfortable feelings you experience.

Try to see any discomfort as a positive sign that your body and brain are healing and going through the essential process of change. Treat those uncomfortable feelings as part of the journey to recovery as you start to evolve into a new and better version of yourself.

When you experience a desire to drink or find something triggering you, instead of acting on the thought try to become curious about where it is coming from. Simply sit with the thoughts and let them pass; don't allow them to control your actions. I recommend writing down any uncomfortable thoughts and feelings as and when they come up and then exploring them more deeply.

Name your feelings and become aware of how long they stay with you by noting down the start and end time. Work on reducing the time they hang around by using the tactics provided.

Tips for dealing with discomfort

Don't hide from the feelings

It is easy to try to suppress the feelings and hide away from them. Many of us have done this for most of our adult lives as a method of avoiding pain. However, by having the courage to face up to them you can learn to sit with the feelings. Get used to writing them down, asking questions about where they have come from and viewing them with a sense of curiosity. You will find that by facing up to the feelings you experience you will manage them far better than hiding away from them.

Be kind to yourself

When an uncomfortable feeling comes up it can be easy to start beating yourself up with negative self-talk. I used to convince myself that I could never be free from alcohol and would find myself right back at the start when I allowed the self-talk to control how I behaved.

When I learned to be kind to myself and to talk to myself the same way that I would talk to a close friend, I stopped giving myself a hard time and instead gave myself the love that I had long been lacking. This made the whole process so much easier as I was able to cut myself some slack and stop putting too much pressure on myself. We will look at negative self-talk in more depth later in the book.

Meditate

There is no better way to deal with uncomfortable feelings than with a few minutes of meditation. There are so many brilliant apps available that can help you meditate easily using your smartphone. I recommend looking up the Calm and Headspace apps, both of which became vital tools for me on my journey to freedom from drinking. You will find a number of useful apps listed in the Resources section at the end of the book.

Talk it out

A problem shared is a problem halved. If you are experiencing uncomfortable feelings and have someone you can talk to, it is very likely going to make you feel much better and more positive about what you are experiencing. If you are part of an online sober group, you can also reach out for support there.

Remind yourself why you are here

Whenever I had urges to drink or I was enduring a tough day and wondering why I was doing this, I would look back at my journal and read the entries I had written in the first few days. These served as a great reminder of how bad things had got with my drinking and reinforced the reasons why I was on this journey. They often gave me just the reminder I needed and helped me refocus on the bigger picture and the goal I wanted to achieve.

Whenever an uncomfortable feeling comes up that makes you think that drinking alcohol would solve the problem, I would like you to answer these three questions:

- What is the reason I believe I want to drink now?
- If I drank alcohol right now, what would it change?
- If I drank alcohol right now, what wouldn't it change?

Answer the questions above right now using the space provided, and whenever you experience uncomfortable feelings refer back to this chapter and ask yourself the same questions. If you have already quit drinking, write down any uncomfortable feelings you have experienced and reflect on the strategies you used to handle them.

Later in the book I will share a number of powerful tactics that you can use to dispel negative feelings. For now, I would like you to pay close attention to anything that comes up and ensure you write them down in your journal. Simply be aware that there is likely to be a level of discomfort in the first week or two after you quit. I don't want you to be afraid of this. I want you to work on your mindset and embrace the discomfort in the knowledge that it is a sign of you growing stronger and healing from the damage that alcohol has inflicted on your life.

Day 8 | You can quit without (much) willpower

The truth is that you will probably need a little bit of willpower and a sense of determination to achieve what you want. But it is important not to rely on this alone because it will only get you so far. When we find ourselves stuck in the cycle of alcohol addiction it is an incredibly uncomfortable place, and I want you to understand exactly how you can end the discomfort for good.

You need to understand why you feel stuck and why it feels painful. When someone has a problem with alcohol and they aren't aware of it, there is no discomfort. They are happily drinking themselves to death in total unawareness. They might still reinforce their false belief that they drink like everyone else, or that nothing is wrong by skim-reading headlines, social media or news articles that speak about the 'benefits' of drinking, but they have become the classic example of the phrase 'ignorance is bliss'.

Can you think of a time in your life when you were living in the 'ignorance is bliss' stage? The fact you are reading this book tells me that you aren't at this stage any longer, but I am sure there was a time when you were. Maybe you were even proud of your drinking abilities and boasted to other people about how you could last the longest during a boozy session.

I recall how I was proud of my tolerance to alcohol and I would laugh at other people who I considered 'lightweights' because they couldn't drink as much as me because they felt the effects of alcohol much more quickly. At that time in my life my conscious and subconscious mind were in harmony; they both had the same viewpoint that alcohol was adding something positive to my life and there was nothing wrong with how much I was drinking. As far as I was concerned, I didn't have a problem and alcohol was bringing only good things to my life.

Use the space provided to write about a time when you were in the 'ignorance is bliss' stage of your drinking.

_____

_____

_____

_____

_____

_____

_____

The problems start when we begin to become aware that we might have a problem with our drinking behaviour. There is usually a trigger, and I believe that once the seed is planted it is impossible to return to a place of ignorance.

In my case, I recall seeing a feature on the TV news about how many people in the UK were drinking excessive amounts at home. The reporter highlighted how much people were drinking on average and explained the risks, including cancer, mental health problems, heart issues, risks of liver disease and the impact of alcohol on sleep. There was an expert guest who talked in depth about how alcohol use at home was an epidemic and explained that many people didn't even recognize that they were putting themselves in huge danger. They discussed the safe daily drinking limits and referred to specific age groups and demographics of the types of people most likely to abuse alcohol at home.

It had my attention. I was a huge home drinker, and everything they spoke about rang so true. I knew I was exactly the type of person they were referring to. I was a problem drinker; the experts had just confirmed it and now it was dawning on me that they were probably right. That was it: the seed had been planted, I was no longer in a state of 'ignorance is bliss', and this is when the pain began.

This single news feature had started a chain reaction in my mind. Once relatively calm and settled, it had become a raging sea of confusion and concern. Suddenly, I had a fight erupting inside my own head. My subconscious mind was firmly fixated on continuing the same old habits and following the same daily path that I always had, but now my conscious mind, which had once been marching to the same beat as my subconscious, was going to war. It realized that my drinking was a problem; it now had an opposing view to its neighbour and friend, the subconscious.

Nothing could drown the noise that was starting to rage in my conscious mind. The news feature had touched a nerve, and there was no going back to a place of peace. From that moment onwards I started to notice more and more information relating to the dangers of drinking. Warnings about drinking now seemed to be appearing everywhere I looked, and, worst of all, I was even searching on the internet myself to try to calm down my racing mind. But, of course, I did have a problem with alcohol, so I found nothing online to tell me that drinking two to three bottles of red wine a day with beers or spirits on top was safe and sensible. I was now stoking up the fire of war that was about to explode in my head.

Before long, the war began. The two sides engaged in a ferocious battle that left a wake of devastation in its path. My subconscious mind that had held firm and steady, fixed to its long-standing habits and beliefs, wanted to silence my conscious mind. It wanted it to stop ranting about quitting drinking and come back to the comfort and safety of believing nothing was wrong and nothing needed to change. But my conscious mind wanted to protect me and was unwilling to submit, no matter how hard my subconscious pushed for it to do so.

The war raged for many years. It destroyed my mental health, my anxiety sky-rocketed and I found myself trapped in a place of complete misery. So, I drank. In fact, I drank more than ever before, because when I drank it was as though someone had raised a flag and called a ceasefire for a few hours. But the next morning the battle recommenced and neither side was taking any prisoners. It was a fight that would last to the death.

You need to know that this war will only end when you follow the advice in this chapter, and that once you have this horrific fight inside your mind the worst thing you can do is try to live with it by doing nothing. You will never be back in the 'ignorance is bliss' state – that is a thing of the past – accept it. If you try to ignore it, then the bombs and guns will rage louder, the battle will become more ferocious, and it will destroy you from the inside out.

You also need to know that your subconscious mind will fool you into thinking that a drink will make everything good, but it is a massive illusion. It is a complete lie that alcohol makes us want to believe in order that it can keep us trapped. This doesn't end the war; it makes it worse and prolongs the suffering.

Please pay attention to this chapter. This information is critical to help you help yourself. If you have this type of internal fight erupting in your head, then you need to understand that nobody can end it other than you.

So what are your options?

You can try to live with the war. This is what I did for around five years after I saw that feature on the TV news. I tried to push it out of my mind, and I kept drinking in the hope it would fade. I even sought the help of professionals to heal my anxiety, meditated and read just about every self-help book I could lay my hands on. But nothing worked. I wasn't dealing with the issue at the heart of the bloody battle inside my mind, and the fight simply carried on. Sadly, some people live like this right up until they die. They are stuck in a perpetual place of internal pain, the war never ends, and they are never happy. All they can do is numb the noise of the fight when they escape for those fleeting moments where they anaesthetize themselves with alcohol to try to drown it all out.

You can quit drinking reluctantly with willpower. When you do this you are essentially accepting that your subconscious mind should be the victor in the battle because the cause they are fighting for is right. But you are still supporting the cause that your subconscious mind is fighting for; you still believe alcohol is a wonderful substance that helps you relax, have fun and sleep, and that you are one of the lucky ones who won't get cancer, have heart problems or die earlier than you should. This doesn't end the war: you are still taking sides, conflict still exists and before long your conscious mind will become noisy. It will start taking shots at your subconscious mind and the fighting will recommence. This usually ends with us reaching for a drink to drown it out and returning right back to the start with the battle still raging inside us.

You can unite the two sides and end the war. I need to be really honest with you here, and I am only able to do this because I have lived with the war in my own head. I have tried every conceivable solution to try to end the battle while maintaining some kind of relationship with alcohol. Nothing worked. The battle continued and I was left a sad, anxiety-ridden shell of the person I should have been. What you need to know is that you won't ever end the war if you keep drinking. Once the fight has started, you can't ever go back to 'ignorant bliss'. You need to accept this – I am giving you some tough love now and telling you that something has to change if you want peace in your life and only you can make that change. The ONLY way you can end the war is if you can get both sides to agree and share the same viewpoint.

Think about why the war started in the first place. Both sides have different opinions. Your conscious mind wants to protect you and ensure you stay safe, whereas your subconscious wants you to stick to your old habits and follow your old routines. Until the two are in harmony, the bombs will keep dropping and your mind will continue to be in turmoil.

Without harmony between the two sides, every time you take a drink you are throwing a grenade or taking a shot at your conscious mind. Whenever you try and quit using willpower you are fighting against your subconscious. You are like a ruthless dictator who leaps from supporting one side to the other, escalating the hatred between the two aggressors in your internal conflict.

Use the space provided to write down any attempts you have made to end the internal conflict and describe what the outcome was.

_____

_____

_____

_____

_____

_____

So how do you get the two sides in harmony?

I am sure you want to stop the conflict. You probably already know how damaging it is and I hope you understand that once you have this fight in your head there is no chance of ending it by staying in the same place. Don't waste your time, because you are going to prolong the suffering and cause yet more damage to yourself. It will only get worse, not better.

Acceptance that you now have to make a change is the most important step towards bringing about peace.

You might be thinking that you could force your conscious mind to drop its viewpoint and get in harmony with your subconscious by accepting that your drinking behaviour is perfectly acceptable. Maybe you can somehow convince it that you don't have a problem, or you could commit to drinking less to compromise and settle it down. But the facts don't lie: your conscious mind knows the truth now and has been seeking out more and more information to support its cause. It won't capitulate; it will never let up because it believes so strongly in what it is fighting so hard for and no matter what you do to try to convince it that some level of drinking is OK, it wants to protect you. It is on your side and it won't let you down. This strategy will not work: you might calm it down for a while but before long the fighting will begin again.

In the past you have probably switched from supporting one side to the other. You begin by siding with your subconscious by convincing yourself that your drinking habits are perfectly acceptable and that everything will be fine. This causes the conscious mind to fight back harder, and it gets incredibly noisy in the process. When this happens, you may have found yourself switching sides again and becoming an ally for quitting drinking for a while. Maybe you had a period of peace at this point, maybe not, because before long your subconscious erupts against you and aggressively attacks in an attempt to pull you back to its way of thinking.

When we find ourselves in this trap, I call it the 'drunken dictator' phase. We move from being the leader of one army, then switch allegiance to the other, then change our support yet again. It can happen over and over, and it causes us to fuel the flames of war without even realizing it. We stir up our own internal conflict when we think we are trying to calm the situation. The battle rages on and on, becoming more intense and more painful. The war never ends while we are stuck in the phase of being the drunken dictator.

You need to adopt the role of an ambassador for peace. The only way to end this war is to hold peace talks between the two sides and ensure that truth and logic prevail. Your subconscious mind needs to keep learning about why alcohol is destroying your life, why you are putting yourself in danger, and it also needs to have a freedom plan so that it can see a way out of the mess so that peace can reign once more. Only then can order and happiness be restored.

Your conscious mind is your voice of reason in this situation. The more you choose to educate yourself, the more your subconscious will pay attention and listen. It will become open to learning more but it needs to understand the facts. It needs to make sense enough for it to realize that it has been wrong in what it believed, and that it was backing a cause that would result in a damaging outcome. Eventually, once it recognizes that it has made a terrible mistake it will raise the white flag and end the fight. The subconscious is open-minded and prepared to change, but it needs to see the absolute logic and reason in the argument being presented by the other side. Sometimes it can resist and continue to fight; it will look for loopholes and will try to exploit situations using its messed-up version of reasoning. There are occasions where you will need to consciously push back against it and reinforce the truth until it falls into line, ends the battle and joins the same side.

When your conscious mind has expanded its knowledge about the dangers of drinking and the benefits of an alcohol-free life, it can then present a solid plan to get you to that place where you start to feel positive about what your future holds. Your subconscious mind likes what it is hearing, and the two sides unite and begin fighting for the same cause. The battle is over: now you can be truly free without the pain of the internal conflict you have suffered.

As you read through each day in this book, we will bring the fighting to a stop and move on to a place of harmony. We all want peace in our lives, and this battle needs to end.

Unfortunately, many of us don't even realize that this internal battle is at the core of our misery. We don't understand it, so we don't know what to do. It is very common to attempt to try to find a compromise between the two sides and spend years playing the 'drunken dictator' by moderating our drinking or quitting for a while before switching again when the conflict continues. We will talk more about moderation later in the book. For now, let's delve into willpower in a bit more detail.

Willpower (or white-knuckling it) is a bit like a muscle: when we rely on it and try to use it to achieve a goal it can become incredibly tired, to the point where it will eventually wear out. Just imagine yourself holding a heavy weight above your head; you can only do it for so long before your muscles can't take any more. Willpower works in a very similar way.

Willpower combined with a positive mindset can serve you well, but if you want to make a lasting change you will need more than this in your alcohol-freedom toolbox, and this book is going to make sure you are fully equipped as you go forward.

Take some time to think of when you (or someone else) have tried to make a change using willpower alone. Write it down in the space provided. What was the change? How did it go? Did it last?

_____

_____

_____

_____

_____

_____

Chances are you have just found an example of how relying on willpower alone doesn't work over the long term. So you need to use a different strategy – you can't just grit your teeth and hope for the best when what you want is complete freedom and lasting peace in your life.

The key in all of this is not trying to find a way to cope with the temptation and cravings to drink. This isn't about putting up with pain. Instead, you need to destroy the desire that is being driven by your subconscious mind and replace your beliefs about alcohol with totally new ones. These limiting beliefs are at the core of what drives your subconscious to fight so hard. By writing a new story and creating powerful beliefs that no longer hold you back and will serve you in a positive way, you can unlock the door to complete freedom.

You are very likely already questioning your relationship with alcohol and wondering if it is making your life better or worse. By exploring and working on your beliefs you can rip the old ones up from the roots and form new powerful truth statements that are going to serve you for the long term. When you change your beliefs you don't need willpower; it becomes redundant because you are no longer internally fighting against anything. Harmony returns and peace reigns.

We dug into your beliefs on Day 3 and looked at how they can hold you back. I recommend having a look over what you wrote down at this point as a reminder to yourself.

Today I would like you to complete an exercise to help you gain an even clearer understanding of your beliefs in order that we can start to pull them up at the roots and stop them limiting you from reaching your full potential. Try to keep in mind that these beliefs are the propaganda that your subconscious thrives on to continue the internal war.

Let's work with the question: What negative thoughts do you have that are holding you back from quitting drinking?

For example:

'I can't stop drinking. I have failed in the past whenever I have tried. I am destined to stay stuck like this.'

Or:

'If I don't drink I won't be able to relax; I will be more stressed than ever.'

Use the space provided to write down what negative thoughts you have that are holding you back from quitting drinking.

_____

_____

_____

_____

_____

_____

_____

What would be the opposite of these negative thoughts, but still totally true? Can you find examples from previous experiences you have had that prove these negative thoughts are untrue?

For example:

'I can't stop drinking. I have failed in the past whenever I have tried. I am destined to stay stuck like this.'

might become:

'Although I have failed in the past, I am learning more all the time. I am much better equipped now, and I am hopeful that this time will be different.'

Or:

'If I don't drink, I won't be able to relax; I will be more stressed than ever.'

might become:

'I have never experienced an extended time without drinking, so I don't know how relaxed I will be, I need to be open-minded and see what happens.'

Below is an example from my own journal:

Negative thought: 'If I don't drink, I won't be able to relax and de-stress each day'.

Opposite of negative thought: 'I have read that not drinking will allow me to relax; sober people have said that they are more relaxed than at any time when they drank. I also know for a fact that alcohol increases anxiety and stress. I am going to experience a period of time without alcohol and decide for myself which belief is actually true.'

Another example:

Negative thought: 'I can't have fun when I go out socially if I don't drink.'

Opposite of negative thought: 'I have never actually experienced going out socially without drinking, so I have only ever seen this from one side. I am going to try a few nights out without alcohol and see how much fun it is.'

Use the space provided to write down the opposite of the negative thoughts you identified above.

_____

_____

_____

_____

_____

_____

_____

It is important that the new statement is totally true as this is what will allow it to begin to form as a new belief for you. Avoid writing opposite statements unless you firmly believe them. In my case, I was able to start making many of my beliefs about alcohol look a lot less convincing simply by educating myself through reading books about quitting drinking and delving into what I believed to be true. But I found that over time, as I experienced things without alcohol in the real world, I began collecting cast-iron evidence that the opposite statements were true and that is when they formed as new beliefs and became really solid.

A great example of a false belief that existed for me was that I couldn't relax without drinking. I truly believed this to be totally true. Alcohol did make me relax; that was a fact. But when I deconstructed the evidence around this I realized that the sense of relaxation was false. After the first couple of drinks I would definitely feel more relaxed as the chemicals numbed my brain. But within an hour or two I would become aggressive, argumentative and snappy. I would drink even more, but any sense of relaxation had long gone.

Eventually I would go to bed. The room spun, and I would often be sick or fall up the stairs before passing out. After a night of broken sleep, I woke feeling tired and irritable the next morning. As I began the new day, my head would be pounding and I would be suffering all the effects of a hangover. I didn't realize it at the time, but my mind had been filled with the thick fog of hangover every day. It wasn't until I quit drinking that I realized I had been in an almost permanent state of being hung-over and didn't even know what a clear mind felt like.

There was no relaxation the day after drinking; my anxiety was worse, my mood was low and I couldn't function or motivate myself to do anything productive. I was simply functioning and getting through the day, with the motivation of drinking again that evening being the only thing that would keep me going.

How can this be relaxing?

After I quit, this false belief was destroyed. I started to experience what true relaxation really was. My anxiety faded, my mood lifted and I started to feel at peace in my life. There was no obsessing about drinking and stressful situations no longer sent me into a tailspin of meltdown. This was real relaxation. I began to find joy in my life and experience new activities that provided deeper relaxation and happiness. It felt so good, and I didn't want it to end.

I also realized that alcohol had ruined many social events that I had attended. In the past I had believed that drinking served to enhance them and it was what made them fun. But my beliefs were destroyed and I could now see the truth. There were birthday parties, gigs, dinner parties, weddings and other celebrations where I would ensure I drank as much as possible because I believed that the more I drank, the more fun I would have.

When I look back at the evidence it is clear that alcohol didn't make any events I attended more fun; they were fun for what they were and, in most cases, the alcohol caused me to either make a fool of myself, do something I later regretted or cause some other form of upset. This is not to mention the after-effects of drinking. This wasn't fun: it was another illusion that alcohol had created to try to keep me trapped. Alcohol really is a master of distorting reality.

I began thinking about other events or occasions where alcohol had ended up making things worse or spoiling it altogether. It even ruined my own wedding night, not that I can remember much of it. I ended up dancing on a table and being forcibly removed before passing out later in the evening. I used my journal and wrote down a list of the times when events had been spoiled in the past through drinking, and I found that this process helped me when it came to forming new positive beliefs and undoing the old ones that I was holding on to about alcohol improving my life. This worked because I explored the evidence and could clearly see how drinking was contradicting what I believed, and the more I was writing down the bigger the contradictions were becoming.

Keep looking closely at your beliefs, observe how true they really are and how they might be holding you back or limiting you. It is essential to form beliefs that allow you to become the best, most authentic version of yourself. You will need to take time to seek out the truth in what you believe and accept that some old beliefs may be totally wrong.

Use the space provided to write down any events or occasions where you feel alcohol ended up making it worse for you or spoiling it altogether.

_____

_____

_____

_____

_____

_____

Use the space provided to write down how these events or occasions you have described would have been different if you hadn't drunk alcohol.

_____

_____

_____

_____

_____

_____

_____

Reflect on your answers in the space provided and ask yourself whether the reasons you believe you like to drink alcohol that you wrote down on Day 1 are still holding true? Or do you feel that your beliefs about how alcohol improves your life aren't looking quite so solid now?

_____

_____

_____

_____

_____

_____

If you have started to find reasons why your original beliefs about alcohol no longer look so strong, you should give yourself a pat on the back – you just had a breakthrough. Don't stop looking; keep asking questions and exploring your own behaviours and beliefs.

You might discover that some things that you used to think were fun start to interest you less. Don't worry if you find yourself feeling this way. You have the power of choice to decide what you want to do, and if your preferences change over time, so be it.

Get into the habit of asking yourself three simple questions whenever you experience uncomfortable cravings, feelings or emotions.

1 What belief is driving the experience I am having now?
2 How true is that belief? Take the time to examine it and explore the reality.
3 What is the opposite of the belief that is causing the discomfort? Ask yourself if the opposite is a truer reflection of reality.

These three questions can serve you well during challenging times, it is worth using them often so it becomes your natural response to any discomfort.

Day 9 | Celebrations and setbacks

Life coach Tony Robbins coined the phrase 'What is great in this?' These words didn't truly resonate with me until a friend of mine was facing a really tough situation with his marriage and I found myself using the same phrase to help him find the good in an otherwise desperate time of his life.

The phrase also served me incredibly well when I quit alcohol. There were days when I felt really down. I wondered why I was bothering with sobriety and thought I would be better off going back to drinking again. But when I got my journal out and wrote down what was great about the situation I always managed to find plenty of positives hiding in the darkness. This gave me strength and motivated me by refocusing my mind on what I was gaining instead of what I was giving up.

Recently a friend of mine told me that his wife had been secretly meeting another man. The affair had been going on behind his back for almost two years before he found out about it after seeing a text message on her phone. He was obviously devastated. After some of the dust had settled, it was obvious that he and his wife still loved each other and they both wanted to put things right and get their relationship back on track.

After a few weeks my friend and I met up for another coffee. He had been experiencing a roller coaster of emotions, so I asked him to consider what might be great about the situation. Initially, he looked shocked, laughed at me and said that absolutely nothing was great – how could anything be great about your wife cheating!

I told him that I believed there was something great in it all and that, if we looked closer, we would find it. So we got out a pen and paper and started to write down all the positives we could find. This is what we came up with:

- His wife has cut all contact with the other man and said she is committed to the marriage; she is still with him and wants to put things right.
- Since the affair came to light he and his wife have talked about things they have never discussed before; their communication and connection had improved beyond belief.
- He has become aware of areas he needs to work on to be a better husband.
- He has realized that both he and his wife had a part to play in the affair happening.
- His wife has shown him a level of vulnerability he has never seen before.
- He realizes how much he loves his wife and how much she loves him.

- He can feel some of the trust starting to return and believes he will trust her again.
- They both believe that the affair will now make their marriage stronger and better than ever.

The point is that, even in our darkest moments, when we feel as though there is no hope and everything is going wrong, we can find something positive. Just make sure you take the time to pause and ask yourself, ' What is great about this?' No matter how bad the situation might seem.

This strategy works brilliantly for the tough days without alcohol, especially if you have a setback and take a drink when you have committed to an alcohol-free period.

It is really important to understand that setbacks are part of the journey. Almost everyone who tries to quit will have a few slip-ups along the path to freedom. So don't beat yourself up about it; instead, look for the positives, get really curious and look at the data so that you can learn from what happened and grow stronger next time.

I can't emphasize this enough – don't beat yourself up if you have a drink after quitting. Instead, speak to yourself like you would talk to your best friend. You wouldn't tell them that they are a failure and will never achieve their goal, so don't talk to yourself this way either. You deserve better than that.

I had so many failed attempts just to get through the first one or two days without drinking. Over and over again I found myself giving into my cravings and ending up right back at the start. Each time I would get my journal out and write down why I chose to drink, what triggered me, and what my emotions were like at the time as well as how I felt before, during and after drinking. This served to help me understand my own behaviour, make changes and grow stronger for next time.

I started to understand my triggers and then I took steps to disrupt the uncomfortable feelings and cravings when they began to rise up inside me. Often I would go to the gym or out for a run to shake off the difficult thoughts. This worked really well. I know other people who take a long walk, listen to music or read a book when they experience thoughts they find hard to handle.

So if you have a setback, don't start blaming yourself or talking in a negative way. Instead, treat the episode like a detective would approach a crime scene. Look at the information and the evidence with an objective, inquisitive eye and write it all down so you can grow and learn from the experience.

Quitting alcohol is like learning a new skill. Often, we have followed the same habit day in, day out for many years. Expecting to be able to change overnight without any setbacks is simply unrealistic in most cases.

Think about a professional sportsperson at the top of their game, for example the tennis player Roger Federer. He wasn't born the best tennis player in the world. He had to practise every day and had numerous setbacks along the way before he made it to the top and mastered his sport. Think about your journey to alcohol freedom as being a bit like this. It takes practice and with practice comes mastery, but don't expect to be a master on day one. Be gentle and kind to yourself and use any slip-ups as a chance to grow and evolve.

I have seen many people give up on their goal of wanting to quit drinking after a setback even though this happens to almost all of us on the pathway to becoming free. It can be easy for our mind to play tricks on us and it can cause people to stop believing in themselves if they allow it:

- 'I can never quit, I am a failure.'
- 'This is how I am destined to be forever.'
- 'I am different, I will never be "normal" like other people.'
- 'This is proof I can't do this.'

If we start listening to this kind of internal dialogue it can be incredibly demoralizing and cause us to lose momentum and enthusiasm. For some people a setback can be enough for them to stop trying. Would you give up on yourself if you had a setback?

It makes much more sense to be realistic about the fact that many people have setbacks. We need to pay close attention to them and understand that there is a big difference between allowing a setback to drag us down and a setback that can help us grow and moves us further forward. It doesn't need to 'set us back'. The only way to approach a setback is to allow it to be a teacher on our journey and use it as an opportunity for growth.

What would that look like for you? Ask yourself whether that has ever happened to you, where a setback (not just with alcohol) taught you something important and helped you grow stronger? If not, what would need to change for these moments to become opportunities to help you learn and become stronger?

This is not about planning for failure. This is about leveraging your most difficult moments into some forward movement, what I like to call 'falling forward', instead of just falling down.

What can you do to ensure you are set for success? So that if and when you have a setback you will get up sooner and come back stronger with as much positive momentum as possible.

Write your own ideas in the space provided and start to learn how a setback can be used as something 'for' you, instead of doing something 'to' you.

Write down your plan to ensure you feel well prepared for bouncing back from setbacks.

_____

_____

Use the space provided to record information about any setbacks you might have experienced in the past or any you have as you go forward. Make sure you also note down exactly what you learned from them and what you need to change to become stronger. You may find that you come back to this later or you may find you never need to return to it again.

Just as we need to learn and grow from our setbacks we should also use our victories as an opportunity to become stronger and celebrate.

I was coaching someone a few months ago who had been 20 days alcohol-free. On the 21st day she had an argument with her partner and, triggered by her emotions, decided to drink. She felt down about it, but did the right thing and learned from the setback. However, we also used this as an opportunity to celebrate her victory. Instead of her resetting herself back to day one and starting again, I explained that a better way to look at her progress was to work out her success score.

The success score was just over 95 per cent based on 20 days not drinking and one day where she had alcohol. By anyone's standards 95 per cent is a victory worth celebrating.

As soon as we reframed her thinking, so that she looked at what she had achieved as well as viewing the slip-up with curiosity and gathering the data, she felt much happier and stronger. She picked herself up from the setback and became even more determined as she went forward with a whole new vigour.

As well as considering how you perceive the information you gather on your journey I also recommend setting yourself some victory goals. When you quit drinking you generally save a lot of money, so it is easy to reward yourself with a nice treat.

I have treated myself to concert tickets, trips to the theatre, meals out and a stay at a nice hotel as rewards for my own progress. These kind of treats can be a real motivator, and it is extra rewarding if you can involve your family or friends so they feel part of the journey with you.

Use the space below to write down what you might reward yourself with at three different points on your journey. You might give yourself treats after a certain number of days alcohol-free or after successfully overcoming a challenging situation (for example the annual work Christmas party or taking your first holiday without drinking). Think about what would motivate you, get creative and write it down. When I did this exercise I gave myself a reward at 30 days, 90 days and 12 months.

_____

_____

_____

_____

_____

_____

You need to remember that you are pretty awesome for exploring your relationship with alcohol. Very few people have the courage to pick up a book like this, let alone face up to their own behaviour and choose to make a change. Be sure to celebrate your achievements and allow what you are doing to warm your heart whenever you think about it, regardless of whether you have the odd setback along the way.

Day 10 | Are you an alcoholic?

These are some of the many searches I used to type into the internet search bar when my internal conflict about my drinking behaviour was at its worst:

- Am I an alcoholic?
- Am I drinking too much?
- How much alcohol is too much?

But when the search engine gave me back the results, I found that I would skim past anything that would cause me more worry. Instead, I would look for articles that would put my mind at ease and tell me there was nothing wrong with how much I was drinking.

This behaviour is called confirmation bias – where we pay attention only to what we want to hear and choose to ignore anything that might cause us discomfort.

I would do the same with my social media accounts. I found myself always 'liking' the posts with pictures of people drinking booze or news articles telling me that wine reduces the risk of cancer. However, if I saw a piece of content telling me that red wine shortens life expectancy, I would quickly scroll past.

I carried on doing this for years, reinforcing my false beliefs in an attempt to calm myself when worries about how much I was drinking came up. Over time, I found the worries were getting noisier in my head and I was struggling to shake them off.

In the years before I quit alcohol I had become very aware that I had a problem and had become dependent on alcohol. I realized that I had to stop kidding myself and face up to the situation so I could work out how to make a change.

So was I an alcoholic? I suppose I was, although I don't really care for this term as a label. We have the power to call ourselves whatever we want, and I don't identify as an 'alcoholic' or 'in recovery'. I know these labels work as motivators for some people, but not for me. I am now passionately sober and have worked hard to be the best version of myself, so I am certainly not in recovery. If I had to have a label, I think it would simply be 'Simon who doesn't drink'.

We often think of an alcoholic as someone on a bench in a park drinking hard spirits out of a bottle in a brown bag. But I believe that all alcohol use problems are on a spectrum, and while some people have encountered difficult times in their lives that may have caused them to end up on the streets, there are even more people who are alcohol dependent and able to function day to day while maintaining their habit.

An alcoholic is loosely defined as someone who does not know when or how to stop drinking and spends a lot of time thinking about alcohol and cannot control how much they consume even when it causes problems with their family, career, health and finances.

This describes my past behaviour perfectly. Sure, I had managed to cling on to my career and functioned day by day with my family, but I was never truly happy and alcohol always came first. Maybe with a few twists of misfortune I might have ended up on that bench in the park. I wasn't really that different to someone boozing daily and living on the streets – I just had nicer shoes.

But I also believe that anyone who feels they need alcohol in their lives is to one degree or another on that spectrum of alcohol use problems, even if it is at the low end of it. They still rely on alcohol and know that they can't live without it.

The good news is that less than 10 per cent of people who drink heavily are physically addicted to alcohol. For the remaining 90 per cent, the addiction is psychological, which means it exists almost exclusively in our heads. If we can change what we think and what we believe, we can break free from alcohol.

The point I am trying to make today is that it doesn't matter whether you are an alcoholic or not. What matters is that you are here and reading this page right now, and that you have recognized that you need to make a change and you are doing something positive and proactive about it. As you keep moving forward your thinking will change and so will your beliefs. Slowly the door to the self-built cage that you have been trapped in will unlock and you will find yourself walking out to enjoy the freedom that awaits on the other side.

So if you have been asking yourself whether you are an alcoholic, forget it. Move on and instead ask yourself if you would prefer to be passionately sober instead. Focus on putting in the work to examine and change your beliefs. This is far more powerful and will serve you in an incredibly positive way.

Society likes to give people labels, but it is up to us to choose which labels we have. It is our own personal choice and we have the power to decide. Alcohol doesn't need to define us. Use the space provided to write down the terms or labels you would like to describe yourself as in the context of alcohol and sobriety. If you don't want to identify with a label, simply write you name, but do consider how you will respond if people use unwelcome terms or labels.

Mine are:

- **passionately sober**
- **sober-rebel**
- **simon who doesn't drink**
- **ex-enthusiastic drinker.**

_____

_____

_____

_____

_____

_____

_____

You may decide you don't want to have any labels, and that is completely fine. In this chapter I want to set you up for success in the future and ensure that you are prepared if and when someone chooses to label you with a phrase that doesn't feel like the right fit.

I can think of numerous occasions where people have asked me if I was an alcoholic, and I always reply by saying that I prefer to describe myself as an 'ex-enthusiastic drinker'. My response always comes off my tongue quickly because I have spent time in the past thinking about what descriptions and labels I am happy to have applied to me. So take the time to consider what feels right for you. You might find that you come back to this chapter and change your answers as you progress through the book.

Personally, I think labels are for jars, not for humans.

Day 11 | How alcohol affects your body

When I was drinking heavily I ignored any warnings about the dangers of alcohol and the risks to my health and wellbeing. I had an attitude that it simply wouldn't happen to me and I would be fine regardless of how much I drank. However, as time went by the whispers in my head about the risks of my daily drinking started to get louder until they eventually turned into a noise I could no longer silence.

I ended up with a divided heart. I wanted to quit alcohol and I still wanted to drink; it was incredibly difficult to deal with, and in the end I found the only way forward was to immerse myself in the alcohol-free life I wanted for myself. I worked on expanding my knowledge about alcohol and made sure I understood all the facts and dangers while at the same time working out which of my long-held beliefs were actually true. Through this process I was able to start taking gentle steps down the path towards freedom.

I also journaled as much as I could and spent time reflecting on my notes so I could learn and grow from my own experiences. At the same time I also connected with people on the same journey in online sober groups and made myself accountable to them by sharing my progress, my goals and my setbacks.

I mentioned on Day 9 that my behaviour had been to reinforce my incorrect beliefs about alcohol by ignoring any articles or social media posts that highlighted anything negative about alcohol. If I saw an article with the headline 'Two glasses of wine a day reduces life expectancy', I would quickly scroll past until I found something that told me the opposite and put my mind at ease. Have you ever done that?

But I knew that if I was going to change my beliefs I needed to face up to the truth about alcohol and understand the facts, even if I found it uncomfortable. By gathering all the information, I was able to make an informed decision as to how I wanted alcohol to feature in my life.

So today I would like you to do the same and start opening yourself up to the facts about alcohol. What follows is an overview of the effects alcohol can have on your body. This information might make you uncomfortable, so acknowledge any feelings that come up as you read. Tomorrow we will look at how alcohol can affect your brain.

You probably already know that alcohol can have a wide range of devastating effects that can impact almost every part of your body. Let's explore the risks we expose ourselves to when we drink regularly over the long term.

The effects of alcohol on your body:

- Hypertension – increased blood pressure
- Arrhythmia – irregular heartbeat
- Heart damage
- Liver damage and disease
- Hepatocellular carcinoma – liver cancer
- Breast cancer
- Colorectal cancer – bowel cancer
- Alcoholic hepatitis
- Mouth and oropharyngeal (throat) cancer
- Muscle cramps
- Sexual performance problems – erectile dysfunction and premature ejaculation
- Streptococcus pneumoniae and other infections of the lungs
- Osteoporosis – thinning bones
- Fatigue and tiredness
- Diarrhoea and stomach pain
- Birth defects during pregnancy
- Risk of stroke
- Pancreatitis.

Other risks we are exposed to:

- Injuries and accidents: According to NHS England, between 12 and 15 per cent of visits to accident and emergency departments in hospitals are related to incidents involving alcohol.
- Violence: every year in the UK there are over one million alcohol related violent incidents.
- Unprotected sex: with lowered inhibitions comes the risk of unsafe sex, and this can lead to unwanted pregnancies and sexually transmitted infections.

Now, I don't know about you, but when I read this list I wonder why I would ever drink a substance that can expose me to these huge and potentially fatal risks. This isn't even a comprehensive list of all the dangers, but it still serves to make it pretty clear that drinking alcohol regularly over the long term can present us with some very serious health problems. It makes me wonder how on earth this destructive substance is even legal. Do you think it would even be allowed to go on sale if someone invented it today?

Write down how you feel about drinking alcohol when you consider the risks to your health and your body in the space provided.

_____

_____

_____

_____

_____

_____

Have you ever had concerns about your health in relation to your drinking? Maybe you have worried about something on this list? Use the space provided to write down any worries you have had in the past about your health and alcohol.

_____

_____

_____

_____

_____

_____

_____

Reflect on your answers and think about how they align with what you wrote on Day 1 when you described the reasons why you believe you like to drink alcohol. You might find some of your beliefs are contradicting each other or starting to feel as though they aren't so true for you any longer.

I recall having a breakthrough moment at this point in my own journey, when I realized how devastating and life-changing the effects of alcohol can be. Yet my original belief was that alcohol was what allowed me to have fun. How could cancer or liver disease ever be fun? Sure, I may have believed I had short-term fun at the times when I drank, but in the long term I could see no fun in drinking, I could see only misery. Alcohol kills more than three million people each year according to the World Health Organisation. It does not discriminate and will happily include you in the statistics.

As my knowledge expanded I couldn't help but challenge my initial beliefs further. The more I learned, the more I questioned the logic of continuing to pour a dangerous poison into my body and expose myself to these awful risks and dangers.

Day 12 | Alcohol and your brain

For over two decades I truly believed that alcohol eased my anxiety and low moods. Even though it was getting worse year on year, I somehow convinced myself that those few hours of relief while I was drinking meant that alcohol was some kind of magical mental health elixir. I should have paused for a moment and looked at the evidence. Sure, I gave myself a couple of hours of relief while I was boozing, but when I wasn't drinking my anxiety was almost out of control. How could alcohol possibly have been helping? How had I never joined up the dots? But I didn't stop to think; I just kept on drinking to blot it all out.

Alcohol is a depressant, which means it acts like an anaesthetic and numbs us both mentally and physically. This can make us feel relaxed, less inhibited and have a higher threshold to pain. When we are sedated we are not the real version of ourselves, we are not in control and we often act very differently. Many people come back to alcohol over and over because of the short-term effects they experience and they form beliefs that alcohol helps them feel more relaxed, have fun, or sleep well. This is an illusion. Maybe we feel this way for an hour or two, but after that we usually end up experiencing the complete opposite of what we believe, yet we continue to live by our false beliefs and ignore anything that dares to suggest they might be wrong.

Alcohol starts to change our brain chemistry not long after we have the first drink. Initially we can feel much happier, even euphoric and more confident as our brain is flooded with endorphins. These are pleasure chemicals that make us feel really good. But not long after this release our brain realizes that things are out of balance and releases a depressant chemical called dynorphin to try to get back to a state of homeostasis, which is the normal balanced state the brain tries to maintain at all times

As we drink more, we enter a cycle of releasing endorphins followed by even more dynorphin and embark on a roller coaster of feelings. Over time, as we become more drunk, the pleasurable effects tend to fade and often become replaced with negative emotional responses such as anger, aggression, irritability, anxiety and even depression. Have you ever ended up experiencing negative feelings or emotions a few hours after you started drinking?

When we drink heavily over a long period of time this continual cycle can become dangerous and we can struggle to ever get back to the original state of happiness that existed before we started using alcohol. Can you remember when you last felt truly happy? When I reflected on my life I realized it was when I was in my early teens, a time when I felt carefree and joyful most of the time, before I had ever experimented with alcohol.

It's not just our mood and emotions that can be affected by drinking. Some people experience blackouts, where they are unable to remember what they did or where they went. These can be frightening and leave drinkers exposed to significant dangers when they aren't in full control of themselves.

I now understand that all the wine I was drinking was making my anxiety and low moods so much worse. It took me many years to discover this for myself, and one of the reasons I am so passionate to spread the word about the benefits of living an alcohol-free life is that the number of people who are unaware of the damage alcohol is causing their mental health is huge and very few manage to make the link between how much they drink and issues with stress, anxiety, depression or their general state of happiness and wellbeing.

I have connected with thousands of people who have cut alcohol out of their lives and seen a huge positive impact to their mental health. People who have gone from daily drinking while suffering from depression, low moods or anxiety to a place of peace, calm and happiness simply by ditching the booze.

My anxiety was so bad that I would have panic attacks and meltdowns, often just from worrying about things that hadn't even happened and usually didn't ever happen. I ended up having to take time away from running my business to find some headspace. Thankfully, this was what put me on the path to sobriety and gave me the blank canvas I needed to explore my drinking and find freedom.

I recall vividly the feeling after a couple of months alcohol-free when the dark clouds of anxiety started to fade away and the sun started shining into my life again. I began to feel happy for the first time in years. I was smiling and laughing again for the first time since I was a child. I actually started to wonder what was going on. Since I quit alcohol my anxiety has never returned, and my mood swings are a thing of the past.

Let's take a closer look at the impact alcohol has on your brain and your mental health:

- **Blackouts and memory loss:** These are fairly common among heavy drinkers, often caused by drinking too much too quickly and resulting in either partial or complete loss of memory while drunk. With heavy drinking our memory can start to suffer and we can struggle to maintain information even when we aren't drunk.

- **Depression, anxiety, stress, anger and aggression:** Many drinkers experience these negative feelings while they are drunk, but for heavier drinkers these issues can become a permanent state. Alcohol stops the neurotransmitters in the brain from working correctly, causing a negative impact on your all round sense of wellbeing. Alcohol is proven to cause depression and worsen anxiety and stress.

- **Hangovers:** As the alcohol wears off we are often left with a variety of side-effects ranging from sickness to pounding headaches. These usually pass after a day, but long-term heavy drinkers can find themselves in a state of permanent hangover and often don't realize it. If you feel tired all the time or have a constant fuzzy head, you might find you are hung-over much more often than you think.

- **Mood changes:** Alcohol can cause mood changes, both during and after drinking. I would find myself becoming snappy, stressed out and irritable, especially when I couldn't have my wine when I wanted it. My mood was low most of the time. If I wasn't drinking, I was obsessing about when I could start. I was caught in a trap of depression, and it overwhelmed me.

- **Impaired thought processing, judgement and concentration:** When we are drunk it is common to lose the ability to concentrate and we usually experience impaired judgement. But with heavy drinking over time this can be the case even when we aren't drunk.

- **Sleeping:** I used to believe that alcohol helped me get to sleep. I now know that I was never getting proper restful sleep because alcohol was preventing me from entering the deep restorative and refreshing state needed to nourish and renew my body and mind for the following day. Heavy drinkers often feel tired and have darkness and bags under their eyes as a result of the poor-quality sleep.

Use the space provided to reflect on the impact alcohol can have on your brain and your sense of wellbeing and write down anything that comes up. Have you experienced any of these feelings? Or maybe you have worried about them? When was the last time you had a hangover and how did it feel? Can you recall the last time you felt truly happy and joyful?

_____

_____

_____

_____

_____

_____

_____

_____

_____

_____

_____

As you reflect on your answers, begin to think about how good your life would be if you didn't have any of these worries or negative feelings. Imagine the joy of knowing you will never be hung-over again or that you could eliminate your anxiety or depression to almost nothing. Think how much you will gain if you made a decision not to drink any longer. Sobriety really is the gift that never stops giving, and I want you to experience this wonderful gift for yourself.

Day 13 | Does alcohol make you happy?

When I started exploring what a life without alcohol might look like I wrote out all the reasons why I believed I liked to drink. One of the first answers I wrote down in response to this question was that I drank because alcohol made things fun and it made me happy. Take a moment to look back again at the answers you gave on Day 1 when you were asked the same question. Did the words 'fun' or 'happy' come up? It is one of the most common reasons people give when they are asked why they like to drink, closely followed by answers involving 'stress' and 'relaxation'.

It is a fact that when we drink alcohol it causes a release of 'feel-good' pleasure chemicals called endorphins. These chemicals create a feeling of happiness which we usually start to experience after the first one or two drinks. But as we explored yesterday, the happy high doesn't last for long and is soon replaced with a roller coaster of feelings and emotions as we drink more and more and our brain frantically tries to rebalance back to its natural state.

I want to be really clear here. alcohol is a drug. As with any drug there has to be some kind of upside or we wouldn't waste our time taking it and keep coming back for more. So, of course, we have a brief period where we feel happier, more relaxed or disconnected from our worries. But you need to pay attention to the price of the trade-off, because alcohol is like a payday loan company with incredibly high interest rates, and what we get upfront is never worth the enormous payback we have to make in return.

What we believe is based on our past experiences and interactions. I used to drink every night and whenever I had fun I attributed it to the alcohol, which reinforced my belief that the drink was what was helping me have a good time and be happy.

I would conveniently ignore the fact that I would often end up unable to speak, struggle to walk and regularly end up being sick at the end of the night. Alcohol was the answer to all my problems and I wouldn't hear a bad word said against it.

Despite all the discomfort I experienced after drinking, I decided it was all worth it for those fleeting moments of false happiness that washed over me before the huge slump that followed as the dynorphin rushed into my brain to bring me back down with a heavy bump. Not to mention the arguments, hangovers and regrettable behaviour that left me full of shame and guilt the next day.

Now I am able to look back at my drinking life with a sense of curiosity, I can see that I was never truly happy. In fact, I was downright miserable most of the time. My mental health was worsening, and my moods were swinging like a huge pendulum; I would be snappy and irritable when I wanted to drink and anything dared to get in the way of me being able to have a bottle of my beloved wine. Alcohol was running the show – I put it in front of everything in my life. This wasn't what happiness was supposed to feel like.

Over the long term, the impact of alcohol on our state of happiness and wellbeing can be devastating. I have met people who have lost their careers, partners, homes – and sadly some people who have even lost their lives – through drinking.

So the only evidence I can find for alcohol making anyone happy is for that short period of time after the first drink or two. Other than that, alcohol causes nothing but negative outcomes, misery and sadness. Yet we keep on drinking, we keep on believing this nasty liquid is somehow adding to our lives and we place a false value on the benefits it gives us.

In order to become free from alcohol it is essential that you create new beliefs that are totally true, beliefs that are based on the facts that will serve to reinforce the lifestyle you want for yourself. Which I hope is one where alcohol no longer features in it.

When you look closer at your beliefs around alcohol I would like you to ask yourself a question: is this belief holding me back, or is it allowing me to be the best version of myself?

If you find a belief you have is limiting you and holding you back, then you should create a new belief that is still totally true but will allow you to thrive and become the person you want to be. I make no apology for repeating myself around beliefs; they are at the core of making a lasting change, and I want to ensure you become incredibly mindful about what you believe and learn how to work on them.

A great example is my past belief that 'I can't have fun without alcohol'.

When I explored this belief more closely I realized it was holding me back, so I wrote down exactly why. These were some of the answers I recorded in my journal:

- This belief holds me back because it means I have to drink alcohol if I want to have fun.
- This belief holds me back because I avoid events and experiences where I can't drink.
- This belief holds me back because I am more focused on getting drunk than enjoying the event or occasion.

Once I had identified the reasons why this belief was limiting me, I worked on creating a new belief that was totally true but would not hold me back. In this example that new belief was:

- **'I have never tried to have fun without alcohol, because I always drink. I am going to experience upcoming social events without drinking and discover if I have fun or not.'**

I wrote this before I quit drinking. At that time I had never experienced an event or night out without drinking, so it was impossible for me to say that I knew I could have fun even if I didn't drink. So I made a statement that was true for me at that point in time. I now know for a fact that I have much more fun without alcohol involved. At parties, gigs, shows, festivals and other events and nights out, I enjoy it so much more when I am fully present, in control and engaged.

I have also realized that some events just aren't fun, and it has nothing to do with alcohol. I can recall plenty of events I attended when I was drinking and they were boring or lacking the fun factor. I would still get drunk but I wouldn't have fun. Can you think of an event or a night out where you drank but didn't have fun?

I have been to two weddings since I quit drinking. The first one was the most fantastic day. I was good friends with both the bride and groom and I knew many of the guests, so I spent all day and night connecting with people, sharing stories, laughing and catching up. The time flew by, and I still hold fond memories of a wonderful day.

A few months ago I was invited to another wedding. The only person I knew was the bride and a couple of the guests. Throughout the day I felt a bit awkward, like a spare part having to make introductions to people I had never met before. I didn't really have fun or enjoy the day and ended up leaving early in the evening feeling a bit flat and slightly confused as to why I didn't have a good time. Maybe I should have put a bit more effort in.

The point I am trying to make here is that it isn't alcohol that makes something fun; it is the event itself and more specifically the people you connect with and your desire to get involved. If I had drunk at the second wedding, I still wouldn't have had fun; and if I had drunk at the first one, I would still have had a great time, although I imagine I would have ended up doing something I would later regret and spoiling it for myself. The fact I wasn't drinking at either event made no difference to the outcome when it came to how much of a good time I had.

Can you think of a time when you have experienced fun without alcohol? It might be from your childhood or more recent times. Use the space provided to describe it.

_____

_____

_____

_____

_____

_____

_____

Can you identify any areas of your life that will be less fun without alcohol in them? Write them in the space provided and describe why you believe they will be less fun.

_____

_____

_____

_____

_____

_____

_____

The fact is that you can have a lot of fun and be way happier when you don't drink. But it's no good if you just hear it from me. I am going to need you to start thinking about taking a step forward and finding out the truth for yourself in the real world.

Chances are that, if you have identified specific events or occasions that you believe won't be fun unless you drink, you have probably never experienced them alcohol-free, so you have given booze all the credit for the fun without allowing yourself the opportunity to learn the truth and form a new belief.

You may feel that drunken benders with your boozing buddies will no longer be fun and I have some news for you, you are right: they probably won't be fun. You will likely find that alcohol-fuelled events become pretty boring when you quit. Right now that might seem alarming. I recall how worried I became at the thought of missing out or not enjoying these events any longer. I worried that people would think I was boring. But a short while after I quit everything started to change as my desire to pursue healthy interests grew stronger. The idea of heading out on a boozy evening started to feel as though the last thing I would want to do; it simply seemed pointless and uninteresting. I was happy to remain friends with the same people I used to drink with, but I didn't share the same interest in this particular activity so I chose not to take part. It felt like I was being authentic and the true version of myself in my decision making.

However, some sober people I know love nothing more than heading out with their drinking friends and staying up until the early hours of the morning before driving everyone home and waking up hangover free after a great night's sleep and a lie in. You need to discover what feels right for you.

You don't need to worry too much about this right now; simply concentrate on working your way through the book and expanding your knowledge about your relationship with alcohol. Later in the book I will ask you to make a commitment to taking a break from drinking. Maybe you could start to give some thought to how you feel about this? Does it feel scary? Exciting? Or something else? Explore what emotions it brings up along with any beliefs associated with your feelings around quitting.

If you are still drinking at the moment, try to do so mindfully and pay close attention to how it feels. Journal as much as you can and become really curious about your feelings and emotions before, during and after drinking. The more data you can gather, the better. Try to get used to naming your emotions and feelings, either by writing them down or verbalizing them to someone who feels safe. Whatever you do, don't leave them lurking in your shadow.

If you have already stopped drinking, a huge well done to you! Keep working through the book and growing stronger day by day and make sure you notice how much more fun you are having in your alcohol-free world.

Finally, I would like you to think about the difference between 'pleasure' and 'happiness'. One of the keys to happiness in life is to ensure we focus our intentions on activities, behaviours and thoughts that will serve our long-term happiness. Pleasure, on the other hand, can be harmful and is usually short-lived and detrimental to our overall sense of happiness and wellbeing. Snorting a line of cocaine might bring about pleasure for a short period of time, but it doesn't serve to improve our overall sense of happiness. Begin to notice the difference and try to remove any harmful or destructive pleasure activities from your life if they are not adding to your long-term sense of happiness.

Day 14 | 12 months without alcohol

Today I want to share what happened to me after 12 months without drinking. My hope is that this will give you a good idea of what your own experience will look like, as well as motivating you as you go forward.

I have an app on my smartphone called I Am Sober, which I use to count the days, weeks, months and years since I quit alcohol. In the first few weeks after I cut the booze out of my life I was looking at this app every few hours, almost as if I was willing it to clock up another day on the counter. I became a little obsessed by it, so I totally understand why some people choose not to use apps for counting the time since they quit.

However, as the weeks turned into months and I gradually moved to a place where I was hardly ever thinking about drinking, I found that I was also rarely looking at the app other than on the big milestones. When I reached 50 days without alcohol I was so proud of myself that I took a screenshot and posted it on my social media accounts. I did the same at 100 days and at other memorable points on my journey. By sharing, I felt like it applied a positive kind of pressure to ensure that I would never go back to drinking, as I had become publicly accountable. Again, this works for some people and others aren't so keen on it, so have a think about whether this is something you would want to do.

The first year of sobriety was amazing, other than the first couple of weeks which felt like I was riding on an emotional roller coaster. After that, so many incredible things happened and new opportunities came up that would never have arisen had I not quit alcohol. Before I knew it, my sober counter app was showing a whole year without drinking; it felt like it had passed me by in a flash. When I reached the 12-month milestone I wrote down everything that had happened to me over the year so I could pay attention to how much I had gained. I think this is an important exercise that we should carry out at regular intervals to remind ourselves exactly why we are here. It is also a great idea to regularly revisit your 'reasons why' from day one to keep yourself firmly focused.

I would like today's chapter to give you an understanding of the incredible benefits that come after a long period without alcohol. I want it to give you hope and to help you see that you can gain so much by making one powerful change to your life. I appreciate that a year feels like a long time, but many of the positive changes I have written about happened after just a few months.

It wasn't all a bed of roses; as I have mentioned, the first month or two were the hardest and I had several setbacks before I managed to make one final decision to quit and cut alcohol out of my life for ever. Even after I had done this I found that in the first few weeks I was thinking about drinking almost all the time. Learning to manage these thoughts and not act on them was an important part of the process.

So what were the biggest changes I experienced over a year without alcohol?

The most notable change was to my anxiety and mental health in general. When I quit drinking I didn't do it solely with a view to getting rid of the anxiety that had plagued me for over two decades, but that is exactly what happened and it felt like I had been given an incredible gift.

I also noticed an incredible change to my face. I had taken a selfie on the first day when I quit drinking and had done the same at various points over the year. I hadn't realized how bloated my face had become and how much darkness I had under my eyes. The improvement was huge, and a few people commented that I looked years younger in the 'after' photos.

As the year went by I found myself reaching new levels of calm and peace in my life that I had never experienced before. The great thing about quitting alcohol is that you become very mindful of your feelings and emotions, and this helps on so many other levels. When you feel discomfort you no longer ignore it and instead take steps to work on any negative emotions or feelings. I now meditate every day, even if it is just for ten minutes in the morning, and I believe this has made a big difference in terms of being calm and at peace.

I also found that I became much more mentally resilient and tough. Things that used to cause me to have an emotional reaction or a childish meltdown just didn't faze me like they used to.

My relationship with my wife, my daughter, my wider family and friends also improved dramatically. I was no longer putting wine ahead of everything and found myself being fully present and engaged. I immersed myself in quality time with the people who mattered to me and felt like my connections went from strength to strength.

There have been so many incredible and unexpected things happen since I quit alcohol that I like to call sobriety the lifestyle that keeps on giving. You will need to trust me a little on this, but I have heard the same thing said time and time again and I guess waking up without a hangover never gets boring!

Take a moment to think about where you would like to be in a year from now, both in terms of your relationship with alcohol and your life as a whole. Use the space provided to write down whatever comes up. You may want to start considering some future goals. We will talk about this more later in the book when we consider a freedom plan, but start to give it some thought.

_____

_____

Day 15 | The marketing myths

Alcohol companies exist for only one reason: to make money. They will use pretty much any tactic they can to sell more units of their product. I used to buy into all the marketing messages and would actively engage with anything I saw that reinforced alcohol as something that would enhance my lifestyle or my health.

But now I have cut alcohol out of my life and educated myself about the bigger picture, I can see the marketing companies and alcohol brands for exactly what they are. I now view their adverts and social media posts with a sense of curiosity and disgust.

I recently met someone who used to work at a senior level for a major alcoholic drinks brand. She spoke about how they would hold senior management meetings to discuss exactly how they could increase their sales by targeting children and underage drinkers. They would brainstorm how to create attractive packaging to entice children into trying these addictive substances and consider strategies to position their drinks on lower shelves in stores to catch the eye of the next generation of drinkers in order to get them hooked early. This goes a small way to enlightening you about how little these corporations actually care about their customers. They want us to get addicted: it makes them more money, and they actively target kids in the process.

I often speak to people who quit alcohol who find the constant bombardment of marketing messages challenging to deal with; they sometimes find booze advertisements become a trigger that makes them feel like drinking. When this happens I urge them to view all the alcohol adverts and social media posts about drinking with more of an observational and inquisitive eye and cut out any emotional reaction.

The tactic I use to do this allows people to deconstruct the marketing messages using the 'Which means' strategy. Let's look at this in more detail so you can use it for yourself.

Let's take an advert for a fictional brand of rum which shows a guy ordering the drink at a beach bar; he then talks to a pretty girl sitting next to him as he sips the drink. Fast-forward to the end of the advert and the couple are now holding hands, smiling and walking along the sand with the caption 'Life's a beach when you drink Ruby Rum'.

So when I see an advert like this I ask the question 'Which means?' I look at the advert and ask myself exactly what message it is trying to give me. What outcome is it telling me I will get if I use this product?

The first message in the rum advert is that, if I drink this brand of rum, pretty girls will talk to me – which means? I will be more popular and attractive to the opposite sex if I drink this brand of rum.

The second message is that life will be stress free; after all, it says 'life's a beach' and is set in a relaxing beach location – which means? I will be less stressed out and more relaxed if I drink this brand of rum.

The final message is that I could find a long-term partner, as at the end of the advert the couple appear to have become an item – which means? Drinking this brand of rum will help me find the partner of my dreams.

You probably realize that all of the messages in this advert are complete nonsense, but we are bombarded by these promises of unrealistic outcomes every single day of our lives. How could drinking a particular brand of rum make you more attractive or lead to a stress-free life. In my experience the more I drank, the less attractive I became and the more stressful my life was. But when do we ever see an advert for alcohol showing someone drunk, with the real effects of the booze taking their toll?

Imagine an advert for the same rum, but this time the guy at the beach bar has been drinking all afternoon; he starts talking to the same pretty girl but her boyfriend who is sitting in the corner (who has also been on the rum all afternoon) takes exception to his advances and an argument follows. Next thing a fistfight breaks out, the police are called and the pair end up spending the night in jail. Such an advert probably wouldn't sell much rum, but would likely give a more accurate representation of the reality and the true outcome.

The fact is that the marketing companies will never tell you the truth about alcohol because they don't want you to know it. They want you to believe that there are huge, life-changing benefits to drinking their particular brand of alcohol and will always ensure there is a subliminal message within the advert that shows some kind of desirable outcome. This is usually something to do with sexual attractiveness, having fun, or a less stressful life.

The product itself takes a back seat; instead, the advertisers prefer to focus the viewer on the false benefits and outcomes. After all, a brown liquid in a bottle isn't exactly appealing, so they need to find a way to make it seem desirable to people.

If you can be mindful and curious when you see alcohol adverts in the future, you will find that they no longer act as a trigger and you can simply deconstruct them using this technique. I often smile to myself when I see an advert and quickly pick apart the 'Which means?' elements and work out what false promises they are peddling.

Find an advert that catches your eye. It doesn't have to be for alcohol. Then deconstruct it using the 'Which means?' process. Use the space provided to describe the advert:

_____

_____

_____

_____

_____

_____

_____

Now apply the 'Which means?' analysis to the advert. What outcomes is the advert promising? Are the outcomes realistic?

_____

_____

_____

_____

_____

_____

_____

As you go forward, try to be aware of the false messages in the adverts and social media posts you see. Think about what message the advert is trying to give you and ask yourself if the outcomes being suggested are actually likely. Try to observe everything with a sense of open-minded curiosity.

There is a reason that alcohol companies don't show drunk people and the real effects of alcohol in their adverts. They know that it will put people off buying their product, which will make them less money. It really is that simple – we need to become curious about the marketing messages and being much more choosy about what we believe.

Day 16 | Is the culture changing?

Recent media stories have reported that one in three young people are choosing not to drink or they are drinking moderately, with many now viewing alcohol as their parents' drug of choice. With the explosion of vaping and marijuana it may be that more youngsters are simply swapping booze for other habits that they perceive to be more trendy. Or maybe, because of the wide availability of information about the dangers of the various easily accessible substances, more young people are armed with the facts and able to make their own choices based on credible information.

It's not just young people. Across the world the number of people who drink has been steadily dropping, and in Europe, where I live, there are now 10 per cent fewer drinkers than there were in the year 2000. These reductions are largely down to people becoming aware of the true risks of alcohol. Many countries have invested heavily in health campaigns giving the message that no amount of alcohol is safe and this has clearly hit home with many people.

You may recall a time when smoking was seen as a cool and fashionable habit. Then the health warnings started to come thick and fast, and we ended up where we are now with smoking having a stigma attached to it. I believe this is where we will end up with alcohol; it is already happening and it won't be long before bottles of wine, spirits and beer carry gruesome health warning labels in an effort to deter even more people from drinking. I firmly believe that alcohol will become more and more socially unacceptable, and the number of people turning their back on booze will continue to rise.

However, governments make huge sums of money from the tax on alcohol; they also spend enormous figures on health services treating people suffering from the short- and long-term effects of drinking. This causes them a dilemma when it comes to putting people off by sharing the truth about the destructive side of drinking, because they want to maintain the revenue from the tax. But as the cost of treatment grows ever higher they will either have to keep increasing the tax or work hard to reduce the cost of health care by lowering the number of people who drink, or both. Just as for the alcohol brands, this is also a profit-making exercise for governments, and as long as the gap between the income from tax and the cost of health care remains positive I wonder how much will actually change.

That said, the tide is already turning. There was a time when being 'sober' was perceived as boring and stuffy. These days 'sober' has become a whole new lifestyle – it is more than just a choice not to drink alcohol, it is a way of life that for many has become a fashionable and hip choice that comes with an amazing journey of self-improvement attached to it. Sober is very much the new cool, and there are now festivals, events, groups and meet-ups for the sober and sober-curious. There has never been a better time to join the alcohol-free movement.

The sober movement has gained such incredible momentum, and there are some wonderfully inspiring people leading the way. Annie Grace, author of *This Naked Mind*, is one of my inspirations; she has helped thousands of people discover a new life through her work (including me) and has become a figurehead for the global sobriety revolution. There are too many others to mention individually here, but in the Resources section at the end of the book you will find a list of some of my recommended blogs where you can find out more and connect with some of these amazing people.

As well as an incredible sober movement, the last few years have seen the rise of the alcohol-free drinks market. There was a time when the only alternative option for a non-drinker was either water, a soft drink or a foul-tasting alcohol-free beer. But everything has changed for the better.

The choice of alcohol-free beers, lagers and ales is now vast, and it can be difficult to tell the difference from the real thing. There are also zero-alcohol wines and Prosecco that taste amazing. Many people love these alternative options, and they can act almost like a placebo and help to fill a void when it comes to having a grown-up drink that isn't alcoholic. However, some drinkers don't get on with them and find that they can act like a trigger and make them want alcohol. Take your time to find out what feels right for you. Part of the fun of sobriety is discovering all the new and wonderful drinks that you probably didn't even know existed.

My favourite drinks have become the incredible zero-alcohol botanical spirits that taste fantastic with a slice of lime and a good-quality tonic water. Some of the brands that I recommend checking out are Lyres, Atopia, Caleno and Seedlip. In the UK a number of options are available in most of the major supermarkets, and while the USA and Canada seem to be a little behind, with good-quality zero-alcohol options being slightly tougher to get hold of, there are new brands springing up every month and the availability is becoming wider globally. It is also easy to find what you want online (see the Resources section at the end of the book for details).

When I quit alcohol I found that in the evenings when I was sitting in front of the television relaxing I still wanted a chunky glass in my hand with something that felt like an adult drink in it. It was probably an old routine from all those years of drinking wine, but I found these alternative drinks helped me so much and enabled me to simply forget that I wasn't drinking alcohol. I have heard the same thing from other people who have quit drinking. Time and time again, I am told that finding new alternative go-to drinks has been an enormous help on the path to cutting alcohol out of their lives.

Think about what you might drink as an alternative to alcohol. Take some time to look at what options are available where you live and make a list of what takes your fancy and what you would like to try. You might be happy with a nice cup of tea or coffee – whatever your preference, consider what will fill the void for you at the times you like having a drink in your hand. Use the space provided to write your thoughts.

_____

_____

_____

_____

_____

_____

Finding a new zero-alcohol drink that feels like it is 'your' own drink can be a major factor in successfully quitting drinking. Begin to look forward to the experience of taste-testing these new and exciting products and start to get excited about what you will discover. You might even want to treat yourself to a special glass to have them in.

Day 17 | Exploring your drinking behaviour

You no doubt picked up this book for a reason. Something has made you stop and think about your relationship with alcohol. Even though it may feel tough at times I want to tell you that you have done something amazing. There is information in this book that you can never unlearn; by the time you reach the end you should be thinking very differently about how drinking features in your life and will probably be considering whether your relationship with alcohol is allowing you to be the best version of yourself or not.

Today I would like you to explore your drinking behaviour and habits in more depth. I used to be an evening drinker. As soon as I had got my daughter off to bed I would break into the red wine and would keep on drinking until I had worked my way through two or sometimes even three bottles. I was also a very secretive drinker – I was good at keeping my habit hidden from people and would go out of my way to ensure there were no clues that I was a functioning heavy boozer who had become dependent on alcohol.

I had a daily routine where I would go to the same shop each day and pick up two or three bottles of wine ready for the evening. Just the simple process of buying the wine would give me a sense of calm and relaxation as I knew I then had it to look forward to later in the day. If I couldn't get to the shop at my usual time, I would start to stress and feel uneasy and concerned that I might not be able to get my supply of booze. No matter what happened I would always manage to make sure I was well stocked up and even kept a backup supply at home just in case.

Yesterday, we looked at what you might drink to fill the void that alcohol once occupied. This can be a huge help when you still fancy a grown-up drink but don't want booze. Today I would like you to think about the times, situations and places that you drink and what steps you can take to prevent these from becoming a trigger.

I worked with a client recently who used to go for after-work drinks with her colleagues in a pub close to her office every Friday. The pub was on her walk home from work, and she couldn't resist the urge to pop inside, especially as she knew her friends were in there.

However, she was serious about cutting alcohol out of her life. She was drinking every day at home and felt alcohol had control over her and wanted to do something about it. She managed to stop drinking at home using the tactics outlined here in the book, but the walk past the pub was still causing her to crave a drink. We agreed that we had to come up with a plan to stop this.

As we talked more, she revealed that she had recently joined a new gym and she loved attending the group fitness classes. I thought that this could be the perfect alternative to the Friday after-work drinks. We ended up agreeing that she would book a class to attend after work each Friday and would head straight to the gym after work. This meant she would no longer pass by the pub and her mind would be focused on enjoying the class instead of drinking.

The strategy worked perfectly and with all the other tactics she learned she has now mastered sobriety and has been alcohol-free for almost 12 months. After a few months without drinking she felt strong enough to attend one of the Friday after-work drinks sessions with her colleagues. She had been upfront with most of them about quitting drinking and they were all supportive of her. She had already decided which alcohol-free drink she would have before she even entered the pub and ended up staying for a couple of hours and enjoying time with friends while she was fully present and engaged. There was no urge to drink as her mindset had changed from feeling like she 'couldn't have' a drink to simply 'not wanting' one.

For most heavy drinkers there are certain places, times of day and situations when the urge for alcohol is greater. It could be when you are cooking dinner in the evening or after the kids have gone to school, or it might be when you pass by a certain shop, pub or location. It is often a habit we have formed from years of the same behaviour.

There can also be specific people in your life who may pose a threat to you staying sober. If you can be really honest with yourself and identify the trigger points, then you can take steps to protect yourself, especially when you are at your most fragile in the early weeks after quitting drinking.

There is no doubt that your environment will play a huge part in you remaining alcohol-free. Read and answer the questions below to formulate a powerful plan for success. Use the space provided to write your answers.

1 Identify people that pose a threat to you remaining alcohol-free and explain why you chose each person.
2 Identify places that pose a threat to you remaining alcohol-free and explain why you chose each place.
3 Make a list of behaviours that pose a threat to you staying alcohol-free and explain why you chose them.
4 Make a list of thoughts that pose a threat to you staying alcohol-free and explain why you chose them.
5 Make a list of feelings that pose a threat to you staying alcohol-free and explain why you chose them.
6 Be totally honest with yourself and write down under what circumstances you would likely use alcohol again.
7 Create a list of warning signs that might be a trigger for you to drink.

_____

_____

_____

_____

_____

_____

_____

_____

_____

_____

_____

_____

_____

_____

_____

_____

_____

_____

Now consider the strategy I explained above. What could you change that would enable you to avoid any strong triggers or urges to drink? This could be changing a particular route you take to avoid somewhere, adjusting your routine or doing something else at the times you find challenging.

By planning in advance you will find you are well prepared to deal with any situations that may trigger you ahead of time. You don't necessarily have to do this for ever, but I highly recommend it for the first few months until you feel strong enough to handle any situation.

Use the space provided to create coping strategies you can implement for each warning sign, person, place, behaviour, thought, feeling and situation you have identified to avoid you drinking.

_____

_____

_____

_____

_____

_____

_____

_____

_____

_____

_____

_____

_____

_____

Later in the book we will make an alcohol freedom plan and will refer back to some of the strategies you have come up with to ensure you are well set for success. For now, just give some thought to ensuring you have a good idea as to how you might deal with any challenging times, people, locations or situations.

Day 18 | Thinking about freedom

You have now spent almost three weeks exploring your drinking habits and learning more about the truth around alcohol. It is time to ask yourself a question: do you want to find freedom from drinking? If I asked you to make a commitment to taking a break from drinking, how would you feel? How long would you commit to taking a break for?

If you are feeling ready to find freedom, then you are reading the right book and I urge you to keep working through the chapters daily. In the coming days we will start to look at committing to taking a break from drinking and creating a freedom plan to ensure you are well setup for success.

When I quit drinking I was at a point where I was so sick and tired of the daily routine that I desperately wanted to be sober. I have found that the more you want to be free from alcohol, the more likely you will be to succeed. I can't force someone to want to quit; I can arm them with all the facts, tactics and information, but ultimately the desire to make a positive change has to come from within.

We know that the journey may include a few bumps in the road. We should be prepared for the odd setback and be ready to learn from them, at the same time as being mindful about not letting emotions and negative self-talk take over. If we can maintain a positive mindset and feel passionate about the new life we are creating for ourselves, then cutting out alcohol is completely achievable and it can even be a fun experience.

If you are not ready to consider breaking free from alcohol just yet, please stick with the book. My hope is that your mindset will slowly start to change to a point where you might consider wanting to explore more deeply how drinking features in your life going forward.

At the end of Part 1 we will make your personal freedom plan, and in Part 2 we will put it into practice and work together each day to ensure you succeed in your new alcohol-free life.

By planning ahead we will ensure you are well prepared for any challenging situations that may arise once you have stopped drinking. The good news is that after the first few weeks without alcohol the entire experience becomes much easier. You will start to notice positive changes both internally and externally, and these often serve as a big motivator and reinforce the fact that kicking drinking was the right choice.

As part of the preparation for making your freedom plan, use the space provided to write down between three and five things that you are worried about when it comes to quitting drinking. Try to give some depth to your answers and explain why you find them a worry.

_____

_____

_____

_____

_____

_____

Now use the space provided to address each concern you have listed. Ask yourself if your worries are realistic, and also write down what you could change in your life or your routine to deal with each specific point that is troubling you.

_____

_____

_____

_____

_____

_____

If any of your concerns have not been addressed in the book yet, it may be worth searching the Be Sober Facebook group for answers from people who have faced and overcome the same challenges. However, I am confident every challenge faced in sobriety will be addressed throughout the book at some point, and I also want to reassure you that you have nothing to lose by quitting drinking. You actually have everything to gain, even though it may not feel like it just yet.

It is natural for us have worries and come up with 'what if' questions when we embark on making a change without knowing exactly what might be ahead of us. I am almost certain that any worries or concerns you have identified will be unfounded and created by your subconscious mind that wants you to stick with your old routines and habits.

If you can create rational and logical answers to address your concerns, you will begin to see the truth behind your fears and will soon realize that you have the power to easily overcome them. You may need to draw on your inner strength at times, but I have no doubt that you have the ability to remove any obstacles out of your way to allow you to continue walking down the path to complete freedom.

Day 19 | You can change, I know you can

On Day 6 we looked at 'who you are' versus 'where you are'. I want to remind you of that as it can be easy to forget. It may even be worth looking back over Day 6 and your notes again to remind yourself that this is 'where you are' at a point in time, as opposed to 'who you are' as a person.

All this can seem like a challenge, and there are going to be some obstacles along the way. But want to make something really clear. You can change! You can quit alcohol and you can find freedom. You can become 'who you are' and you should feel very excited about that. Don't feel afraid to get excited either – if you knew what amazing gifts were coming your way from living alcohol-free you would probably be like an excited kid on Christmas Eve!

I have helped thousands of people quit drinking, and most of them find the hardest part of the process is getting through the first few days and feeling fully empowered in making a final decision to be alcohol-free. As soon as you have made that decision you will be on the path to forming new habits and the more you practise the new habits, the sooner they will start to become your new normal way of doing things. It gets easier and easier as time passes; often the first few steps are the toughest to take.

Now I already know that you can do this. I know you have the inner strength, the determination and the courage to stand tall and that you want to be the best version of yourself. I also know that you want this badly, for you, your family, your friends, your health, your career and, above all, your happiness and wellbeing. You wouldn't be reading this book otherwise.

The reason I know you can do this is because I have worked both one-to-one and in groups with thousands of people and I have seen them change. I have witnessed their struggles, and I have watched in awe as they find new levels of resolve, mental strength and self-determination that emerge when they become hungry for the incredible new life that awaits them. They smash obstacles out of their way, they sit with uncomfortable thoughts and cravings in the knowledge that they will pass, they trust the process and they experience change. They understand that there is no running away from this and that they have to go through it to come out stronger and better on the other side.

They stop making excuses, they take responsibility for themselves and their actions and they own their new life choice with complete pride and passion. Don't worry if you don't feel quite like this just yet, I just wanted to let you know that I believe in you. I am almost certain that I have worked with people who have drunk more than you did, who have ended up in worse situations than you are in right now and believed they could never change. But they have done it, they have broken free, and I often see posts on social media that say 'If I can do this, so can you' – and believe me, this is so true.

I have worked with people who have had tears streaming down their face, who have suffered appalling childhood trauma and formed a firm belief they are destined to stay stuck and addicted for ever. Yet they have found the determination and belief within themselves and committed to learning how to break free before going on to create a new and happy life for themselves.

When we have removed the outdated stigma of 'alcoholic' and people understand how much they stand to gain, how good life can be and how wonderful the community is that they are about to join, they see hope, they start to feel positive. They see others believing in them, and they begin to realize that they really can do this.

Confidence starts to grow. 'I can't' shifts to 'maybe I can'. One foot gently steps in front of the other, and they begin to walk down the path to freedom. Not alone, but with the support of an entire global movement holding their hand, willing them forward and knowing they will make it.

Once the first week or two are out of the way, 'maybe I can' shifts to 'I absolutely can' with the added words 'and nothing is going to stop me'. I have personally witnessed these changes, and that is how I know that, no matter how tough it feels right now, you have the ability to change and that your time to do so is right now. Let's write a new story and change your life in ways that you never thought possible.

This is why I have been asking you to put in the pre-work and planning before we look at making a decision to either take a break from drinking or to quit alcohol altogether. By exploring topics including what alternative drinks you will have, what challenging situations you might face and how to handle them, you will be well prepared and set for success. Winston Churchill said that when we fail to prepare, we should prepare to fail. The sentiment of this statement is right, and it is your responsibility to put the work in and to be fully prepared for whatever comes up. I can't do that for you. I can show you the way, but you need to take ownership in this. Just like a soldier heading into battle, make sure you complete your training, have the right equipment and a team around you that you can trust with your life. Thankfully, we are not heading into war, but we are sure to face a few battles on the journey.

The key in all of this is your mindset. If you can get yourself into a positive frame of mind and see ahead of you a new life free from alcohol, you will find it will make things so much easier. Instead of feeling like you are losing something, think about how many incredible things you will be gaining. Think of that soldier who failed to prepare – what is their mindset when they are about to head into battle? They will probably have huge doubts; they know that the enemy is stronger, better equipped and able to exploit their weaknesses because they haven't prepared – either physically or mentally – for what is ahead.

Again, you aren't going into war, or anything like it, but it seems like an apt analogy when it comes to highlighting the importance of being prepared and taking ownership and responsibility for yourself.

I would urge you to keep looking at the reasons why you picked up this book, the reasons why alcohol is holding you back in your life, and know that you will be unleashing the very best version of yourself by making the decision to cut drinking out of your life. These can serve as excellent reminders, especially if you feel yourself having a wobble or begin feeling like taking a drink will help.

At any point, if you start to feel as though an area needs more work, don't ignore it, go back and refresh yourself, research it and work on it until it sticks. Use your journal to identify any areas of weakness that come up as you go forward, be totally honest with yourself and take the time to put the work in. There is no rush and you are under no pressure, so take your time to feel confident in all you learn.

Make it a habit to think before you act on your thoughts and feelings. Just because a thought comes into your head it doesn't mean you need to respond to it. We have around 60,000–80,000 thoughts every day, but when one relating to alcohol pops up after we have quit it seems to be louder than the rest. Learn to observe the thoughts, then let them pass you by.

Try to feel your feelings instead of reacting to them or overthinking them. Once you have recognized that an uncomfortable feeling has arrived, take the time to identify specifically what it is. Can you label it? Is it, for example, anger, loneliness or sadness? When you can identify how you feel you can try to release it. The worst thing you can do is to try to suppress it; you need to *feel* it. Work on building a list of methods that allow you to feel and release your feelings. Below are a few examples of things I have done to feel and release my own feelings rather than use my energy dwelling on them.

- **Anger:** Shout it out loud, punch a cushion, or jump into some vigorous exercise. I even purchased a stretchy toy that I can twist and pull when I feel angry.
- **Sadness:** Hug someone close, meditate, exercise.
- **Fear:** Do something courageous. Laugh in the face of your fears.
- **Shame/guilt:** Talk openly and honestly about it. Share your story with someone close to you.

An excellent strategy is to use your journal to write down what you are feeling at three different times during the day – morning, midday and evening. This will help you to form a habit of naming your feelings, acknowledging that they are with you and bringing much more awareness to them to help you end avoidance and suppression.

Use the space provided to list which emotions tend to trouble you and which ones you experience the most often.

_____

_____

_____

_____

_____

_____

_____

Now I want you to think back to your past. Was there a time, perhaps during childhood, where any of the emotional responses you have identified were formed? For example, if you experience shame often, was there an episode that involved you feeling overwhelming shame? Have you carried it with you into adulthood? Use the space provided to explore your emotional responses and their roots further.

_____

_____

_____

_____

_____

_____

_____

When we bring awareness to the root of our emotional reactions we can start to understand them better and begin to catch ourselves when the emotions stir up inside of us. By bringing this out into the light you can also take steps to heal any past trauma, neglect, hurt or pain that you might still be holding on to from the past.

Can you think of a time when you have moved from being caught in an overwhelming spiral of emotion and something or someone has caused you to step out of it and return back to your usual self? Sometimes it can be the words of another person, or it might be an action you took to dissipate the strong emotions. It can feel as though a switch has been flicked and we are almost instantly no longer emotional, rather like we have been snapped out of it. If you have experienced this, write it down in the space provided.

_____

_____

_____

_____

_____

_____

_____

Another excellent technique for managing emotions and overwhelming thoughts is to close your eyes, breathe slowly in and out through your nose, and, as you relax, visualize yourself standing alone holding a helium-filled balloon. Then imagine that the thought or emotion you want to let go of is in the balloon and feel yourself releasing the balloon and watching it float up into the sky. It gets smaller and smaller as it floats higher. Once it is out of sight, the thought is gone. Play this like a movie in your mind. The more you use techniques like this, the more power and choice you will have over what thoughts you act upon. You will start to feel much more in control, especially if you have a noisy brain like mine.

I also recommend doing a short daily meditation – even a ten-minute daily exercise is enough to bring about a feeling of relaxation. The more you meditate, the better you will become at keeping your mind calm and still   it is well worth putting a bit of time and effort into this.

Although it might feel as though you are alone on this journey, this is far from the truth. Make sure you connect up with Facebook sober groups, share your story in these safe spaces and engage with other people who are going through the exact same experience as you. I am confident you will find this a real help.

Another brilliant habit to learn is reframing the way you talk to yourself. When you hear unhelpful talk in your mind, use it as an alarm bell and quickly rework unhelpful statements into something that is totally true but also positive and in line with your goals.

Here is an example of my own unhelpful self-talk around the time I quit drinking:

'You can't do this; you need wine or you will never be able to relax and have fun.'

I would reframe something unhelpful like this into:

'I don't yet know if I can do this, but I am going to give it my best shot and I am also going to discover if I can relax and have fun without alcohol involved.'

It was early days in the process, so I couldn't say with certainty at that point whether I could reach my goals or whether I could experience fun and relax without drinking, so I needed to ensure the statement was totally true while still being positive in its tone.

As time passed by, that statement changed to:

'I now know I will never drink again. I am having more fun and feel more relaxed than ever before without alcohol in my life.'

But it had to be true and I had to have felt things change in order to be able to make a statement like this, and that took a little time because I had to experience it for myself in order for it to become a reality.

Just be mindful of how you talk to yourself internally and keep working on maintaining a positive mindset. I often think how choosing an alcohol-free life is a little like the liquid version of becoming vegan. When someone is vegan they are incredibly passionate about it. They don't feel deprived because they can't have meat and dairy products; they have chosen a lifestyle that they want for themselves and they are incredibly proud about it. If you approach sobriety with the same attitude and see it as a journey of self-discovery and growth, not just quitting drinking, you are likely going to love your new life. So start thinking like a 'liquid vegan' and you can smash sobriety and have fun at the same time.

Think about someone you know who is really passionate about something they do. What are the characteristics of that passion? What can you learn from their passion that you could use in your own journey of self-improvement?

I have mentioned people who choose to be vegan – they are often passionate and proud of their lifestyle choice and excited to be part of a movement that they feel part of. Take a moment to think about the elements of sobriety that you feel passionate about. Maybe it is the sense of joining an awesome community or the feeling of becoming a sober-rebel or liquid vegan?

Use the space provided to write down everything that excites you about sobriety alongside anything you can think of that would make you feel proud and passionate about being alcohol-free.

_____

_____

_____

_____

_____

_____

_____

Use your answer to light the fires of passion to help ensure you are motivated, positive, energized and excited in an alcohol-free life.

Don't worry if you struggle a little with this exercise; just write down whatever comes up. But do ensure you spend some time thinking about your attitude towards a life without alcohol and work on being as positive and passionate as possible. If you need extra help with this, there are a number of motivational videos on the Be Sober YouTube channel that will help (see the Resources section at the end of the book for more details).

I am not looking for you to falsely convince yourself that an alcohol-free life is wonderful. You need to truly believe it for yourself by approaching the whole journey with an open mind and paying attention to the positive changes and improvements you will notice as you gain momentum on your own journey.

If you can adopt an attitude of being part of an incredible and powerful community and become really proud of your achievements, it will make a huge difference in terms of how you approach a life of sobriety.

Day 20 | Negative self-talk

I have mentioned self-talk several times already. Today I would like to explore it in more depth and ensure that you feel fully equipped to deal with any negativity that might arise in your mind.

I used to beat myself up internally by constantly being self-critical and talking to myself in a negative way. I would often tell myself that I could never succeed at quitting drinking and that there was no way out of the trap, so I was destined to endure a lifetime of addiction.

This constant internal dialogue of negative self-talk would get me down; I would allow it to control how I felt and how I behaved. I could find myself in a terrible mood for several days as the result of even a single negative thought that had entered my head, which I had then latched on to and acted upon.

Thankfully, I was able to break free from alcohol, despite telling myself on numerous occasions that I couldn't do it. I also learned so much about being mindful of the way that I talked to myself. I want to share what I learned in the hope that it serves to make you more aware and stronger as you go forward.

I don't know many people who don't experience negative self-talk to one degree or another. We have already seen how we have around 60,000–80,000 thoughts every single day, most of which we simply allow to pass us by without acting on them. Negative self-talk is just another one of those thoughts – we think we can't do it, we think we are a failure, we think we aren't worthy. But these thoughts can touch a nerve and usually stand out among all the other thoughts passing through our minds. They often get our attention, and then we grab hold of them and start to believe them to be true and react emotionally as a response.

If you feel as though negative self-talk is holding you back, then I recommend you explore the strategy that I use to overcome it and take back control. The first step is to fit yourself with a 'virtual alarm' system. What I mean by this is that you need to ensure you have a method of alerting yourself when a negative thought arises or unhelpful self-talk starts happening in your head. My alarm was to say out loud to myself the words 'negative self-talk'. This did attract the odd strange look when it happened in the middle of the supermarket, but it worked. It meant that I was now very aware of the thought that had the potential to disrupt my state of wellbeing.

Then, once you have become aware of the negative thought, ask yourself whether you would talk to your best friend in the same way. In almost every case the answer would be no, I would never talk to them like that.

For example, you had a long streak without drinking and then had a drink after 30 days of being alcohol-free. The negative self-talk in your head is calling you a failure and telling you that you can never achieve a life of sobriety. As soon as you notice the thoughts, write down exactly what the negative statements are, so you have complete clarity on them. This process alone can enable you to see them in a more rational light, especially if it is clear that what you are thinking is completely untrue.

Then ask yourself what you would say to your best friend if the situation was reversed. I doubt you would call them a failure or tell them they can't achieve their goal. The likelihood is you would tell them to learn from the setback and reinforce how well they had done. You would then reassure them that they can achieve sobriety and explain that setbacks are an opportunity to learn and grow stronger and this is just part of the journey to freedom.

So when you hear the alarm going off in your head, get really clear on what the negative self-talk is saying to you and then reframe it to exactly what you would say if you were talking to a good friend. This can be an incredibly effective way of quickly snuffing out any unhelpful comments created by your own mind. If you can use your journal to do this, all the better. Learn to become your own best friend and talk to yourself with the loving kindness you deserve.

If you experience negative self-talk in a place where you are able to sit quietly and close your eyes, I also recommend a visualization exercise. As you sit quietly, close your eyes and breathe steadily in and out through your nose until you feel relaxed. Concentrate only on your breath, and try to allow your mind to become free of any thoughts. Allow calmness to wash over you.

If any thoughts appear or you find your mind wandering while you are doing this exercise, simply acknowledge them and then bring your attention straight back to the breath flowing in and out through your nose. Use your breath as your anchor.

Next, visualize yourself sitting on the bank of a fast-flowing river of rapids. The rapids and rushing water represent your thoughts. Sit in stillness and simply observe them passing you by and away into the distance. Continue to sit and watch them as they come and go. Don't get into the water and allow them to wash you away. As you sit with your thoughts and observe the fast-flowing river of thoughts, you will find your mind calms down. As it does so and you have fewer thoughts passing through, try to slow down the speed of the water, ideally to a point where it becomes still, just like your mind.

You may need to practise this, and it can take around ten minutes to completely still your mind. The more often you do it, the better you will become and you will be able to experience a feeling of complete calm by using this exercise.

Use the space provided to give some examples of how you have talked to yourself in a negative way in the past.

_____

_____

_____

_____

_____

_____

Now, using the same statements you have written above, write down what you would say to your best friend if they approached you for support in the same circumstances.

_____

_____

_____

_____

_____

_____

Earlier in the book we talked about how our inner child often has a part to play in our actions in adulthood. Negative self-talk is often driven by our inner child. As you know, my inner child reacts badly at the slightest hint of being abandoned or rejected, and I noticed how my negative self-talk tied in with this. When we experience pain, hurt or trauma as a child we try to soothe ourselves, but we can't process the emotions and generally end up deciding that we must be to blame. We can carry this sense of blame throughout our lives and we often overcompensate by trying to overachieve, pleasing other people and struggling to say no, all of which can lead to internal discomfort and unhelpful self-talk.

If this sounds familiar, please take the time to learn how to show your inner child that they are safe, loved and cared for. As with so many areas of sobriety, this all starts with noticing and becoming more mindful. In this instance, try to catch yourself when it is the child talking instead of the adult.

Here is an example of my own negative self-talk after my wife declined my invitation to go out to dinner one evening. 'Why would she say no? She has rejected you! She obviously doesn't love you. Why would she turn you down if she loved you? She just isn't interested in you any longer. You have been together for such a long time she is probably bored of you by now.'

You can see the link between my fears of being rejected and abandonment and the negative self-talk over what was a polite 'Not tonight, I don't feel like it' from my wife. I know that this was my inner child speaking, and we owe it to ourselves (and our child) to work on bringing both versions of ourselves into harmony with each other. Just like inner conflict around alcohol, when these two aren't on the same team it can cause a painful sense of disruption.

There is an excellent book called *Growing Yourself Back Up* by John H. Lee. If you are noticing that your inner child is causing discomfort, I strongly recommend you read or listen to this and explore your internal relationship deeper.

Can you identify how your own negative self-talk links with your inner child? Think about events or behaviours (especially those of your parents) from the past that may have left you feeling hurt. Maybe you were ignored, felt unloved, were insulted, shamed or abused. Be gentle with yourself – I don't want you to stir up painful memories; I simply want you to see if there is a connection with the way you talk to yourself and your inner child. Use the space provided to write your thoughts and identify whether there are specific triggers.

_____

_____

_____

_____

_____

_____

_____

_____

_____

_____

_____

So is it the adult who is doing most of the negative talking or the inner child?

Negative self-talk is often described as cognitive distortion. Psychologists use this term to describe unrealistic or inaccurate explanations for what is going on that leads to unwanted emotions and moods.

Most people talk negatively to themselves at times. You can use this to your advantage by starting to notice when other people display cognitive distortion. Often when we are talking negatively internally we will also express it verbally in an attempt to seek reassurance from others. Listen when people are speaking to you and notice any negative self-talk you hear, as this will help you become skilled at paying closer attention to yourself.

Another simple tactic is to pause when you notice any internal dialogue that is causing discomfort and say 'Cancel, Cancel, Cancel'. This is an excellent way to become really mindful at the same time as disrupting the chatter in your mind. In many instances, it will enable you to move on by distracting yourself as the internal talk weakens.

I have also managed to silence negative self-talk by intentionally changing my internal voice tone. Think about how the tone of voice that people use can affect the way we feel. If someone uses a sarcastic tone, it can make us feel embarrassed or ashamed, for example. If you can apply a label to your internal tone of voice, for example 'judgemental', 'angry' or 'disappointed', then you can quickly change the tone. A soft tone that sounds caring, empathetic or loving is not going to impact you in the same way. Try practicing this technique.

You deserve to be positive and happy. Pay attention when negativity creeps in. Catch it early and use one of these tactics to get back in control. Most of the time our internal dialogue is so far from the truth that it is laughable. If you need to take steps to calm your mind, use meditation or visualization until you find stillness. If this is a major problem for you, spend some time learning more about overcoming the problem. You might like to read the book *The Self-Talk Solution: The Proven Concept of Breaking Free from Intense Negative Thoughts to Never Feel Weak Again* by Stuart Wallace.

One other tactic you might like to try is called PASSES. The reason I called it this is because that is what always happens: it passes. No state is permanent, and you will soon move beyond it and find that the negativity ends. When you find yourself engaging in negativity use this word, say it to yourself and make sure you have the following process close to hand. You might want to consider keeping it on your phone so you can easily access it.

The PASSES process

P – Pause This is the most important step as it allows you to disentangle yourself from the web of uncomfortable feelings and will allow you to make a conscious choice about what to do next.

A – Acknowledge Instead of attempting to suppress the feelings, welcome them in and acknowledge they have arrived. When we try to resist, the feelings persist and get stronger. Simply accept them, regardless of how they make you feel.

S – Slow down and breathe Begin breathing slowly and steadily in and out through your nose. If you can find somewhere to sit quietly, it is beneficial. Focus only on your breath. Follow it in and then follow it back out of your nostrils. If your attention moves away from your breath, bring it back again without any judgement or self-criticism.

S – Stay where you are Stay until you experience the discomfort weakening and fading away. This usually takes a few minutes, but don t rush. Take as long as it needs and don't try to force it.

E – Exhale As you feel yourself becoming calmer, try to notice where in your body you can feel the discomfort the most. I often feel mine in my heart or my stomach, but we can carry it in many different locations. Once you have pinpointed this, take a slow deep breath in and then exhale out from the area where you are holding the feeling. Visualize it leaving your body and floating away as you let it go.

S – Show yourself the truth Once you have completed the exercise, take the time to look at what caused you to feel this way. Explore your beliefs and the truth around whatever pulled you into the discomfort. It might be that you need to reflect on your journal entries or dig deeper to get clarity. It is important that you put the work into understanding the truth around any limiting beliefs you might hold and taking steps to change them permanently.

If the talk is coming from your inner child, learn to pause. Recognize that your child has taken control, and as the adult reassure your inner child that you will take care of the situation and you will protect them. Remind them that they are safe and loved. When we bring this increased level of awareness, it often quickly snaps us back into being the adult and we become more rational and much calmer very quickly.

Day 21 | Is your heart divided?

As you have been reading through the chapters, you may have still been hanging on to beliefs that alcohol might still benefit your life in some kind of positive way. Maybe part of you still believes that drinking really is the key to relaxation, having fun and living a stress-free life. If so, be totally honest with yourself and keep reading. I want those false beliefs to vanish, and I want you to keep reminding yourself that they are not only wrong but are also holding you back from experiencing a life-changing transformation.

Have you ever experienced a divided heart? The feeling of wanting two things at the same time that conflict with each other? It is a painful and uncomfortable state to find yourself in. The wife of my friend who I talked about on Day 9 had a divided heart. She had feelings for the guy she was having an affair with and also loved her husband; she wanted both of them but knew she could never have what she desired and live in peace and happiness. This caused her to lie and sneak around, which may have enabled her to get what she wanted for the short term, but in the end it all came crashing down and she had to make an incredibly difficult decision and end the pain at the same time as dealing with the fallout from her self-destructive behaviour.

In the last few years before I quit drinking I felt exactly like this. My relationship with red wine had lost the sparkle it once had; it had become toxic, yet I felt like I still needed it in my life as I firmly believed it was helping me with my anxiety and I couldn't have fun without drinking. At the same time I had started to become curious about a life of sobriety. My head had been turned by the promises of what might await me in an alcohol-free life, and my heart was becoming more and more divided. I felt like half of me needed to drink and half of me wanted to be sober.

As we have explored previously, this internal conflict can be a very uncomfortable experience. You can end up feeling like you don't know what to do for the best. I often found myself drinking more just to silence the guilty thoughts and negative self-talk about drinking. It sounds ironic, but it made sense to me and it felt like the only logical solution at the time.

In the end I did make a choice and decided that I had to end the pain that alcohol was causing me to feel. But it took me a long time to work it out for myself and get where I wanted to be. I am happy to tell you that if you have feelings of a divided heart you don't need to sit with them for long; you can do something about it and end the pain and discomfort for good.

With hindsight, I wish I had acted as soon as I started to have the feelings of a divided heart. I should have acknowledged the feelings and then decided that if my head was being turned towards sobriety I would take a break from alcohol and see how it felt, but it didn't even cross my mind.

Then at the end of the break from drinking I should have made a further decision as to whether I needed booze in my life any longer or not. But I didn't do that. I kept on drinking and tried to blot out the discomfort I was experiencing. It was the only solution I had for dealing with feelings and emotions after spending most of my life running away from them.

We talked earlier in the book about inner conflict and how the only way to end this is by creating harmony between the two sides that have gone to war in your head. I make no apology for repetition on this point. It is the single most common reason people go back to drinking after they have quit, and I want you to become acutely aware of any conflict that exists inside your mind.

You have to keep reminding yourself that there is simply no point in drinking; all you are doing is stoking the fires of war by taking sides. You may believe that you will go back to the place of blissful ignorance, but it has gone: it no longer exists and you can never return. Don't waste your time or your energy by finding out the hard way.

Do you have a divided heart? Use the space provided to write down any conflicting feelings you have. Then reflect on them and get curious about which of these conflicting feelings will serve you best and which are holding you back.

_____

_____

_____

_____

_____

_____

There are a number of tactics that I recommend using to end the feeling of having a divided heart once and for all. Read through these, and then apply them by working through the questions that follow.

- **Work on obtaining new information that makes your current beliefs untrue:** In my case I was telling myself I needed to keep drinking as I believed it helped ease my anxiety. But after some time without alcohol I knew this belief was completely untrue. Look closely at your beliefs and search for new information so you can find the real truth about them.

- **Reduce the importance of one of the beliefs that is causing you pain, while increasing the importance of the other:** For example, you could consider the long-term damage that alcohol causes and recognize how important living a long and healthy life and seeing your family grow is to you. This reduces the importance of the first belief and increases the importance of the second one.

- **Change or eliminate one of the behaviours or beliefs that is causing you pain:** This can present short-term problems for people as it can seem difficult to change habits that have become engrained for a long time. Hopefully, you are already wondering how much truth your beliefs hold and whether your behaviour is holding you back from being the best version of yourself. As you keep moving through the book and exploring your relationship with alcohol more deeply, my hope is that you will feel ready to commit to making a decision to cut alcohol out of your life and make the change you want.

In the space provided, record any new information you have obtained that is making you feel as though some of your beliefs are untrue.

_____

_____

_____

_____

_____

_____

Now think about how you could reduce the importance of one or more of your beliefs about alcohol, while increasing the importance of those that conflict with them. Record your thoughts in the space provided.

_____

_____

_____

_____

_____

_____

Have any of your beliefs or behaviours shifted, changed or been eliminated already? Write down how they have changed in the space provided.

_____

_____

_____

_____

_____

_____

_____

Don't worry if none of your beliefs or behaviours have changed yet. While it would be wonderful if you have felt a change, it is still early days and we have a long way to go. I wouldn't expect them to have completely shifted just yet.

However, if you have felt changes already, then make sure you celebrate this as a breakthrough. No matter how you feel, just write down whatever comes up for you when you consider the questions.

Day 22 | The habit of change

We are fast approaching the end of Part 1, and I will soon be asking you to make a personal commitment to taking a break from drinking. Today I would like you to think about what changes you might need to make in order to protect yourself and stay alcohol-free during your break from booze.

Do you need to change the places you visit?

Do you need to change the people you engage with?

Do you need to change what you have in your home?

By removing obstacles, it is possible to make the process of quitting drinking much easier. Imagine if I left an open box of chocolates unattended in your kitchen. You would most likely eat one, right? But if the chocolates weren't there in the first place, they would never pass your lips.

Change can feel like a scary prospect, especially when we start to convince ourselves that we might not achieve the goals we have set. People often stay stuck where they are and put up with discomfort rather than face the fear and uncertainty of changing something in their lives. Stop any negative thinking right now. If you have followed the steps in the book so far, then you are well on track to be set for success as you go forward.

Don't be that person. Making change in your life is much easier than you think. Stop telling yourself stories about tomorrow and forget the past that you can't change. Stay present and focus on today. You can start to learn the habit of change by making small adjustments to your life that feel manageable and achievable.

It can be all too easy to fall into habits that don't serve us in a positive way. Only recently I found myself working incredibly long days. I wasn't allowing any time for myself, and I was neglecting my family by putting my work in front of them; it was starting to feel similar to my behaviour with alcohol, which used to come before them all the time. I knew that I needed to make a change.

The first step was to become aware that something needed to be different. By keeping a daily journal it becomes very easy to identify any areas of your life that might need adjusting. Once you have brought the areas of discomfort out into the light, you can then make a decision about what you should do for the best. You need to be honest with yourself – if you play it down or convince yourself everything will be fine if things stay as they are, then you are only fooling yourself.

In my case I decided that I needed to impose some personal boundaries. Rather than start work half an hour after getting out of bed at 7am, I would keep my phone and computer off until 9am. I would use this extra time to enjoy the company of my wife and daughter. I also set a strict finish time as I often find myself working until beyond 7pm in the evenings. Going forward the computer would be shut down no later than 6pm so I could prepare the evening family meal and hear about how my wife's and daughter's days had been.

You might think that this seems like a simple change to make. It was, but until I had recognized that I didn't want my work hours to stay this way and that I needed to impose some personal boundaries, I would have stayed stuck in the same place with the same routines – burning myself out, increasing my own stress and feeling like I never have time for myself or my own family.

Change is simple. We need to become aware, consider our options, then make a firm decision and stick with it. By using a journal and writing out the pros and cons of a change, it can give us the insight we need to reach the best final choice for ourselves.

You may have heard of 'microhabits' – a microhabit allows you to bring small changes into your life with the minimal level of difficulty. For example, you may want to get fit but the prospect of visiting the gym on a daily basis seems overwhelming, so instead you could commit to working out at home for ten minutes each day. Slowly, over time, you start to reap the rewards of the change you made from your new and healthy microhabit. You might decide to increase the amount of exercise you do over time or you might even begin to venture to the gym as your confidence grows.

Micro-habits can be the catalyst for change, and they can also ease us into the habit of making more powerful and lasting adjustments to our lives. These are a few examples of small adjustments that are incredibly easy to make and will help bring about a habit of change.

- Commit to working on a project, hobby or activity and create the time to do it.
- Clean up immediately as you go (I need to start doing this!).
- Stop complaining and radiate positivity.
- Set your alarm earlier.
- Make healthy food choices or swaps.
- Exercise for ten minutes a day.
- Sleep on the other side of the bed.
- Meditate for ten minutes daily.
- Take on some extra household chores.
- Stop comparing yourself to others.
- Read more.
- Stop doing things to please others – practise saying 'no'.
- Drink more water.

I want you to get out of the mindset that this is all too hard and that you will be making your life more difficult by 'going through' change. Adopt a positive mindset that any change you choose to make is positive and that you are doing it in order to improve your happiness and all round wellbeing. There is no downside; you are only limited by your own mind and any false beliefs you might be hanging on to.

I also want you to keep in mind that you are doing this for the future you. Take a moment to visualize yourself in five years' time. Can you see what that person looks like? Do you want them to be stuck with the same habits and routines? Or does something need to change in order to remain on track and fulfil the visions you have for yourself?

How would you feel if I asked you to make one small change to your life today? What would it be? Would you stick to it?

If you feel ready to embrace change in your life, use the space provided to write down what you want to change right now. Don't make it too hard. Try to keep it simple and adopt the microhabit approach to ensure you don't feel overwhelmed.

_____

_____

_____

_____

_____

_____

_____

The goal is for you to recognize that you can easily make changes to your life if you want to and it really isn't as difficult as you think. You have the power and you are in control.

Would you be willing to make one small change every day for the next week? If so, make a commitment right now and write your daily changes down in your journal. Make sure you track your own progress and notice if you begin returning to your old habits or neglecting your new commitments.

You may be saying to yourself that making small changes is easy, but when it comes to the bigger things you feel as though you are stuck and unable to switch out of your old ways. Just like small changes, you can also make bigger ones, even if it feels difficult to do it. Try not to lose sight of the fact that we have the power of choice in everything we do in our lives. Sometimes the choices can feel limited or there might not be an obviously positive one, but the fact remains that the choice remains our own. We can either run away from the fear of making a decision or we can step up with courage and embrace change in our life.

I strongly suggest taking a little time over your decisions when it comes to bigger changes. Try to avoid running with an idea immediately just because it entered your head. Remember what I said about us having over 60,000–80,000 thoughts a day: you don't need to act on them all and should take the time to thoroughly consider which ones you give your time and attention.

To succeed with change you need to ensure you set up your environment for success. For example, if you want to learn to play the guitar but the nearest instrument is kept at your friend's house who you only visit once a week, you simply won't be able to practise or play enough to make any significant progress. Whereas if you keep a guitar close at hand along with anything else you need to learn to play, you will find yourself practising more and progressing far more quickly.

Equally, by surrounding yourself with anything that reinforces your old habit you will keep yourself stuck. This is why I encourage people to remove all alcohol from their house at the time they choose to take a break or quit drinking altogether.

Successful change also requires education. If you are learning to play a new instrument, you will need some tuition or you probably won't get very far. That might be from a tutor, a friend, books or online video tutorials. Try to align yourself with people who share the same interest as you and can help you progress further and faster.

If you try to go it alone, the chances are that you will struggle; if you surround yourself with a supportive team who truly want you to achieve your goals, you will feel encouraged, supported and accountable.

You can turn your small changes into big ones. I have seen many people who have started an exercise programme with just a few minutes of commitment each day and then moved on to a more rigorous training schedule that has seen them smash their goals and become fitter than they have ever been.

If you don't make time for change, you will probably struggle. Think about how much time you will need available to fully commit to what you want to achieve and then work out where that time can come from. Maybe you could spend less time on social media? Or ask your partner or a friend to help with some of your other commitments?

Finally, it is important that you hold regular 'progress meetings' with yourself. You need to track your own performance and be honest with yourself when it comes to looking at the data you gather on your journey of change. Your journal is the perfect way to document your progress and you can reflect weekly to assess if you need to make further adjustments in order to stay on track.

Don't be fearful of change; begin to embrace it. If you have found yourself stuck in the same loop of behaviour for years, then now is your time to change. Start by proving to yourself today that change is possible, no matter how small and then build on this with confidence.

Use the space provided to write down what bigger changes you want to make to your life and what obstacles you might need to overcome in order to achieve them.

_____

_____

_____

_____

_____

_____

If you have identified obstacles and they feel like huge obstructions blocking your path to change, you need to plan how you will move them out of the way. Sometimes this can mean making difficult choices and you should be careful not to keep yourself stuck because you don't want to confront something uncomfortable. This may seem like the easy choice, but over the long term it is actually much harder as it impacts us in many different negative ways.

Staying consciously stuck will lead to pain and conflict in your mind. The fact is that courage is the only antidote to fear. This might be your time to show yourself that you have more inner strength and courage than you have given yourself credit for and that you can bring change into your life whenever you want.

Use the space provided to write down how you will overcome any obstacles you have identified.

_____

_____

_____

_____

_____

_____

When you feel ready, stand tall and make the changes you want for yourself. Let go of the fear, don't procrastinate, enjoy the journey and embrace any uncertainty. Put yourself first and start moving forward in the knowledge that you hold all the power in your life and can change anything you want, whenever you want.

Day 23 | What won't you compromise?

I used to put alcohol ahead of the most important things in my life. It had complete power over me, and I would always place drinking in front of everything else – it quite simply ruled my world. If there was a chance that I might not have an ample supply of wine in the cupboard ready for the evening, then I would become stressed out and irritable and would do whatever I needed to ensure I wouldn't miss out on my beloved drink.

If I was out in the evening and couldn't get my hands on wine, I would become moody and would generally leave early so I could get home and start drinking. I was never engaged or fully present. My mind was constantly thinking about wine and how long it was until I could get my hands on it. Everything else took second place; the wine always came first. There was no compromise.

There were so many occasions where I would choose drinking over family outings, nights out with friends and even date nights with my wife. All I wanted to do was sit at home and drink wine. Nothing else provided me with the same feeling and this daily routine had become all that mattered to me. I didn't care if I was drinking alone, or drinking with others, I just had to ensure I had my fill of wine.

I also believed that nothing else could ease my inner turmoil in the same way that wine did. The sense of relaxation and the warm fuzzy feeling after the first glass gave me the belief that I was benefiting so much from drinking. But as the years went by I built up such a tolerance that I could drink an entire bottle before I started to feel any effects from it.

I have no doubt that my drinking behaviour had a negative impact on my relationships with both my daughter, my wife and my circle of friends. The more I drank, the more I pushed them all away in favour of getting drunk. Since I quit drinking everything has changed. I now feel as though we have never been closer, and I am so much more present, engaged and excited at being involved in every aspect of their lives. These days my wife, daughter and I go out together regularly and I have never had so much fun. I used to feel as though I was being dragged along and would begrudgingly join in if I really had to. Now I look forward to spending precious time together, and I am often the first one out of the door raring to go somewhere together as a family.

Those feelings from the drink that I believed I could never find elsewhere are now found in the magical moments with my daughter, my wife, my family and my friends. The laughter, the silly pranks we play on each other, holding hands and sharing stories with my wife on a long walk in the woods – these light up my life like never before and fill me with a sense of joy that I didn't know existed inside of me. That joy had been locked away in a cage and the wine held the key. Once I was able to cut the booze out of my life the cage was unlocked and the joy was unleashed back into my life.

It would be easy to fill myself with a sense of regret and shame about my past behaviour, but I refuse to do that. I want to live in the present rather than dwell on the past; I know I had a problem, I made a change and I put things right. There is no need to beat myself up about past events that I have no power to change. I have apologized for specific episodes and moved on.

Tomorrow we will be making your personal freedom plan, which will help to guide you – it will be your roadmap on your route to peace and happiness. But for today I want you to think about what you are no longer willing to compromise in favour of alcohol.

For me, it was my wife and daughter. When I quit drinking I made a vow to myself that I would never again put alcohol in front of them both. I knew that this meant I could never drink again because I would immediately be back in the grip of alcohol and putting it ahead of them both. But what is it that you are no longer prepared to compromise for alcohol?

Use the space provided to write down what important areas of your life you have put alcohol ahead of in the past.

_____

_____

_____

_____

_____

_____

I would like you to make a commitment to yourself: what are you no longer prepared to put alcohol ahead of? Write your answer in the space provided.

_____

_____

_____

_____

_____

_____

_____

Now ask yourself if you are willing to stick to this commitment? I want you to really mean it and be confident in the commitment you make here. Don't make any false promises – this has to be a true and honest commitment to yourself.

Once you have made a true and firm commitment, you might want to put it somewhere prominent to remind yourself. Maybe that's on your phone, or even on a sticky note on your fridge. Think about what would work for you.

Day 24 | Making your freedom plan

On Day 14 we explored where you might want to be in 12 months from now, both in terms of your relationship with alcohol and your life as a whole. Today I would like to expand on that by making a freedom plan that will help you stay focused and ensure you have the best chances of succeeding in reaching your goals.

You may have found quitting alcohol to be a real struggle and at times felt helpless believing that you can never change, but please trust me and know that you absolutely can. Take heart that the feeling of not always having control is totally normal and that the good news is that you really can break free. With so much focus on alcohol it is very easy to forget about the many areas of your life where you do have true power and complete control. Think about what those areas are: Where do you hold the power in your life?.

Some of these areas of your life where you have total control are likely to positively influence your ability to quit alcohol, but it can be easy to forget to pay attention to them. By focusing on what life changes you could make that will create a difference to you personally, you can, over time, take some big steps towards claiming back the power from drinking.

Making a freedom plan is a process of brainstorming what you could change in your life that will help you become the person you want to be and what you need to do in order to get there. Think about anything that comes to mind – it might be habits, behaviours, relationships or routines that are holding you back and preventing you from feeling truly fulfilled in your life. But don't stop there. Consider every element of your life and ask yourself if you are totally happy with it as it is, or whether something needs to change.

Consider what is really important in your life: what do you need to thrive? What lights you up and brings you joy? What do you look forward to?

You should also think about your personal core values. Your values highlight what you stand for and guide your behaviour, rather like a personal code of conduct. By identifying your top ten values you can ensure that what you do in your life aligns with them. When we fail to honour our values we can fall into bad habits, negativity and behaviour that doesn't reflect the person we really are.

I have provided a comprehensive list of the most common personal values. Read through the list and circle the values that are true to you. Then refine the list, leaving the most important values so you have ten remaining that are the most meaningful to you. These are your core values.

Abundance	Decisiveness	Humility	Punctuality
Approachability	Dependability	Humour	Reflection
Approval	Devotion	Impartiality	Reliability
Awareness	Dignity	Independence	Resilience
Accessibility	Directness	Integrity	Respect
Accountability	Discipline	Intelligence	Security
Achievement	Discretion	Intimacy	Self-control
Action	Drive	Inspiration	Self-reliance
Adventure	Duty	Joy	Significance
Agility	Effectiveness	Justice	Simplicity
Altruism	Empathy	Kindness	Sincerity
Ambition	Energy	Knowledge	Skill
Appreciation	Enjoyment	Leadership	Solidarity
Approachability	Enthusiasm	Learning	Spirituality
Approval	Equality	Liberty	Spontaneity
Awareness	Excellence	Liveliness	Strength
Balance	Excitement	Logic	Stability
Beauty	Fairness	Love	Structure
Being the Best	Faith	Loyalty	Success
Belonging	Fame	Mastery	Status
Calmness	Family	Mindfulness	Teamwork
Care	Fidelity	Modesty	Thankfulness
Certainty	Flexibility	Money	Tolerance
Cheerfulness	Frankness	Motivation	Tradition
Clarity	Freedom	Nature	Tranquility
Comfort	Freedom of	Open-	Trust
Commitment	speech	mindedness	Trustworthiness
Compassion	Friendship	Optimism	Truth
Competition	Frugality	Order	Understanding
Confidence	Fulfilment	Originality	Uniqueness
Connection	Fun	Passion	Unity
Consistency	Generosity	Patience	Valour
Continuity	Gratitude	Peace	Variety
Contribution	Growth	Perfection	Vigour
Control	Happiness	Persistence	Vitality
Courage	Harmony	Philanthropy	Warmth
Creativity	Health	Power	Wealth
Curiosity	Honesty	Privacy	Wisdom
Determination	Honour	Professionalism	Wonder

My freedom plan

I invite you to start brainstorming the short-term and long-term life changes that come to mind for your freedom plan. Write down everything that comes to mind. You can refine the freedom plan as you go forward, and we will review it later in the book. There are no right or wrong answers, and you may find that, as you give more thought to your plan over the coming days, you come back and make further changes.

Trust yourself as you brainstorm – this is your freedom plan. Believe in your own intuition to guide you towards what you need to do to move into a place of complete freedom and happiness. Think about everything you have read in this book so far, any advice you have been given from people you trust, and any other information you feel will add value to your plan.

As you write your freedom plan, be sure to ask yourself how everything aligns with your personal values. You may even decide to write which personal values apply to each specific entry in your freedom plan. If you find that an entry in your freedom plan does not align with your personal values, you should dig deeper and ask yourself whether it is really true for you and whether it should be included or not.

Take heart in knowing that by making this plan you will start to focus on creating a true change for the better. Even the smallest life changes can expand into big steps along the path to freedom.

Tips for writing your freedom plan

- Consider your hopes and dreams – think about what you need to do to identify them and achieve them.
- What matters to you? What is it that you really want to achieve? How do you plan on achieving it?
- What are your short- and long-term priorities?
- Map out your vision for the year ahead, but also think about where you want to be in five and ten years' time. Look at the bigger picture and work backwards to learn how you can achieve it.
- Break down your biggest goals into smaller more achievable steps. For example, rather than simply stating that you want to buy your own home, create milestones such as:

  1 Begin saving for a deposit.
  2 Research and decide on a location.
  3 Speak to mortgage providers to ensure you can get the finance you need.
  4 Contact real estate agents and begin to conduct viewings of potential properties.

- What challenges might you need to overcome to achieve the outcomes you want?

- Create clear goals that reflect what you want to achieve along with the small steps that you can take to reach them. Create a freedom plan that allows you to take small, consistent steps forward so that you can remain on track and build momentum.

- Ensure you clearly define the benefits of achieving your goals. Be totally clear on the reasons 'why' you want to make them into a reality. If you ever face a tough time, you should reflect on these reasons in order to draw motivation and restore your focus.

Consider all the areas of your life and how satisfied with them you currently are and how important they are to you. You might want to score each area out of ten both in terms of satisfaction and importance. What might you need to change in order to improve your scores in the areas that are most important to you? The areas to consider might include:

- work and career
- self-care
- family
- intimate relationships
- leisure activities and hobbies
- caregiving and helping others
- community involvement
- money and finances
- personal development and education
- friendships
- religion and spirituality
- health and wellness.

Write down the short-term and long-term changes you want to include in your freedom plan in the space provided.

Short-term changes

_____

_____

_____

_____

_____

_____

_____

_____

_____

Long-term changes

_____

_____

_____

_____

_____

_____

_____

_____

_____

Return to your freedom plan as often as you wish, make adjustments and changes as you see fit. But, above all, start making those small changes and moving towards achieving everything you have outlined.

Day 25 | Making a commitment to yourself

Today is the last day of Part 1. Hopefully, you have learned something about yourself and feel ready to find out even more. If you haven't stopped drinking yet then today is the day, I want you to make a firm commitment to yourself. Let go of any fear, try to be excited about discovering what awaits you on the journey ahead.

Now is the perfect time to reflect on everything you have read and the answers you have provided. I find it particularly helpful to spend time reminding myself of the reasons why I wanted to stop drinking in the first place. So you may want to take a few minutes just to go over the answers you have written in the previous chapters to refresh yourself.

Part 2 is designed to be your day-by-day support companion from the first day that you decide to put the bottle down. So if you aren't ready to make a commitment to taking a break from alcohol right now, you should return to Part 2 only when you feel ready. There is no judgement. I want you to take a break when you feel totally ready, and if that means you need some time to prepare yourself then that is completely fine. Please don't start Part 2 until you are ready to begin your break.

Of course, my hope is that you do feel ready to take a break from drinking. In fact, I wonder if you feel excited to find out what happens to you without booze interfering with your life? Have you wondered whether you will feel happier, less stressed out, whether your skin and face changes or whether your sleep improves? Remember to continue journaling and gathering data and noting down everything you experience going forward.

It is important that you don't treat this as a challenge. A challenge sounds like something we can either fail or succeed in; it is black and white and there is no failure here, only learning and growth. Look at it more as a journey of discovery that you will be approaching with an open mind, curiosity and interest. There will no doubt be ups and downs, no matter what happens, but learn from it and grow stronger as you go forward. Nobody is judging you, and there is no need to judge yourself.

It is up to you how long you want to commit to taking a break from alcohol for. I recommend 25 days initially as this ties in with the remaining number of days left in the book. It also allows enough time for you to get through the first week or two which can be the most challenging and begin to experience some of the positive changes. Don't feel pressured, though – if you want to do more or less, that is your decision. The book will guide you day by day through the next 25 days and will provide you with the tools and tactics you need to go forward from there.

So are you willing to make that commitment to yourself right now?

Use the space provided and write down an honest commitment that you know you will stick to. This is a promise to yourself, and you need to be completely truthful and certain you will commit to it. Use a wording along the lines of 'I commit to taking a break from alcohol for the next 25 days, and no matter what happens I will stick to this promise'.

Take a moment. Do you feel ready? If not, put the book down and come back when you do.

However, if you are ready, grab your pen and let's do this!

My personal commitment to taking a break from alcohol:

_____

_____

_____

_____

_____

_____

_____

Once you have made your commitment, you should give yourself a massive well done. It is incredibly powerful and you have just taken a huge step towards claiming back the power that alcohol has taken from you. How liberating does that feel?

You may want to put your commitment somewhere prominent to remind yourself of it, or you may choose to keep it private – it is entirely up to you. Now you have made your commitment, let's move on to the first day without alcohol tomorrow. Or, if you would prefer to make today your first day without drinking, you can read on right now.

Part 2
How to stop drinking

Before you begin …

I am so happy that you are reading this page. It means you have made a true commitment to yourself to take a break from alcohol and that you are really serious about making a positive change and discovering what happens to you when you choose not to drink.

The second half of this book will guide you day by day over the next 25 days and will provide you with the support you need as you experience your break from alcohol. I would like you to continue to read one chapter each day and keep on completing any exercises with total honesty and openness. It doesn't matter if your first day without drinking is now or if you have already quit drinking and started your break from booze… No matter what, just keep on reading a chapter a day and working through the book.

Don't read beyond this point until you have made your personal commitment to taking a break and you are ready to begin your first day alcohol free.

Continue to update your journal every day. Use it to write down anything (and everything) that comes up. This can be positive or negative and might include feelings, emotions, experiences or challenges you faced (and hopefully overcome). You may decide you would prefer to use an online journal rather than traditional pen and paper – choose whatever works for you, but make sure you write daily and gather the data as you go forward.

Now is also a great time to take a selfie. In the weeks ahead I will ask you to take another one and to notice the changes that have taken place to your face. Commonly, we experience bags and dark circles around the eyes fading away, less facial bloating and 'glowing' skin as blotchiness begins to vanish. I often see 'before' and 'after' photos where people have quit drinking and they look five to ten years younger in the 'after' photo, all that from simply cutting out alcohol. Who needs Botox!

I also recommend weighing yourself and making a note of your current weight. You may well notice changes to your weight in the weeks ahead, but don't get hung up on losing weight. I want to manage your expectations with weight loss – it can take a bit of time. Noticeable changes to weight usually take between three and six months, so don't expect overnight miracles; just know that you are heading in the right direction.

As well as continuing to read a chapter of the book each day I also recommend doing all you can to educate yourself and expand your knowledge about the alcohol-free lifestyle. You might like to watch the videos on the Be Sober YouTube channel or connect with sober communities on social media to gain some extra insight and inspiration. Try to immerse yourself in the new world that you are exploring and the incredible community you are becoming part of (see the Resources section at the end of the book for more ideas).

Approach everything that happens with a sense of curiosity, rather than being swept away by emotion or allowing negative self-talk to take over. Simply try to question everything – keep on asking yourself 'why?' Learn to explore your experiences as deeply as feels comfortable and possible. Try to look at everything that happens during the experience as if you were an outside observer with no judgement and no emotional attachment. Start making factual and logical observations about what is happening and why. Become aware when your emotions start to run the show and pay attention to when your inner child is reacting instead of the adult you.

Finally, as we get closer to the end of the 25 days that the remaining chapters of the book will guide you through, we will explore whether a further break from alcohol would feel right for you. Many people experience so many positive changes during their break that they can approach the end of it feeling like they never want to drink again. We will also look at what to do if you have taken a break but still want to drink.

Most importantly of all, I really want you to enjoy the ride, be positive and get motivated about what you are doing. This is an incredibly powerful journey of self-growth and personal discovery. If you could see all the wonderful and amazing changes that will happen to you over time without alcohol in your life, you would be jumping for joy about becoming the future version of you.

So let's get started and move into Day 1 of your break from alcohol.

Day 1 | Alcohol-free

Today is your first day alcohol-free. You might be feeling excited, nervous or even scared of the journey ahead. It is common to experience a combination of all three. Please don't worry – we are going to do this together.

Know that there is likely to be an element of discomfort in the form of cravings and unstable emotions at times, but the feelings will always pass and you need to experience the feeling of them arriving and then leaving so that you can draw strength from the knowledge that you have the power in these situations.

Continue to work through one chapter a day and stay strong in the face of any fears, emotions or challenges that come up. No matter how difficult they feel at the time, you need to sit with them until they fade. Every time you allow discomfort to pass without reacting, you will become stronger. This is part of the process, and it is what will set you up for long-term success as you go forward.

Throughout the book we have examined our beliefs about alcohol and how it features in our lives. I make no apology for repeating myself on these points as I firmly believe that, if we can form new beliefs and do away with the ones that are holding us back, we can unlock the door to changing our mindset.

If we can change our mindset about alcohol, we can quit drinking without huge amounts of willpower or any sense of loss or frustration. We can actually enjoy the life choice we have made for ourselves and have fun at the same time.

We want to move from a place where we feel a sense of deprivation that we 'can't have' a drink to a feeling that alcohol is unimportant and insignificant and that we simply 'don't want' a drink. The way myself and thousands of other people have made that shift is by unlocking limiting beliefs and finding new, healthy beliefs that are not holding them back from being the person they want to be.

I was totally obsessed with drinking for over two decades, and after I quit I became a little fixated on sobriety and the new life I had created for myself – it felt so good that I knew I would never drink again. But I didn't see sobriety as simply 'Simon doesn't drink'. It was a complete lifestyle choice that I felt empowered in making and the start of a wonderful journey where I would go on to find out things about myself that booze had kept hidden away from me for years.

I often have people asking me how they know if they are truly free from alcohol after they have quit, and I ask them to picture a scenario where they have just pulled up in the car outside a house where their friends are throwing a party. I tell them to visualize themselves walking up to the door, hearing the music and the muffled voices inside, maybe even smelling food from the grill wafting outside. Then as they step closer to the door I ask them to pause for a moment and ask themselves which of these they feel:

- **Fixated:** At this point, standing outside that door, the drinking version of me would have been thinking about how soon I could have my first sip of alcohol. Getting my first drink would have been my biggest priority, and before I had even finished my first glass I would be thinking about the second.

- **Liberated:** After my beliefs had changed and my mindset had shifted I actually went to a friend's party similar to the visualization I have described here, and as I approached the door I wasn't thinking about drinking or obsessing over how quickly I could get the first drink down me. I was thinking about the people I was going to connect with, the laughter, the dancing and the fun that awaited me. I also found myself wondering about what food they would lay on and what music they would play. I decided I would view drunk people with curiosity and interest and would make a mental note of what I observed. The next day I wrote it all down in my journal: everything I experienced, how much fun I had, who I connected with and how it all felt being alcohol-free. I used to look back at this entry regularly as it was a night that served to help me grow stronger.

I wanted to be liberated, because to me liberation meant complete freedom and peace in my life and I wanted that so badly for myself. Once we feel liberated from alcohol we become totally free, alcohol is irrelevant to us and we engage, connect and become fully present without thinking about drinking all the time. Of course, we will still have the odd thought about it, but we know that these are simply thoughts; we don't need to act on them. Instead, we allow them to pass us by like clouds moving across the sky and away into the distance.

When we quit drinking we move through different stages. It can take a little time to feel totally liberated and free, so don't worry if you don't feel as though you are there just yet. It just means you are at a different point in the journey, but you are travelling in exactly the right direction.

Below are the stages to alcohol freedom.

- **Unawareness:** This is where someone has a problem with their alcohol use but doesn't acknowledge or even care about it. They just carry on with their behaviour regardless of the impact it is having on their life. Sadly, this is where most people stay stuck, often because they (wrongly) believe their life will be worse without alcohol in it. This is ignorant bliss.

- **Awareness:** This can be the most painful part of the journey to freedom. I found it really uncomfortable and stayed at this point for around five years. I had become aware I had a problem, and part of me felt that I should do something about my drinking, but all I did was drink more to blot out the thoughts. I lived with internal conflict around my drinking, stuck in a place where I knew I had to do something but not knowing what to do for the best. The good news is that most people don't usually live with the discomfort for as long as I did and end up deciding that change is the only positive way forward.

- **Education:** Once we have become aware of the problem and decide we need to do something about it, then we start to learn about the tools, tactics and support that will help us get to where we want to be. Sober books, podcasts, blogs and videos all helped me expand my knowledge and educate myself, in turn helping me form new beliefs and change my mindset.

- **Practice:** While we can write down new beliefs that we feel are true and honest and reflect the life we want for ourselves, we also need to put them into practice. Just like learning a new skill, sobriety takes a bit of practice in order to move on to complete mastery. For example, if you believe that you can't have fun without drinking and write down a new belief to stop limiting yourself from only being able to have fun if you can have alcohol, at some point you will need to get out into the big wide world and prove to yourself that you really can have a great time without having drink involved. As you engage in more and more experiences alcohol-free, your new beliefs become rock solid and totally true because they are now based on factual evidence that you can't argue with.

- **Mastery:** The more you practise, the stronger your new beliefs will become and as you spend more time alcohol-free the less you will think about drinking. I found that after four or five months I was in a place where I felt like I had mastered a sober life. I was rarely thinking about drinking and found myself so much happier as well as being fully present and engaged in the new healthy activities I had become involved in. It can take time to get to this stage, but it gets easier and easier with every day that passes.

Today is the first day on your alcohol break that you committed to yourself, and I want you to stay really focused on your beliefs and your mindset as you go forward. Use your journal to write down everything that you experience, especially when it comes to these two important areas.

Use the space provided to write down where you feel you are at in your own journey along with what challenges you might face before getting to the stage of mastering sobriety.

I regularly have clients tell me how 'it feels different this time'. Whenever I hear someone say this I know they are experiencing a shift in their mindset. Try to notice if anything feels different for you and write it down.

_____

_____

_____

_____

_____

_____

_____

Above all, make sure you congratulate yourself, because, whatever stage you are at, I know that you are way further forward than you were when you started this book. You have put the work in to get this far, and you are continuing to move forward. Be kind to yourself – you deserve it.

Day 2 | Reward or penalty?

On Day 9 of Part 1 we explored how you might reward yourself when you reach different points on your personal journey. Take a moment to look back at what you wrote, because I want you to feel really motivated about what you are doing and hopefully get excited about the rewards that await you alongside the positive changes to your life.

If you find the prospect of a luxury spa day or a meal out at your favourite restaurant motivational, then make sure you remind yourself about what is in store for you. Just think how proud you will feel when you are making that dinner reservation at the same time as having the joy of knowing you will enjoy that meal out fully present, clear headed and, best of all, hangover free the next morning.

I like to describe this kind of reward as a dangling 'carrot' type of motivation. You know a prize is on the horizon and it strengthens your resolve to reach the personal goals you have set for yourself. It works incredibly well and has served to motivate thousands of people when they quit drinking.

We outlined the rewards you might give yourself on Day 9 (Part 1), but you may want to add more context to those now we are further down the path and consider which milestones in your journey will trigger them for you. For example, you might state that 'After 30 days alcohol-free I will reward myself with a trip to the theatre with the money I have saved from not buying wine'. Do whatever works for you but try to ensure you are really clear about the goals you have set yourself. There is space at the end today's chapter for you to be more specific.

You may also choose to set some goals and rewards based around your personal freedom plan and these may well not be linked to your use of alcohol. This is completely fine – it is your journey and you can do whatever feels right to ensure you are as motivated as possible to make the changes in your life so you can truly flourish and start thriving instead of simply surviving.

However, sometimes as well as a carrot we also need a stick. Unlike the carrot, a stick doesn't present us with a reward for achieving our goals; it gives us some kind of penalty for not reaching them. Giving ourselves a stick can be equally effective, and I find that most people tend to favour one or the other, but a handful of people like both. There is no right or wrong way of doing this; you can decide what works for you.

So let's talk about the stick. I was working with a client who had given herself rewards as goals at various points on her path to alcohol freedom, but she kept having setbacks and drinking. For some reason the rewards just didn't motivate her. We spoke at length about this and discovered that when she was a child she was far more responsive to the threat of a punishment than the promise of a prize.

So we decided to adapt her plan slightly and replace the carrot with a stick. She had committed to taking a 30-day break from drinking, and we agreed that if she was to drink during this time it would add a further week to the length of the break, a second setback would add two weeks and a third would add three weeks (and so on). She loved this idea and told me it was the right fit for her in terms of motivation. She went on to go through the first 30 days alcohol-free with no setbacks and at the end told me her mindset had changed about alcohol to the point where she never wanted to drink again. To date she never has.

Personally, I respond to rewards as opposed to punishments, but we are all unique and different things motivate different people. So give some thought to what you think might motivate you. It might be the carrot, it might be the stick or it could be both.

Another client who I worked with was having real trouble being open with her teenage daughter about how alcohol was having an impact on her life. She was worried her daughter would think badly of her, and that she would lose her respect if she told her she had a problem with drinking. This couldn't be further from the truth. The fact is that our children can become incredibly inspired by what we do; they tend to do what we do, not what we say. When we quit alcohol our children can't help but take notice and learn from our behaviour. My own daughter has been on my journey with me and has learned things about alcohol that have changed her own thinking about drinking for ever. We will talk more about our children later in the book.

We agreed that she would have an open and grown-up conversation with her daughter to tell her about her relationship with alcohol and her decision to try to no longer drink. We decided that we would make it fun, instead of it becoming a difficult, serious conversation. We used the carrot-and-stick approach, which she shared with her daughter so she could involve her and make her part of her support team. Her daughter loves clothes shopping, so it was agreed that if her mum had a 30-day break from alcohol they would head to the mall for new clothes and the daughter would have a £50 budget. However, if mum had a setback during the 30 days the budget would be doubled to £100.

This strategy made the conversation so much easier, and they both thought it was a really fun idea. Before long her daughter was supporting her mum and urging her on to success. She went through 30 days easily with the loving support of her daughter the entire way. They had an awesome shopping trip and Mum remains alcohol-free.

Have a think about whether you prefer the carrot or the stick approach, or a combination of both, and in your journal today map out a clear plan for how you could best reward (or penalize) yourself during your break from drinking.

Write down your reward plan in the space provided. Take some time also to write down anything else you are feeling today – any emotions, concerns, successes or thoughts you may have along with anything that you have noticed about yourself or the experience you are having.

Day 3 | Uncomfortable thoughts and cravings

You are now three days into your break from alcohol. How does that feel? Take a moment to reflect on where you were and how far you have come. I can clearly recall a time when I couldn't imagine even one day without drinking, let alone three days. You are doing brilliantly, and I want you to regularly remind yourself of that and celebrate.

How about sharing your success by posting in one of the online Facebook sober groups? Or, better still, reach out to me directly and tag me in a post on Instagram using @besoberandquit. I would love to know how you are getting on. You could post a photo of you with this book, or an image that reflects your current mood and then tag me to ensure I get notified. Post as often as you need; it is a great way of staying accountable and feeling connected.

It is also incredibly important for you to know that the first couple of weeks are the toughest part after you quit drinking. The more time that passes, the easier it gets. Take it from me. I wondered when (if ever) I would stop thinking about drinking, but as the weeks passed, and as my mind and body recalibrated and I found new routines, enjoying the activities that I used to deprioritize for alcohol, it didn't take long for the thoughts to become less and less frequent.

I am going to be brutally honest now: almost every client I work with tells me that days three to five are the hardest. Once they get through this phase they start seeing light at the end of the tunnel; it gets easier. Now is your time to stand in the storm and sit with any discomfort. Use the tactics you have learned when you need them and stay strong. If you have support around you, make sure you use it. If you belong to any online sober communities, reach out if you are having a tough time. Avoid feeling alone and ensure you have whatever you need around you to ensure you stay safe in your sobriety.

Just like everything in life, this is temporary, it will pass. Dig deep and get through anything that comes up. Alcohol is not going to help; it will put you right back where you were previously and will leave you in that awful place with more internal conflict than before. I can clearly remember the 'wine witch' whispering in my ear over and over in those first few days, trying to convince me that it was the solution to the discomfort I was experiencing. I had to stand strong. I knew that if I were to drink I would never get out of the trap, and I was very aware that alcohol wanted to keep me well and truly stuck. It is the master of illusion; it will play tricks on your mind and do all it can to convince you that it can help, that it can take away any pain you feel. Do not believe it. I want you to call it out for the liar that it is and see through the smoke and mirrors.

These days I barely ever have uncomfortable thoughts about drinking or cravings for alcohol. But in the first week after I stopped drinking, the thoughts and feelings were hitting me several times an hour, like huge waves from a rough sea crashing in, before fading away only to return stronger and harder next time around. It can be really tempting to succumb to them as it can seem like an easy way out. Yes, it ends the uncomfortable feelings for an hour or two, but it also sends us right back to the start and back into the pain of being stuck. I make no apology for repeating myself here: please ensure you keep in mind that these thoughts and feelings will pass, and today I want to share some tactics that worked for me when it came to dealing with them, and keeping the choppy sea at bay so the waves didn't knock me down.

If you are anything like me, then you might feel as though someone has pulled away your cherished comfort blanket, the blanket (in my case, red wine) that makes you feel safe, secure, warm and loved. The blanket also makes you relax and washes away your stresses and anxieties when you are snuggled underneath it. Even though I desperately wanted to experience life without this fake comfort, I also knew it was very easy for me to get my hands on another blanket – all I had to do was head to the shop. Nobody would even know, so this was down to me. So I had to use a little willpower to stop myself simply going straight back to my old ways.

During the first week I made sure I regularly paused and took the time to remind myself of all the reasons why I knew my life would be better without alcohol in it. I also reflected on what my life looked like when I was drinking and this helped to strengthen my resolve. I would also regularly look at the list of things I was not prepared to compromise for alcohol. Whenever I read this I knew that drinking would immediately destroy the commitment I had made and I would be breaking the promise I had made to myself. Whenever I came close, this 'integrity check' always helped to put me back in the right place.

But the biggest tactic that helped me during those first few weeks was awareness. Instead of allowing myself to become overwhelmed by the thoughts and feelings, I instead treated anything uncomfortable that came into my head as an incredibly noisy fire alarm. Then, instead of simply latching on to the thought or feeling and allowing it to dictate my behaviour, the sound of the fire alarm in my brain allowed me to pause for a moment, then step back, take stock and make a decision about what to do next.

Try to practise this process. Start to become really mindful of any uncomfortable thoughts or feelings, as you become aware of them allow your internal fire alarm to ring loudly. You will find it to be a powerful way of claiming back control over your thoughts and feelings. That fire alarm will stop you in your tracks; it will help you stop latching on to a thought or a feeling that causes discomfort and running away with it.

The next step is to make a choice. The easy way out is to give in to the thoughts, but you wouldn't be here if you wanted to do that – and I am pretty sure you aren't the type of person who takes the easy option. So, instead, you can use a number of brilliant tactics to work through the thoughts and feelings.

Try to experiment with the following tactics – some will work better than others. Treat it a bit like trying on new pairs of shoes: test them out, see how they feel and spend a little time with them until you find something that fits perfectly that you feel really comfortable with as your post-fire alarm tool.

The tactics I outline here work well for dealing with uncomfortable thoughts and feelings as well as handling cravings to drink. Mine were like a voice in my head saying things like:

- 'Go on, Simon, have some wine, you deserve it, you had a tough day at work.'
- 'Three days with no alcohol, Simon, well done! You should have a drink now; you have proved you can stop any time you like now.'
- 'Well done, Simon, you achieved so much today; you should celebrate with a glass of wine.'

The thoughts were so easy to latch on to; they would impact my mood and my sense of wellbeing and I had to put the work in and practise the art of pausing when my internal fire alarm rang out. Don't worry if you don't master it the first time around. It is like learning a new skill: just keep practising and it will become second nature.

Once that alarm rang inside of me, these were the options I had in my toolbox:

Acknowledge the thoughts and feelings – the elephant tactic

The worst thing you can do is try to push away the thoughts and feelings. Don't try suppressing them; all it does is give them energy and power, and it will make them come back even stronger.

You are far better to acknowledge your thoughts and feelings – face up to them and you will remove their power. Always try to name your feelings and emotions.

You can try this tactic with your eyes closed while sitting in a quiet place, or just use your mind's eye if that isn't possible. Start by imagining that you are sitting calmly in your favourite room at home, somewhere that you feel really comfortable and relaxed, maybe your living room or your kitchen. Then start to visualize those difficult thoughts and feelings as an enormous elephant that has just come crashing into the room.

This elephant is huge, hairy and rather angry-looking. She is trampling all over your floor and lifting her trunk and making loud trumpeting sounds to get your attention. Your sentimental family photos are sent crashing from the shelf as her huge frame brushes against them before she finally settles down and simply stands there, refusing to move from the centre of the room. There is no hiding from this beast and she smells a bit, too; there is no ignoring that either.

You could also give your 'elephant' a name – mine was called Sabrina, like the Teenage Witch I used to watch on television when I was younger. I have no idea why I named an elephant after her, and I should take this opportunity to apologize to the actress Melissa Joan-Hart who played Sabrina the Teenage Witch as she has absolutely no similarities to an elephant. But it worked for me, and giving my elephant a name made this tactic much easier to work with.

You could try to push your 'Sabrina' out of the room so you can simply ignore her, but this would require a lot of effort and the chances are that she will just come lumbering back in again feeling angry at your attempts to suppress her. You can't match her strength and you can't control what the elephant does. So this really isn't a viable option.

Instead, what you should do is acknowledge the elephant, look her straight in the eye and then say out loud, 'Hey, Sabrina the elephant, there you are. I was wondering when you would show up. How are you?' I wasn't reacting or becoming emotional; I was simply accepting that these thoughts and feelings had come into the 'room'.

Then I would calmly say (you can say it out loud or just say it in your head): 'I am not coming on a ride with you, I am busy right now.'

By doing this, I would feel the power of the thoughts and feelings significantly weaken. Most of the time the elephant in my head would get bored because they had failed to get my interest and would simply wander off to wherever they came from.

Occasionally, the elephant would continue to just stand there, ignoring what I had said. So I would say it again, which usually did the trick. But if it didn't, I would move on to one of the other tactics below.

Play it forward like a movie in your mind

This tactic is brilliant and worked incredibly well for me. It is simple but highly effective.

When those thoughts and feelings come to mind and your alarm is making a noise, take a moment to pause before you choose how you react (yes, you have a choice in this, always remember that; it is very powerful yet incredibly easy to forget that it is you who has the power of choice).

As you pause, take a moment to get into your mind's eye. I find this best done sitting with my eyes closed, but I have also done it sitting at my desk in a busy office, on an aeroplane, in a café and while walking around a busy supermarket (where the wine shelf caused some uncomfortable cravings).

All you need to do is simply visualize what will happen if you latch on to the thoughts. Mine were mainly thoughts along the lines of 'Simon, you should have a drink; you deserve it, my friend', so I would take a moment and hit the play button on a virtual movie of the next 12 hours in my mind.

My internal (horror) movie would look like this. It is a Friday afternoon. I am walking around the supermarket and eventually give into my thoughts telling me I need a drink. So I pick up a bottle of wine from the shelf in the store and I feel a strong sense of guilt because I have let myself down as well as my wife and my daughter. I promised them both that I was now living an alcohol-free life, and now I am putting booze ahead of them again.

I also feel like a failure. Shame washes over me as I reinforce my belief that I can never quit drinking, and I am destined to be controlled by alcohol until the day I die. I try to wrestle with these thoughts and provide myself with comfort in the knowledge that the wine will blot them all out when I start drinking later.

As I push my trolley away and walk towards the checkout, I stop in my tracks and turn around. I head back to the shelf and get two more bottles of wine. There is no way one would ever be enough; I need more.

I pay for my groceries and wine, and then I head to the car and drive home. When I get home my wife is in the kitchen. She is in a great mood and excited about the plans we have over the weekend. I sheepishly tell her that I have brought some wine and will be drinking this evening as I can't control the thoughts any longer.

She is so understanding (she always is) and tells me that it is my choice if I want to drink and that she will support me no matter what. But I can see the disappointment in her face. I also see something else. I look closely and I realize that what I can see is fear; she is scared for me. She knows I am hooked on alcohol and she is genuinely worried for me. Her husband, the addict. She isn't trying to make me feel guilty. I can see that she is truly worried about what I am doing to myself.

After this exchange I feel like a complete loser, but once again I remind myself I have my old friend back in my life. I know that Ms Shiraz will take away all these uncomfortable feelings as soon as I open the bottle.

As evening approaches, my teenage daughter emerges from her bedroom (a rare occurrence these days); she wants to go to the movies with us both. I totally forgot about the film she wanted to see and this has caused me a dilemma. I am now dead set on getting stuck into my wine. My head is like a washing machine, with thoughts and feelings whirling around, and drinking now feels like the only way I can stop it.

I don't want to go to the movies – the wine is coming first – so I tell my wife and daughter that I won't be joining them and make excuses about watching sport on the television. They are both so disappointed. My wife knows the real truth and I have just sunk even lower in her estimations of me. But she covers for me to my daughter and they head off to the cinema.

So I sit on my own and I drink. The first bottle of wine lasts no more than 40 minutes; by the time they come back I am well into the third. Yes, the feelings I had earlier have been put on hold, but I know they will be back tomorrow, probably much louder and clearer, alongside a banging hangover.

My wife calmly tells me that she feels really disappointed that I chose to stay home and drink ahead of going out with her and our daughter. The wine has made me snappy and irrational. We argue and I am unreasonable and say things that I know I will deeply regret and would never say sober.

The argument escalates and we have a major falling out. She tells me to sleep in the guest bedroom as she doesn't want me near her. With that she storms off to bed, not before reminding me that I am ruining what could be a wonderful life with my alcohol abuse.

I stay sitting downstairs, feeling sorry for myself and continue drinking until the wine runs out. I am full of anger and frustration. Even though I know I am in the wrong, I refuse to accept or acknowledge it and instead blame my wife for being unreasonable and my daughter for wanting to go to the movies at an inconvenient time. My alcohol-infused brain decides that they have upset me on purpose.

Once the final bottle has been drained I start to make my way to the guest room, but not before I throw up in the downstairs toilet. Some of it went on the wall and floor, but I can clean that up tomorrow (the reality is that I will just forget about it and the cleaning fairy will take care of it).

As I climb the stairs, I stumble twice, almost toppling right back down. That could have been a nasty accident. Thankfully, I make it to the landing without sustaining a serious injury. Eventually I get into bed; I am fully clothed and I can smell the booze and vomit on me. I shut my eyes and I feel as though I am on a ship on the roughest of seas: everything is moving, the whole room is spinning, it feels awful.

After this I can't remember much. I must have passed out or gone to sleep.

The next thing I know it is 10am and my wife is in the room pulling back the curtains and reminding me that we need to take my daughter to her badminton class. She seems to have moved on from the argument last night. Why is she so damn nice! I can't even remember what I said – I wish I could. I tell myself that I am a bad person. Who would treat their own family like this? My head is so fragile and I still feel drunk. The last thing I want to do is drive to a sports hall full of noisy kids, but I know I need to try to make amends.

I take a shower and realize just how awful I feel. Not only do I have a pounding headache, I also start hating myself for not being able to control my drinking. I call myself a failure, I beat myself up, and then I cry. I hate myself right now. I can't escape this cycle of drinking, so why do I even bother to try?

On the way to the sports hall I have to pull over to be sick, causing my daughter to ask all sorts of questions before she announces that I have a life-threatening disease she learned about in her science class. The irony is that I actually do have a life-threatening disease; it's just not the one she thinks it is.

Then the cravings come back, and my mind is full of thoughts, fears and emotions. So I decide the only thing for it is to console myself by deciding to get some wine later. It wasn't just one more drink; it was straight back to a lifetime of addiction.

And that is where my movie would end. This is actually a fairly accurate reflection of many nights that I spent drinking – it makes me cringe with embarrassment as I visualize it.

Playing this movie at the point an uncomfortable thought or feeling comes along and just watching how it will all unfold in my head gives me exactly what I need. It serves to show me that those thoughts and feelings just want to lead me down a different path and that I should simply acknowledge that they are there, but no way should I ever latch on to them and allow them to dictate my behaviour.

Use your own 'mind-movie' to visualize how your story would play out if you decided to drink. I am confident it will be enough to stop you in your tracks.

Meditation to make the thoughts and feelings fade away

I used to turn my nose up at people who meditated. I thought it was reserved for hippies and 'perfect people' who posted pictures of themselves on Instagram in stunning locations as they sat cross-legged in a zen-like state, facing a sun-drenched turquoise ocean.

Once I started to practise meditation for myself I began to see the true power it could harness in my mind.

Just like so many things on the path to living an alcohol free life, meditation takes a bit of practice. It doesn't take long to start finding your feet, and once you give it a chance it will enable you to empty your mind and learn to appreciate sitting in stillness while enjoying the feeling of complete calm.

I can still clearly recall the first time I managed to meditate to a point where I felt really deep calm and complete relaxation. It was a revelation for me. I felt like I had a new superpower that I could use to control my mind when it became overwhelmed. On top of this, meditation enabled me to feel much more at peace in my life on a daily basis and has become one of the best habits I have ever picked up.

I started out using guided meditations. These are fantastic for beginners because they give instructions on what to do throughout the process. Commonly, these kind of meditations are between ten and twenty minutes in length, meaning they don't take up huge amounts of time and can be practised early in the morning to provide the perfect start to the day.

Alongside guided meditations I also use timed meditations. These have no spoken instructions; instead, they generally have soothing sounds and a bell at the end of the allotted meditation time. When I first started using timed meditations I struggled a little as thoughts kept coming into my mind, but I worked on staying anchored to my breath and allowing the thoughts to pass. They always pass, and I am always able to reach a state of complete calm.

I use two meditation apps on my smartphone, Calm and Headspace. I tend to use Calm more than Headspace, but they are both excellent and I highly recommend you try them for yourself. Calm has a ten-minute 'Daily Calm' guided meditation with a different topic each day. I listen to the 'Daily Calm' and meditate using it most mornings (including this morning) and always feel great when I finish the session and remove my headphones.

If you have a little time and a suitable space, meditation is one of the best ways of emptying your mind and learning how to allow uncomfortable thoughts and feelings to pass by until you find a place of complete peace.

Turn it around

A powerful tactic that can help bring clarity to our discomfort is to turn a statement around and then explore it in more depth. This is a process of discovery to investigate whether a different perspective on your belief will allow you to address it with an alternative solution.

For example, you might feel down because your partner hasn't been supportive of your sobriety. As the days have passed, you have been convincing yourself that they can't love you otherwise they would have been there for you much more than they have been. You find yourself in a seriously bad mood.

If you can create a statement that reflects exactly what you believe is causing the discomfort and then write it down in your journal, you can carry out the process of turning it around and exploring it.

In this example the statement might be:

'It makes me sad that Paul doesn't support me. He doesn't love me. If he did, he would be there when I needed him.'

Once you have written down the statement, write the complete opposite. Replace the person you are projecting your emotion onto with yourself. This statement might become:

'I make myself sad when I don't support myself. I don't love myself. I am not there when I need to be.'

The point of writing the opposite statement is to explore whether you should be looking inwards, rather than projecting negative feelings outwards.

While the message in the new statement may take some time to unravel, this process usually throws up a whole new perspective around the discomfort and enables us to become far more self-aware in terms of the source of our own feelings and emotions. Very often, we will project negativity onto others when the source of the discomfort lives within us and it is ourselves we need to work on.

Breathing exercises

Similar to meditation, breathing exercises can be a great way to calm down quickly, while taking control of thoughts and feelings and finding stillness.

The process of breathing slowly and focusing only on your breath takes your mind away from any other thoughts or feelings; it also slows your heart rate down, which enables you to experience relaxation and calm.

There are hundreds of different breathing exercises you can do. I often search on YouTube to discover new techniques I like the look of and will then plug in my headphones so I can listen through my smartphone. Almost always I will finish a short session of breathing feeling way more relaxed and at peace than before I started.

When my anxiety was at its worst I went to stay with a Japanese lady named Etsuko Ito. She is an expert in relaxation, yoga, life skills, meditation, healing and healthy living. Etsuko runs a retreat for anxiety sufferers in the New Forest here in the UK (details in the Resources section at the end of the book). I found her to be one of the most inspirational people I have ever met, and we ended up becoming friends. Over the time I have spent with her she has opened my eyes to many new ways of thinking and helped me change my life in many positive ways.

One of the rules of the retreat is that guests cannot use smartphones and are not allowed to drink alcohol. The first time I went to stay at her retreat I am surprised she didn't hear the wine bottles clinking in my travel bag, at the same time as my phone was pinging with new notifications in my pocket.

So yes, Etsuko, I admit that I did sneakily drink red wine while I was in my room at your retreat. I can't justify my behaviour other than to say I was addicted. But this was part of my journey, and I remember cringing when I had to make a decision whether I should break the rules of the retreat or not. To a heavy daily wine drinker there was actually no decision to make: I had to drink.

I didn't ever discuss my alcohol problems with Etsuko until after I quit. The reason I am mentioning the anxiety retreat is that while I was there Etsuko taught me a technique called 'Brain Breathing', which fast became my favourite breathing exercise and one that I would definitely recommend you try.

When she first informed me that we would be practising brain breathing I thought she had taken leave of her senses, but after the experience I couldn't believe how calm and at ease I felt. It was a sensation of being almost carefree, at the same time as being fully grounded and in tune with my mind and body.

The process is fairly simple, but it requires a little imagination. The first step is to sit with your legs crossed, your back straight and your eyes closed. If your back aches in this position, rest it against a firm surface such as a wall or a chair. You can also kneel if it is uncomfortable.

Once you are settled, start to breathe slowly in and out through your nose. As you breathe, focus only on your breath, watch it coming in and observe it flowing out. If your mind drifts away, don't worry – simply bring your attention back to the breath, treating your breath like an anchor to bring you back from thoughts that try to pull you away. The more you practise, the easier it becomes.

Once you feel settled, you can start the process of brain breathing. There are six steps, which I have outlined below. While working your way through the steps, stay in a relaxed posture with your eyes closed. You can also try this while laying down, although I often fall asleep when I do this. So I sit upright so I am alert and connected at the same time as being relaxed.

Step 1: Visualize breathing in through the very top of your head, into the centre of your brain. Make the breath slow and deliberate (but try to avoid snatching at the breath, but allow it to flow freely). Then breathe back out through the top of your head. Keep your focus on your breath at all times, almost as if you are watching it with your mind's eye. If you find that your focus drifts away, simply pull your attention back to your brain breathing.

Step 2: Visualize breathing in through the centre of your forehead right into the centre of your brain, feeling the breath move through you and watching it as it does. Then breathe out from the same spot.

Step 3: Visualize breathing in through both of your temples into the centre of your brain. Keep your focus only on the breath and watch it move from your temples to your brain. Then breathe out from the brain and out through the temples.

Step 4: Visualize breathing in through the point in between your eyes right into the centre of your brain, then breath out again through the exact same spot. Watch the breath as it flows in and back out again.

Step 5: Visualize breathing into your brain from the point between your nose and upper lip. As before, stay focused on the breath and watch it flow into you. Then breathe out from your brain through the same spot below your nose.

Step 6: Visualize breathing up into your brain from the top of your spine on the back of your neck. Feel the breath move through you and up into your brain and then breathe out following the same route.

Repeat the process two or three times, or more if you wish until you feel a state of complete calm and relaxation.

I approached this crazy-sounding process with an open mind, and by the time I had tried it a couple of times I had discovered an amazingly powerful technique that could help me calm down and relax in a matter of a few minutes.

If you search on the Be Sober YouTube channel you can find a video where I explain the process of brain breathing in more detail.

Focus on the hands

As if breathing into your brain wasn't stretching your imagination far enough, this method of letting go of uncomfortable thoughts and feelings also requires you to slightly suspend reality.

The good news is that this method works in just about any situation. I have used it when driving, walking, in the cinema and even midway through a half marathon when some unwelcome thoughts entered my head at mile five.

The tactic is really simple. All you need to do is be aware when something uncomfortable comes to mind, then pause and take a moment. At this point you need to focus all of your attention on the tips of your fingers; don't think about anything else. If your attention drifts away, pull it back to your fingertips, no matter how many times your focus slips. Keep coming back to the fingers over and over.

At the same time breathe slowly in and out through your nose, watching your breath as it flows, but then switch from watching the breath in your nose and instead try to imagine that you are breathing in and out through your fingertips. You will know it is working when you feel a pleasant tingling sensation in your fingers.

You can do this exercise for as long as you need. It is very easy to jump in and out of it, and there is no need to close your eyes unless you want to.

Do the opposite – write a new story

I firmly believe that the more positive energy we radiate, the more we will receive back in return. Trust me, I have seen this from both sides during my lifetime and I know with absolute certainty that projecting positivity is so much more rewarding than being negative.

It might be simple acts of kindness such as allowing a car to turn ahead of you, or helping someone in a store, right up to bigger gestures such as making a charitable donation or giving up your valuable time to help others. The fact is, you will receive way more smiles when you make it your intention to give out positive energy. When you receive more smiles, it becomes an almost self-fulfilling process as you end up being nicer and kinder out of habit.

Many people forget that we have choices available to us with almost every situation we experience in life. This is why I always recommend pausing for a moment when something that causes discomfort comes up – this short pause allows you time to consider the choices.

I was recently speaking to a wonderful lady who I have coached to help quit drinking. She had spent four days without drinking and then experienced a really tough day where a combination of episodes caused her irritation, anger and frustration that culminated in her feeling overwhelmed and deciding she needed wine to take the edge off the feelings she was experiencing.

She is a keen road cyclist, and the most challenging incident happened when a car drove past her while she was on her bike. The driver of the car was too close to her, and he had to brake sharply as he passed to avoid hitting her; his car skidded as he dramatically screeched to a stop, causing her to fall off her bike and leaving her on the side of the road feeling very shaken up and emotional at what had nearly happened.

The car pulled away; the driver didn't get out or check to see whether she was hurt. She saw that the driver had turned into a nearby golf club and she was now feeling incredibly angry and wanted to give the motorist a piece of her mind.

She got back on her bike and rode into the golf club. The car was nowhere to be seen, so she went into the club shop. Shaking with rage she asked the shop assistant to help her locate the driver so she could confront him and tell him exactly what she thought of his awful driving. But the shop assistant had no idea who the driver was and in the end the search for the mystery motorist was abandoned.

As I spoke to my cycling client the day after this episode and we went over the chain of events that led to her feeling overwhelmed, I asked her to think about pausing when challenging moments arise, and to consider if she could do the opposite of what she would normally do.

Initially, she was taken a back, but I explained that, instead of seeing things like this as a source of irritation or anger, she should see it as an opportunity to give out lovingkindness.

At this point I would like to state that I am in no way suggesting that we allow people to walk all over us or treat us as doormats; I am simply talking about a change of approach.

So my client and I replayed this incident, and this time we changed the story and she did the opposite of what she originally intended. We assumed she managed to find the driver in the golf club and the conversation went like this:

Cyclist: 'I am so glad I found you. I saw you had to brake hard in your car and skidded when you almost hit my bike. I wanted to ensure you were OK?'

Car driver: 'Yes, I am fine, thank you. I am sorry if I caused you to wobble on your bike. I misjudged the gap on the road; it was completely my fault. I hope you weren't hurt?'

Cyclist: 'No, I am fine thank you. I did have a wobble, but there are no injuries. I actually wanted to ask if I could buy you a drink as a thank you. Moments like that make me glad to be alive.'

Car driver: 'Wow, thank you. Yes please, let's go get a coffee.'

OK, so we suspended reality a little in this example, but the point here is that, by doing the opposite and changing the story, you can change so many situations from being a source of annoyance or pain into an opportunity to give and receive positive energy.

I encouraged my client to spend the next 48 hours doing the opposite in any suitable situation that came up in her life, and I am pleased to say that after this period she told me that it felt so empowering it was as though she had control of the situations. She also said people were smiling more and being so much nicer to her, as though her energy was infectious.

You need to consider a situation before you take the 'opposite' approach. For example, if a mugger smashed me over the head and stole my phone and wallet, I probably wouldn't chase after him to see if he needed any extra cash. However, I do believe there is lovingkindness to be given to some extent in almost any situation. You may have seen people in the news who forgive the people who murdered their loved ones. They often speak about the sense of peace it gave them and how they were finally able to let go of some of the painful feelings they had held on to by doing this.

Just like my advice to my client with the bike, I would urge you to try mindfully adopting this approach for a couple of days to see how it feels, and to see what changes for you. Write it down in your journal and then consider whether it is something that should feature more often in your life.

Lovingkindness costs nothing, and it is often the biggest gift you can give to another person as well as to yourself.

Pay attention to your inner child

Earlier in the book you may recall that we looked at how our inner child can be the root cause of why we use alcohol to deal with past pain and hurt. This really is an important area to pay attention to. Even the process of noticing when our inner child is being triggered can be a big step towards preventing emotions overwhelming you and becoming a cue to drink alcohol.

When you find yourself in the midst of a craving or uncomfortable feelings, try to take a moment to address the root cause and find out whether your inner child is playing a part in how you feel.

It may be worth reading the chapter again and ensuring you are writing down any inner child experiences in your journal. Treat this as an information gathering exercise that will allow you to build a clear picture as you go forward.

As I mentioned previously, if you find that looking at past events is causing too much discomfort, please stop immediately and revisit this at a time that feels right. Instead, use a different tactic to calm your mind or release any discomfort.

Disrupt

Another great way of weakening discomfort is to disrupt it. I would often do this by going to the gym or heading out for a run. You can use any activity that works for you. Take the time to discover what produces the best results and know that you have this in your toolbox whenever you need it.

Use your senses

This tactic is a great way of focusing your mind away from any discomfort. It works best if you can write your answers down or type them into your phone, but if this isn't possible you can run through it in your head instead.

5: Notice FIVE things you can see around you. It could be a pen, a spot on the ceiling, or anything else in your surroundings.

4: Notice FOUR things you can touch around you.

3: Notice THREE things you hear.

2: Notice TWO things you can smell.

1: Notice ONE thing you can taste.

Change the word

If you find yourself saying things like:

'I can't calm down I need wine'

or:

'I won't be happy unless I have a drink',

switch the word to what you really need at that time. In my case it was often a hug from my wife or a chat with a close friend, so I would change those statements to:

'I can't calm down I need A HUG'

or:

'I won't be happy unless I have a CHAT WITH MY FRIEND'.

Another great tactic is to use the word 'BUT' and add it onto the end of any statements similar to these, for example:

'I can't calm down, I need wine'

would become

'I can't calm down I need wine, BUT I know that going for a run will help me feel better.'

Or:

'I won't be happy unless I have a drink'

would become

'I won't be happy unless I have a drink, BUT if I meditate it will probably weaken this thought.'

PASSES tactic

We looked at this tactic on Day 20 in Part 1. It is designed to allow you to pause and calm down whenever you feel that you need to get back in control. It is fairly easy to remember but you might want to keep it on your smartphone so you have it to hand as and when you need it. Take a moment to remind yourself of the process so you can use it whenever you require.

Countdown tactic

All of these tactics can serve you well, but one of the biggest problems I encountered was when I felt down or overwhelmed by emotions there were occasions where I simply couldn't motivate myself to move from my place of misery to using a tactic. It felt as though I was sitting with my terrible mood on one side of a vast canyon and the tactic that I knew would set me free was on the other side. There was no way of getting from one side to the other. I needed to build a bridge, and the countdown tactic is exactly that.

This tactic is incredibly powerful yet unbelievably simple. It is intended to propel you from a state of feeling low to enable you to jump into a suitable tactic by acting as your bridge across the vast canyon.

Follow the steps below if you struggle to move from negativity into a tactic.

Step 1: The first step is to decide what tactic you would like to use. Take a moment to choose one that you believe will serve you best based on how you feel at the time.

Step 2: Breathe deeply and slowly in and out through your nose, close your eyes and empty your mind of any unwelcome thoughts. Once your mind is clear, move on to step 3.

Step 3: Once your mind is empty, focus on the tactic that you want to do. Let's say you want to go for a run because you know it will dispel the negative feelings you are holding. With your eyes still closed and your breath remaining calm and steady, focus all of your attention in your mind's eye on what you need to do to start running. Visualize the process of getting changed into your running kit, putting on your running shoes, lacing them up and stepping out of the front door and then putting one foot in front of the other as you begin your exercise.

Step 4: When you feel ready you should start to count down, rather like the countdown you hear when a space rocket is about to blast off from the launchpad. Keep your eyes closed and begin at ten and count back all the way to one. You can do this in your head or say it out loud. As you reach zero you need to say to yourself 'MOVE'. This is your signal to launch into action.

Step 5: When you say 'MOVE' after the countdown ends, you need to instantly leap into action and carry out the process you visualized in order to begin the tactic that you feel will work best for you.

This tactic is rather like a mental kick up the backside, something we all need from time to time, and it works brilliantly. Give it a try the next time you feel stuck even though you know what you should do.

Tactics bowl

Once you have experimented with the different tactics and learned which ones work best for you, it can be fun to write each one on a piece of paper before folding them and placing them all in a bowl. If you use a goldfish bowl, please remove the water and re-home the fish first.

Next time you need to use a tactic to deal with discomfort, pick one of the pieces of paper at random from the bowl and surprise yourself with whichever solution you pull out. This makes the process surprisingly fun. As strange as it sounds I even found myself looking forward to the discomfort arriving in order that I could put my hand into the lucky dip bowl.

I can't emphasize the importance of filling your sober toolbox with the tactics that serve you best. Take the time to test them and practise the ones that work so you know that they are there to help you whenever you need to call on them.

Day 4 | The biggest mistakes when we quit drinking

Today is your fourth day without alcohol. There is every chance that you will be experiencing cravings for drink and that your emotions will be up and down; some people describe it like a roller coaster. Please keep reminding yourself that this is a temporary stage you are simply passing through.

I also want you to remember how alcohol will try to fool you into thinking it will end any discomfort you are experiencing. This is a complete illusion. If you need reminding why you can never return to the place of 'ignorant bliss' and that drinking alcohol will cause you more pain and suffering, go back and read the chapter from Day 8 in Part 1 right now.

Once you reach seven to ten days without alcohol, your mental resilience will have significantly improved and your emotions will have started to stabilize. Even if it feels tough right now, hang on in there. You will thank me later and you will also feel incredibly proud of yourself.

Working as a sobriety coach I see people make the same mistakes time and time again. I want to share some of the most common mistakes with you in order to set you up for success. These are the errors that I often see when people quit that usually cause them to struggle on the path to alcohol-freedom.

Not sticking with it

I am not going to sugar-coat it, the first few days after we quit drinking can be hard. Our emotions can be unstable: one minute we feel like crying and the next we are laughing out loud and wondering why we feel so happy, and at the same time as experiencing thoughts about drinking and fighting cravings. This is usually the most challenging part of the journey. Thankfully, it passes and it doesn't last too long. We have to learn to stand in the storm and be able to allow it to pass in order to grow stronger.

You may have heard of GABA (*gamma*-Aminobutyric acid) – it is a receptor and chemical in our brain which, among other things, helps regulate our emotions. In simple terms, it stops them flooding out of our heads and keeps everything in check. Imagine if I was talking to you about a friend of mine who you had never met, and I told you they had passed away. A normal emotional reaction might mean that you feel a sense of sadness. Without keeping those emotions regulated, you would probably find yourself with tears streaming down your face and wondering why you had become an emotional wreck.

When we drink regularly, GABA becomes affected; alcohol starts to take over the job of regulating our emotions instead. Imagine GABA as a set of brakes on your emotions. It knows when to press down so they don't run riot. It is a delicate and complex system. With regular drinking we allow alcohol to take over the emotional braking controls (and often the entire driving seat of our lives) and GABA no longer fully carries out the duties it is meant to. This can cause some serious issues.

When you quit drinking, GABA remains out of whack for a while despite the fact there is no longer any alcohol in your system.

We can find ourselves in floods of tears, in low moods, and yet within a few hours we can be jumping for joy. Make sure you are aware of this. Become curious about how you feel and write it down in your journal. Treat it as though you have an assignment to collect all the data that comes up with your emotions over the first two weeks and notice how it improves as the days pass by.

You may not experience the levels of emotional disruption I have described, but it is unlikely you won't have some level of discomfort. You need to be prepared; you know you need to go through this. Think of it as if you are running a marathon over that first week. At the start you feel fresh and excited about the 26.2 miles ahead of you, but as you get a few miles in you start to have moments where you wonder if it will ever end. You question your own ability and determination, but you keep going, you continue to put one foot in front of the other. Your mood swings from high to low, the cheering crowds spur you on, you notice painful blisters growing on your toes from the expensive new running shoes you decided not to train in, and your vest is chaffing under your arms. As you continue, the support seems to have faded away, it starts to rain, it feels positively gloomy and your mind is filling with doubts.

But even while your head is swimming with negative thoughts, you continue. You keep on moving forward. Eventually you hit the 20-mile marker. You feel lifted, you start truly believing you will finish this beast of an event. The rain eases and the sun begins to shine and you feel the warmth on your face. There are crowds of people now, they are shouting your name, willing you to keep going. Someone passes you water, you feel refreshed and energized. You have got this, you will do it, you believe in yourself and nothing is going to stop you. After what seemed like a monumental amount of time you have less than a mile remaining, your feet hurt and you have given everything you have both mentally and physically but nothing is going to prevent you from passing the finish line.

The people lining the route are practically in a frenzy. You pick up speed – you didn't realize you had these incredible resources, such inner strength and the ability to keep going when it feels so hard. Before long you see the finish, you cross the line with your arms held high, and as the medal is placed around your neck you experience more pride in yourself than ever before

Please don't think I am trying to paint a picture of doom and gloom. You have found yourself in the exact same cycle that I and millions of other people have ended up in. Staying stuck is no longer an option; you have to understand that the internal conflict won't ever end unless you take positive action. You need to go through this to come out the other side. But, believe me, it really is worth it and the rewards you are going to discover will change your life. That has to be worth a week or two of discomfort, so please keep moving forward, no matter how much it might hurt at times.

On top of feeling like you are riding an emotional rollercoaster, it is common to experience disrupted sleep, especially during the first week after you stop drinking. During the first few days of my own experience, heading off to bed seemed like the perfect way to escape the discomfort I was experiencing. Yet when I rested my head on the pillow I found that I was wide awake. I tossed and turned for hours before eventually dropping off. I woke in the morning with sheets that were cold and damp from sweating in the night and felt even more tired and drained than when I had gone to bed the night before.

The disrupted sleep lasted for three or four days before settling down. I remember the first night that I actually fell asleep quickly after getting into bed instead of lying awake for hours: I slept right through until the morning and woke up feeling fully refreshed and energized. It was a feeling I hadn't experienced before, and it felt wonderful. The as-yet-unknown joy of proper sleep rhythms awaits you.

After we quit, it doesn't take long before we start to experience sleep that truly refreshes and renews us. We enter all the cycles of sleep and our mind and body feel energized when we wake. This kind of sleep is essential. It helps us heal and reboot: without it we constantly feel tired, irritable and anxious.

I compare it to a computer. Have you ever had multiple website browser tabs and applications open on your laptop? I have 16 open on this one, right now. As you may know, this impacts performance — it can slow the computer down. But I often forget to shut my computer down at the end of the day. I leave it turned on with all of the tabs and programmes open and running. Over time, the computer slows down, it can't process all the information, it gets tired and needs a reboot, and eventually it will crash because it can't cope. Our minds work in a very similar way: we need to fully shut down at the end of the day in order to refresh and reboot. When we drink alcohol it is the equivalent of leaving the computer turned on overnight.

I see so many people get partway through the challenges of the first week and they convince themselves that alcohol is the only answer; it just feels too hard and they begin to believe drinking will solve it all and end the pain. This is an illusion. How will alcohol help? All it will do is put you back at the start and you will find yourself in a place where you have much worse inner conflict than before you started. Your subconscious mind will be trying to convince you that drinking is the solution, and your conscious mind will be trying to tell you that you need to quit. I need to make this clear – once you have that tug of war in your mind, it won't ever go away. Whether you drink or not, thinking alcohol will make it better is a complete fallacy which will test you and try to keep you stuck in the loop of that first week.

There is no peace found in deciding to end the short-term discomfort in favour of drinking. You have to stand in the discomfort; you need to be strong. Just work on getting through the first week. After that, you will start feeling better.

The great news is that you will wake up early one morning to find your mood is surprisingly good and you sense things have started to change. You will feel proud and thankful that you didn't give up after three or four days. You will start believing and will realize you have stepped outside of the loop of pain. You don't need to return to the start and keep trying to get through it over and over again; you can stop convincing yourself that you can never do it and believing that the tough period will never end. It just has, it is over: it is all positive from here.

It does end, and it ends much quicker than you might think – you need to know this. But many people make the mistake of not allowing themselves to get beyond the first week and experiencing how much better they feel. Don't let that be you. There is no comfort, cure or relief in going back to the start; all you will find is even more pain. No matter which choice you make, you are going to have to go through some tough times to come out on the other side.

So make your choice: do you want the short-term pain or the eternal mental pain of the tug of war that will never end? It seems like an obvious choice to me, but it is one that only you can make.

Learn to stand strong and dig your heels in when it starts to feel tough. This is the time when you might need a bit of willpower and the ability to draw on your inner strength. Believe me, it really is worth going through the short-term challenges for the long-term gains you will experience.

Not putting in the work

It can be all too easy to read a book or join a programme and believe that you have done enough to breeze into a life of alcohol-freedom, and, for some people, this absolutely turns out to be the case. But for the vast majority it is a case of putting the work in: we need to expand our knowledge and navigate a journey of growth; we get out what we put in.

Very few people master a new skill without learning about it and practising. Sobriety is no exception.

Don't assume that just reading a book is enough. Take the time to create a strategy that will allow you to continue building your knowledge and understanding. Start to put what you learn into practice and experience it in the real world. Gather that data, get really curious and explore what comes up in your experience; journal everything and reflect on what you write.

I am not saying you need to be reading sober books every day for the rest of your life or journal daily for years to come. But do take the time to discover different perspectives, hear new stories and learn new approaches to quitting drinking. Listening to podcasts, watching videos and connecting with others in sober communities are a great way to do this.

Failing to find support

I often work with people who have quit drinking for a period of time and found it a real test of their willpower. Often, they have made the decision and kept it to themselves, or only shared it with a small number of people, and they have failed to reach out to anyone for support.

Willpower doesn't last; it wears out over time and under pressure. You might recall that we explored this on Day 8 of Part 1. Take the time to review what you learned about willpower if you need to refresh yourself.

When we make ourselves vulnerable with other people they usually want to do all they can to help us. Not only do we end up with someone supportive on our side who we can turn to during tough times, but we also make ourselves accountable and have a sense of not being on the journey alone.

Be careful who you choose for support and accountability. Make sure you completely trust them and that you feel they are someone who will be completely supportive of what you are doing and will be there for you when you need them.

Another danger of trying to make a lasting change on willpower alone is that we often fail to explore tactics that will help us get through periods of discomfort that we often experience in the early stages of sobriety. This puts huge amounts of pressure on the willpower and it can send many people right back to the start.

Boredom

It is important to spend some time exploring pastimes and activities that bring us true joy. These might be activities or hobbies from our past that we gave up on many years earlier in favour of alcohol. It can be all too easy to sit around feeling bored, unproductive and unfulfilled. This can be a recipe for disaster. It impacts our state of mind and overall sense of wellbeing, and before we know it a drink can seem like the only solution.

A great trick for identifying a hobby or activity that brings you true joy is to make a list of the things that cause you to lose track of time when you do them. One of mine is writing; in fact, I have been at my desk writing these pages for over three hours and I thought it had only been an hour! This is because writing brings me joy. It focuses my mind and I lose myself because I become immersed in what I am doing and it is one of my true passions.

Same old habits

I often have people ask me how they are going to visit the pub after they quit drinking. My answer is always 'How do you know you will want to visit the pub after you have quit?' My point is that when we get sober and discover a new version of ourselves, we start to pay attention to the things that bring us true happiness and joy and the idea of sitting in a pub tends not to tick the boxes any longer.

It is dangerous to keep to old habits. We need to be kind to ourselves in the early period of sobriety and move obstacles out of our own way. Make swaps for healthy activities instead of joining in with boozy nights out and trips to the pub. Maybe when you feel strong enough the idea of a visit to the pub might appeal from time to time, but I strongly suspect you will have very little interest in going very often.

There is a saying that goes 'If you sit around in a barbershop long enough, sooner or later, you are going to get a haircut'. What I am saying is that we should avoid the barbershop, and save ourselves the headache. It may well be something that concerns you right now, but I would urge you to be open-minded and see how you feel about it after a break from alcohol.

Use the space provided to write down any areas you can identify in which you may need more education or more practice. Once you have identified these areas, make a commitment that details what you plan to do to ensure you are as strong as you can possibly be. This might be listening to podcasts or watching videos on specific topics, or possibly changing your mindset or routines so they fit with your new lifestyle.

_____

_____

_____

_____

_____

_____

Don't ignore any areas that might not yet be as strong as others. Ensure you are really honest with yourself and identify them in order that you can target your learning to develop your strength in all areas to ensure you don't feel exposed, regardless of whatever arises in your life.

Day 5 | Partners, kids, families and friends

Your partner, children, family and friends can become your biggest sources of support, accountability and encouragement when you quit drinking, and I would urge you to ensure that you don't deny yourself the opportunity of tapping into this incredible resource.

Our children often pick up on the signs of addiction, no matter how hard we try to hide it. They can feel wary about which version of their parents they are going to be dealing with, and this can cause them to experience stress and anxiety that often leads to issues with emotional neglect and bonding as they grow older.

I can clearly recall how I would often behave like I was two different people. It was as though I was asleep on the job when it came to being a proper father to my daughter. Thankfully, quitting alcohol allowed me to wake up from my slumber.

I know that she was left feeling insecure because of my unpredictable nature as she would never know if I had been drinking or whether my mood was stable. If I already had my supply of alcohol ready for the evening and felt a sense of relief that I would soon be drinking, then I would usually be fairly happy and act like a proper parent. But there were many negative experiences mixed with the positive ones. Usually when I was cranky, hung-over or drunk, I would be snappy, dismissive or rude, and over time these mixed messages played havoc with her confidence around me.

I recently recorded a YouTube interview with my daughter where she told me that she would never have opened up to me about the challenges she had faced around her gender identity and sexuality when I had been drinking, and how, since I had quit, she had felt confident and trusted me so much more than previously to the point that she was able to talk openly to me about what was going on in her life.

Since quitting I have been invited into her world, and we often share personal challenges that we work on together as a loving team. She trusts me now; she knows she isn't having to worry about a Jekyll and Hyde character who acts unpredictably and irrationally. Stability, safety and calm have returned, and our relationship has transformed.

At the time I stopped drinking I made myself vulnerable and was open and honest with my wife and daughter about what I was doing. They both supported me and were always there for me whenever I faced any difficult moments. My wonderful wife was never far away, with a huge hug waiting as well as wise words of advice and comfort whenever I needed it, and my daughter would constantly encourage me by checking how many days I had been alcohol-free and ensuring I was staying on track.

It felt like they were both proud of me. I had made myself accountable to them both and I wasn't going to let them down. It can feel hard talking to the people you are closest to about something so personal, but you owe it to yourself to have the right support around you, and very often the love and encouragement you need will be right under your own nose.

I didn't tell my wider family straight away. I wanted to have at least a week or two alcohol-free under my belt before I opened up. But when I did, the reaction was the same – I received nothing but support, love and encouragement, although my mother was alarmed to hear how much I had been drinking and wondered how she had never noticed. I smiled to myself and thought, Mum, you have never noticed anything I do, good or bad; that neglect is part of the reason I ended up drinking so much.

The 20/60/20 rule

In terms of my friends, I like to use what I call the '20/60/20 rule' because it seemed so apt when I announced my sobriety more widely.

- **20 per cent were overwhelmingly pleased for me. They asked questions, encouraged me and offered support. Some even approached me asking how I managed to stop drinking as they were worried about their own relationship with alcohol.**
- **60 per cent didn't seem bothered one way or the other.**
- **20 per cent reacted negatively, with a couple making unhelpful comments.**

Expressing my friends in percentage terms sounds like I am some kind of social butterfly with hundreds of buddies. This isn't the case, but this rule of thumb definitely seemed to apply even to the small number of people in my own circle.

It was quickly obvious that those who had reacted negatively were the people I had a relationship with where the entire friendship was based around drinking. Alcohol was the glue that held the friendship together, and as they probably had their own concerns about how much they drank, I imagine my announcement had probably touched a nerve, so I wasn't going to take it personally. I would urge you to do the same if you encounter any strange reactions.

They may also have felt that if I was no longer drinking we might no longer be friends, which I am sure caused some upset. The fact is that I was more than happy to remain friends; I just didn't want to take part in booze-based events any longer. If they wanted to meet for lunch, go out for dinner or coffee, then they could count me in. However, an evening sitting in a boring pub just didn't appeal to me any more. This wasn't personal; it wasn't about them, it was about me. I was on a journey of self-growth and developing a new awareness about what I had been doing to myself, and nothing was going to stop me.

I drifted apart from a couple of my friends, but with everyone else my bonds grew stronger as I became far more interested in connecting and spending quality time together instead of sitting at home drinking. I was also so much more present and found myself enjoying moments with my friends that had previously felt like an interruption.

The biggest change I noticed was my new-found desire to get out into the real world and explore activities and hobbies. This enabled me to make new friends in environments that weren't based around drinking. Sure, most of the people at the fitness classes, Pilates sessions and online groups I joined might have been drinkers. But the activities we were taking part in weren't about drinking. Alcohol wasn't at the centre of the show and was irrelevant. The new level of connection I was making was different to any friendships I had experienced previously, and I am thankful to my sobriety for allowing me to create some wonderful friendships that would never have happened had I not stopped drinking.

I also made hundreds of friends in the sober-community. These were with people who understood my own struggles and had battled their own demons. Some had been bigger drinkers than I, and others hadn't drunk as much; it didn't matter, because we all understood each other. There was no competition or judgement. I found the friends I made in the sober-world to be some of the most humble and caring people I had ever met.

I often coach people who find themselves leading a lonely existence. They might not have a partner and don't have many (or any) friends in their lives. They worry that life will be even more boring without alcohol, until they realize that it is drinking that has been keeping them trapped and holding them back from feeling motivated to get out into the big wide world.

I have witnessed so many people move from a place of loneliness to experiencing a new energy to connect with other people and proactively pursue their favourite hobbies and activities. It doesn't take long before they are forming bonds with new people and regarding them as friends. It can often be a case of facing a little fear at the start and calming down any 'what if' thoughts by drawing on their reserves of courage to go ahead and do it anyway, knowing that it is the right path to follow.

I was overwhelmed by the support offered my wife, my family and my friends: almost all of them had my back. I didn't encounter many people who were negative, and it is quite rare not to have loving support all around you once you open up about what you are doing.

However, it is important to be aware that there can be certain types of people who may not want you to quit, and it is almost always because they believe that if you don't drink it will negatively impact their own life in some way. This is selfish and often controlling behaviour, and I want you to keep your guard up and look out for any 'enabling' behaviour that you notice. If you experience any of these traits, you may start to question your relationship and ask yourself if this person truly has your best interests at heart.

An enabler is someone who makes it easy for an addict to return to their old ways. They might create situations or say things that cause this to happen. If we love someone, we should protect them from self-damaging behaviour and support their decision to stop drinking, but an enabler will do the opposite.

Even though an enabler may love someone and truly care, they can still hinder them by allowing their self-destructive behaviour to continue without boundaries, support or guardrails in place. Sometimes it can seem like an enabler is acting from a place of compassion, for example telephoning their partner's workplace when they have a raging hangover to make an excuse so they don't have to go in. But this allows the addict to avoid facing up to the consequences of their actions and makes it all too easy next time around.

An enabler might also fail to talk about the issue or minimize it so that it doesn't seem like a problem. By denying that there is an issue that needs to be addressed, it can give the addict the message that there isn't anything to worry about and that it is fine to keep on drinking.

Enablers can also behave in a selfish manner, and I have seen cases of partners who don't want their significant other to quit drinking because they don't want to drink alone or because they want to maintain a level of control in the relationship. So they might buy them wine or tell them that 'one drink won't hurt' until they finally give in.

If you find someone is attempting to enable you, then the best strategy is to tell them straight that their behaviour is not helping you reach your goals and explain calmly how this makes you feel. There is no need for this to become a confrontation, and it is far better approached from a place of vulnerability where you reach out with a view to explaining exactly what you need from them and making it clear what your expectations are.

Often, enablers will believe that they are trying to help, especially if they have seen you struggling with difficult feelings and emotions in the early stages of sobriety. They might think that offering you a glass of wine is exactly what you need when you are in the middle of a craving. It is very likely that their actions come from a place of love and that they simply need it making abundantly clear what the boundaries are and exactly what you expect from them.

Taking this one stage further, it makes sense to ensure that the people closest to you are also very clear in terms of the roles that you expect of them. You might have poured all the alcohol down the sink, but what will your partner do if you are begging them to go and buy you a bottle of wine from the store? What will it take for them to give in to your demands?

You need to be really honest with yourself and think about how far you would be willing to go in terms of pushing them to enable you. Use the space provided and write down what the conversation might look like. Would you shout, cry or become violent? What would you want your partner to do in that situation?

_____

_____

_____

_____

_____

_____

_____

I recently worked with a client who had a wonderful loving husband. He wanted her to quit drinking and supported her in her quest for sobriety, but she had never defined his role and what her expectations were of him. It didn't take long before she experienced some cravings and discomfort, and when she spoke to her partner about how she was feeling, his solution was to offer to go and buy a bottle of wine.

There was no malice here; he simply didn't know any other way of helping her. As we reflected on the incident and spoke in some depth about what had happened, we agreed that she would write down what she needed him to do if this were to happen again. She knew how far she might go and even considered a worst-case scenario of her physically shaking him and pleading for him to get her alcohol. But she was adamant that she wouldn't want him to enable her even if she was begging on her knees. She needed him to stand strong in the face of her requests, and he needed to understand what his role was.

That same day she spoke to her partner and explained that no matter how much she cried, begged or pleaded that under no circumstances was he to capitulate and buy her alcohol. She handed him her debit and credit cards so she couldn't buy it herself and she also handed him a letter. The letter was one that I had asked her to write to herself; she was only to read it if the discomfort became really hard to handle, and her partner was to hand it to her in a sealed envelope if she became emotional and continually insistent on him getting her alcohol.

The letter went like this.

Dear Jennifer,

If you are reading this letter, you are in the middle of a challenging moment and I need you to take a breath to pause and digest what is written here.

This is the rational, sober version of you speaking now, you need to pay attention. Wipe away any tears and listen up.

You know that alcohol is not going to help. It will simply put you back right where you were at the start and you have come such a long way. There is no going back to that place of ignorant bliss because it no longer exists. That place has gone, and if you believe it is somewhere you can get to by drinking, then you are sadly mistaken.

I am proud of my sobriety and how far I have come. I don't want you ruining this just because you can't sit with some discomfort. You will feel awful if you give in and drink. You might think it is the perfect solution right now, but tomorrow you will be devastated, full of shame and wondering why you threw it all away.

You aren't doing this for the current version of you; this is for the future version of us. Think about how you want our life to look in five or ten years from now. Do you still want us to be addicted and controlled by that awful substance that has ruined our life?

I want to make this very clear: the feelings you are experiencing right now will pass. They will fade and you will soon be back in your usual positive headspace.

Right now, you need to snap out of it, stop asking Harvey to buy you booze, and use one of your tactics from your sober tool box instead.

How about you also get your journal out and write a reply to this letter? By the time you have finished I am pretty sure you will be feeling a lot better.

Think about how you will feel if you were to drink. You will be even sadder than you are now. You will feel disappointed, and you will start to believe that you can never quit drinking successfully.

Love, Jennifer

This is a very powerful tool, and when you combine it with a partner who understands what they need to do when the going gets tough it works exceptionally well. It can have even more impact if you include a photograph that reminds you of the significance of your decision to quit drinking. This could be an image of your children or an occasion where you were drunk that you would sooner forget.

Jennifer didn't drink, and instead lay on her bed for an hour reading the letter over and over. She cried a little and felt sorry for herself, and then she wrote a reply in her journal. Before long the feelings began to fade before she walked back into the kitchen, hugged her husband and thanked him for not sending her right back into the alcohol trap. Had she failed to communicate this to him and made it clear what he needed to do, there would very likely have been a different outcome.

Use the space provided to write down what you might need to put in place to protect yourself and ensure that those around you are able to support and protect you if you experience any challenging times.

_____

_____

_____

_____

_____

_____

_____

If you decide that writing a letter to yourself would be useful, why don't you write it now? It is an incredibly powerful tool that will only serve to help you further down the line.

Take the time to ensure you take whatever action is necessary to protect yourself and those around you so you can get through any difficult moments without resorting to drinking.

You won't regret taking these steps, and they will serve to keep you on track so you can sit with any discomfort and learn to know that it always passes.

Day 6 | Becoming authentic

I often refer to myself as an all-or-nothing type of person. Whenever I do something I am either all in or all out, there is no middle ground, and this same trait seems to apply to just about every area of my life.

I recently invested in a Peloton bike after my much loved hobby of long-distance running was cut short due to a horrible knee injury. The Peloton bike is essentially an exercise bike with the added feature of allowing riders to work out live together. There is an element of competition while you exercise as you try to go faster than other riders and move higher up the rankings.

Just like my running had extended to ultra-marathons, my indoor cycling started heading the same way; it was almost addictive. I was finding myself on the bike daily, sometimes twice a day. I was pushing myself to go faster, ride further and finish in the highest position in the standings. Sure, it was a healthy pursuit but it was all-or-nothing behaviour in a nutshell yet again.

Had I started to swap one addiction for another?

Many of the people I work with describe themselves as having an all-or-nothing personality. There isn't really anything wrong with that until you mix it with unhealthy activities or an addictive substance, then it becomes dangerous.

But these personality traits can run deeper: why are we all-or-nothing with so much of what we do? Where does this come from?

Once again, we need to look to our inner child. On Day 4 of Part 1 we saw how, when children experience trauma, stress, hurt or pain, they are unable to rationally process the situation and will often end up deciding that, because it is a bad situation they must be to blame. Children can carry that blame and feeling of not being good enough through their entire lives.

In an attempt to compensate for our shortcomings, which only exist in our own minds, we can try to get the attention we crave, or the love, validation and acknowledgement we believe we truly need. We often do that by overachieving, working extra hard in school, excelling in sports, taking in part in extreme challenges or building brilliant careers before buying bigger houses and more expensive cars. We often try to show off our achievements or please other people rather than face up to the real version of ourselves.

Does any of this ease the pain or the hurt? Not for me it didn't, especially when I didn't feel acknowledgement for my adult life achievements from the people I was subconsciously trying to gain approval from. None of the people I was trying to impress were there as I crossed the finish line at my first London Marathon, and even this amazing achievement ended up feeling like yet more rejection. Nobody was impressed with bigger houses and fancy cars, the shine soon wore off and I was right back where I was beforehand.

Since I began exploring my all-or-nothing nature more deeply, I have found so much happiness in learning to simply be the authentic version of myself. I do this by questioning my decisions, pausing for a moment and asking if I am doing this for me or for someone else. I also check in with my inner child and ensure that it isn't Little Simon driving the decision to ride on my bike for an extra ten miles or to go ahead and purchase something new and shiny.

I even take a moment before replying to messages or responding to emails, especially if they stir up feelings of rejection. I want to be honest and authentic, and if that means I have to say no and disappoint someone, so be it. It is far better to be authentic than to live behind a mask hiding from our childhood insecurities.

I want you to start questioning the choices you make. Begin asking yourself if you are making a choice for you or for someone else. I want you to care less about what other people think and start taking care of you and your inner child. It will probably throw you outside of your comfort zone, but you will also feel a sense of joy that you are being totally true to yourself.

Use your journal to keep a log of how many times you say 'no' each day over the next two weeks. Try to train yourself to get into the habit of saying 'no' instead of agreeing to things just to please others, and avoid posting on social media if you think you are doing it to seek approval.

Being authentic is not about being different from other people, and if you are truly an all-or-nothing person, make sure you celebrate that and embrace it like a superpower. There is no need to compare yourself to anyone else – you don't want to disconnect in the pursuit of authenticity.

Simply put, being authentic is about being true to what you believe, letting go of your image and being strong enough to express your genuine opinions and feelings when you feel it is right to do so. The idea is to connect with our true identities and make the way we behave on the outside match the way we feel on the inside.

To become more authentic it is important that you:

- **Become more self-aware:** True authenticity is a goal you should work towards and is part of your journey of self-growth. We are under constant pressure not to be authentic. If we can start to become aware of when we are wearing a mask, being fake or trying to please others with our words and actions we can start to take steps to change.

- **Learn what masks you have:** A classic 'mask' we wear is how we present ourselves on social media and how we try to impress other people. We might behave differently in front of certain people at work or when we are socializing. By knowing which masks we wear, we can start to consider why we wear them and, more importantly, begin paying attention to our true identity.

- **Find out why you wear masks:** We avoid authenticity because we want to hide who we really are. If we know our flaws and accept that nobody is perfect, we are being true to ourselves. When you find yourself wearing a mask, take a moment to understand what you are hiding from. Maybe you are fearful of what other people will think of you, or perhaps you have a strong need to feel liked which overpowers your desire to be authentic. Once you have clarity on this, you can start to change.

- **Experience the honesty:** When we are authentic, honest and genuine, other people generally behave the same way as us. When we wear masks we are far less likely to experience honesty from others. If you are unable to share your true feelings, or you pretend to be someone you are not, then it is wrong to expect the same from other people. By being authentic, you will experience honesty and respect from others, and you will learn to grow from your new and true experience of the world.

Use the space provided to write down examples of times when you have been truly authentic.

_____

_____

_____

_____

_____

_____

_____

Can you identify any people, places or events that cause you to struggle to be truly authentic? Think about times when other people's expectations have made it challenging for you to be who you want to be and when you might have worn a mask.

_____

_____

_____

_____

_____

_____

You can give yourself permission to change. Don't get stuck in your own story. Instead, start to understand that our true identity changes over time along with our interests and opinions. Use the space provided to write what you could change in order to stick to being who you are and become truly authentic.

_____

_____

_____

_____

_____

_____

Embrace the path to true authenticity as part of your journey of self-growth. Enjoy the experience and notice how much better your life becomes when you pay attention to being the authentic version of you. Trust me – you will feel so much lighter when you drop the masks.

Day 7 | Review your freedom plan

It has now been seven days since you made a firm commitment and took the decision to quit drinking. I am sure you have experienced many different thoughts, feelings and emotions, and I hope you haven't found it too uncomfortable when you have had to sit with anything challenging.

Now you have come this far I can assure you that things will likely start to get a lot easier. As I have mentioned previously, the hardest part of the entire journey tends to be between days three and five. From here your mental toughness builds and you start to feel yourself growing stronger, calmer and more grounded.

It can be common to feel tired as you move into a new and healthy type of sleep rhythm. Continue to be gentle with yourself and notice whatever comes up. Avoid becoming sad, angry or frustrated, and instead try to adopt an approach of noticing and journaling while continuing to remind yourself that discomfort is very much a sign of healing and moving to a better place.

Throughout the remainder of the book we will continue expanding your knowledge and addressing specific challenges that are likely to arise, but for now you can relax. You are sober right now, and you have everything you need to keep things that way.

If you have experienced a setback, there is no need to give yourself a hard time; all you need to do is refer to Day 9 of Part 1, where we discussed celebrating your victories and learning from your setbacks and make sure you follow the steps to ensure you use a setback as an opportunity for a huge comeback.

Make sure you also consider using one of the suggestions we looked at previously around how you frame a setback in the context of counting days. You don't need to go back to 'day one' if you don't want to.

Today I would like you to spend a little time revisiting the freedom plan you made on Day 24 of Part 1. It is an opportunity for you to review the plan and reflect on what progress you have made. Maybe there are some areas that you need to adapt based on what you have learned or experienced since you created the plan.

Hopefully, there are also a number of areas of your freedom plan that you have actioned and made progress with. But if not, don't worry – today is a chance to revisit, review, and if necessary, renew your plan.

When you made your freedom plan I asked you to consider habits, behaviours, relationships and routines that were holding you back, along with any other areas of your life. Use the space provided to write down what the main areas were that you felt needed to change.

_____

_____

_____

_____

_____

_____

_____

Now write down what actions you either needed to take or have taken already in order to address the areas you identified. Keep these as two separate lists, 'done' and 'to do'. If you have already completed some of the actions, give yourself a big pat on the back. Don't forget to include the fact that you have committed a break from drinking. That's a monumental positive life change.

_____

_____

_____

_____

_____

_____

_____

Finally, identify the top areas you want to address that you haven't yet actioned. Keep the list to no more than five points to ensure you aren't overwhelmed with areas to change in your life. If there are more than five, keep a separate list of these alongside your freedom plan to ensure you don't lose sight of them.

You may still feel unsure about how to deal with certain specific issues, and some of them may relate to wider areas of your life that are not covered in this book. If so, ensure you methodically do your research, avoid becoming emotional and take advice from people who understand the best way to approach things in order to achieve the outcome you want.

As you write out the list of priority areas you want to address, I would also like you to note down exactly what outcome you would like from each of them.

_____

_____

_____

_____

_____

_____

_____

Keep a fluid approach and open mind as to your freedom plan. You have already made excellent progress, and there is no rush to change things right away. You might even want to consider putting a 'to do by' date next to the areas that still require your action or attention.

Use the final space provided to make any further notes about your freedom plan. Consider anything you want to edit, add or remove as well as reflecting on your progress to date.

_____

_____

_____

_____

_____

_____

_____

Day 8 | Sparks of joy and social media

Well done! You are heading towards the end of the toughest part of quitting drinking. I am sure you have experienced many different emotions and learned to stay strong when the going gets tough. You probably also know by now that you have the ability to sit with cravings and discomfort and that they will always fade, often quite quickly, and that the more you do this the weaker they seem to become.

You are starting to regain control. The 'wine witch' in your head is starting to lose her power. Alcohol is like oxygen to her; the longer you deprive her, the weaker she gets, and before long she will be starved to a point where you can no longer hear her voice.

Do not drink now – you have come too far. Focus on completing each day and remaining strong in your new-found sobriety. Trust me, it will get a whole lot easier very soon.

Today I want you to give some thought as to how social media features in your life. Start paying attention to how often you check your smartphone and find yourself liking posts, reading comments and updating your status. Do you find yourself reaching for your phone at every opportunity? Do you use it as a place to hide when you are faced with uncomfortable situations? Start to become mindful as to when, how and where you are using your phone and, in particular, social media.

If you have an iPhone, you can use the 'screen time' function to monitor how long you spend on specific apps. If you use an Android device, you can do this by looking at 'device usage'. Start to become aware of your use of social media and consider whether you think your consumption of this type of media is healthy, just right or harmful. If you use a journal, you could log the time over the next few days and take steps to adjust it to what you feel is a healthy amount of time.

If you feel that you should cut back on your social media usage, you can limit or restrict your access by using the inbuilt functions on your smartphone.

Social media can be a very powerful tool when it comes to quitting drinking, but I would like you to start today by checking in with yourself and considering whether your social media use needs changing. If so, make that change today.

I want you to bring a sense of awareness into your life in everything you do. Know that you can make adjustments and change your behaviours when you decide it is right to do so.

Facebook, Instagram, Twitter and YouTube all have thriving sober communities, and they can be a fantastic place to find support, accountability and tactics to help you thrive in an alcohol-free life.

It makes sense to be part of a private sober group on Facebook. None of your friends will be able to see that you are a member, and they can't read anything you post. This can be your safe space online and will allow you to connect with other people following the same journey.

If you haven't done so already, carry out a search on Facebook and identify which groups you want to join. I recommend joining no more than two or three to avoid your newsfeed becoming overwhelmed with posts about quitting drinking.

Make a note in the space provided of which groups you joined and why you joined them. You can find my own Facebook group by searching for 'Be Sober' on Facebook and then clicking 'Groups'.

_____

_____

_____

_____

_____

_____

_____

If you are already a member of some Facebook 'quit drinking' groups, you may have noticed that some members can post comments that might stir up uncomfortable feelings. If you are new to Facebook groups, I want you to be aware of this.

I often have people tell me how posts from other group members who have had a setback and are calling themselves a failure for finding themselves back at day one can feel triggering. My advice is to scroll past these posts, or unfollow the group or specific members who make them. Right now it is important to surround yourself with positivity, and you should keep your social media house in order to create an environment that works for you.

This aside, Facebook sober groups really are an excellent tool, and I would urge you to enjoy the journey of finding a tribe that allows you to feel part of something special. Remember, we are not losing anything by quitting drinking; we gain so much and this gives us a glimpse of the new world we are lucky enough to be entering into.

I have found Instagram to be another fabulous sober social media tool. I often urge my clients to create an anonymous Instagram account when they stop drinking and make a daily post sharing how they feel with complete vulnerability and openness. There is no need to share any specific personal details if you prefer not to do so. It's your account; you can make up the rules.

If you decide to explore the sober-community on Instagram, it is worth following plenty of other people who speak about sobriety, provide inspiration and help others. If you have made a new account, try to make yourself vulnerable, be totally honest and stay accountable with what you post. This will also help ensure you start getting people following you back.

Some brilliant sober accounts to follow are:

- <@besoberandquit> (this is mine)
- <@thisnakedmind>
- <@carlybbenson>
- <@soberexperiment>
- <@soberdave>
- <@alcoholexplained>
- <@the_sober_sessions>
- <@thesobersenorita>
- <@sobergirlsociety>
- <@thealcoholfreeco>.

If you are using your Instagram account mainly as a sobriety tool I also suggest the following:

1 Choose a strong profile photo. If you are keeping your account anonymous, select something eye catching that represents your vision of the authentic you. Pick a username that reflects who you are and one that you will be happy to keep long term.
2 Write a strong bio. This will help your profile get found in searches and will tell other users what your account is about.
3 Keep your account public if you are happy to do so, especially if you are posting anonymously. This will ensure you grow a following and build a community of your own fairly quickly.
4 Post daily, be vulnerable and be honest. Don't try to impress anyone or be fake; this is a place for you to be totally authentic and raw with what you share. By posting daily you can use Instagram a little like an online journaling tool. You can also look back at your posts and see how far you have come.
5 Finally, no matter what social media platforms you use, take the time to give them a regular spring clean. If there are people, pages or groups that post content that rouses your inner child or causes you any kind of distress or emotion, unfollow, block or delete them.

As Marie Kondo, the house-tidying expert says, if it doesn't bring you a 'spark of joy', put it into a pile, thank it for being part of your life and then put it in the trash.

It can be all too easy to allow negativity to creep in and for us to just put up with it. I'm not just talking about that pile of old VHS tapes that you haven't touched in over a decade; I mean everything from the people, possessions and places in our lives, right through to the media that we choose to digest in its many forms. There has never been a better time to carry out a spring clean and I recommend you do so regularly to help maintain mental wellness.

Can you identify any elements of your life that don't spark joy? Write them in the space provided (and then put them in the trash with the VHS tapes).

———————————————————————————————

———————————————————————————————

———————————————————————————————

———————————————————————————————

———————————————————————————————

———————————————————————————————

Maybe some of them are impossible to put in the trash. If so, what positive changes can you make to minimize negativity and surround yourself with joy? When it comes to people, I like to use the plumbing analogy of 'radiators' and 'drains'. If someone radiates positive energy, they are a 'radiator'; if they drain your energy, they are a 'drain'. In the non-virtual world we can't unfollow, remove or block someone in the same way we can on social media, and it isn't always possible or practical to put them in the trash.

Use the space provided to write down how you can minimize any negative energy in your life without putting people in the trash. Consider what boundaries you could put in place.

———————————————————————————————

———————————————————————————————

———————————————————————————————

———————————————————————————————

———————————————————————————————

———————————————————————————————

If you feel ready, maybe you could start to make changes right now? If you find yourself making excuses and delaying, consider the reason why – is there a specific fear or concern? If so, where is it coming from?

I want you to start embracing change. You have the choice and power to make change whenever you desire it. Tomorrow we will talk more about getting into the habit of change. But for now I will leave you to put the trash outside.

Day 9 | Deprivation or inspiration

One of the biggest surprises I experienced in sobriety was how excited I became about the journey that was ahead of me. The more I read, heard and saw about the incredible new community I had discovered, the more I wanted to be part of it.

I found myself nodding my head as I turned the pages of books like *This Naked Mind* by Annie Grace, *Alcohol Explained* by William Porter and *The Sober Diaries* by Clare Pooley as their personal stories resonated so strongly with my own. I began to realize that this wasn't a problem that was exclusive to me. I really wasn't alone in this as I thought I was before; I was becoming part of something really special.

As I watched inspirational speakers sharing their stories of addiction on YouTube, I could see myself in them. I knew exactly what it felt like when they spoke of their struggles and the pain of being firmly stuck in the alcohol trap. I saw hope, real hope, that I could change. So many people had spoken about their stories, and they gave me such great motivation. If they had been where I was and changed their own lives, then there was no reason I couldn't change just like they had.

They spoke about how their lives had transformed in so many positive ways – they were happier, had defeated mental health problems, improved their relationships and fallen back in love with themselves. I wanted that for me, I wanted to be just like them. I felt like I had discovered a hidden treasure, and the more I dug into it, the more valuable and beautiful it appeared to be. I soon convinced myself that being alcohol-free was the right fit for me. It seemed to reflect my values as a person and align with the lifestyle I wanted for myself.

Without the inspiration of others and investing time in my own education, I don't think I would have got very far. I would have felt like I was going it alone and hanging on in there with nothing more than willpower.

I also believe that, if I had failed to change my mindset to one of excitement and positivity about everything I would be gaining, I would have felt like I had lost something important in my life. It would have been as though I had been deprived of the one thing that I truly believed helped me relax and have fun. Nobody had ever challenged my beliefs about alcohol and forced me to take a long, hard look in the mirror at my own behaviour before spending time identifying what I really wanted for myself. I soon learned that alcohol was doing so much more harm than good. I no longer loved it; in fact I started to hate it, and I wanted its toxicity out of my life for ever.

I can't state strongly enough how this change in my attitude helped me, and I make no apology for repeating it throughout this book. It felt like the change that gave me the key to the door of a prison that I had been stuck in for over two decades. I held that key within me the entire time, but I didn't know where to find it. You hold that very same key within you.

You have to understand that it really is true: when you quit alcohol you become part of something very special. Not only do you embark on an incredible journey of self-improvement and growth, you also join a wonderful community that makes you feel part of something much bigger. Your whole life changes in the most beautiful way; you become self-aware, calmer, more rational and grounded. Problems that used to cause a meltdown seem much less stressful, and you feel fully equipped to face just about any challenge that comes your way.

I often use the term 'sober rebel'. As I mentioned previously, I don't identify with labels like 'alcoholic' and 'in recovery'. In my opinion they have a stigma attached to them and feel negative. Whereas 'sober rebel' is the complete opposite. Do you want to be a rebel?

Only around 5 per cent of people in the Western world choose not to drink through their own conscious choosing; this is excluding people who don't drink for religious reasons. So us rebels are very much a minority. Combine that with the fact that we have been faced with a lifetime of social conditioning to reinforce the belief that drinking alcohol is what we have to do to celebrate, commiserate or use for just about anything in between. Alcohol is everywhere. It has become the done thing and has turned into the only drug on earth that people feel uncomfortable about not taking. Why should we need to justify our personal choices to anyone? Can you think of a reason why you have to provide a justification for the choices you decide to make?

Probably not, because we don't need to justify ourselves. This is our journey. Forget wanting to fit in, doing things to please other people and the fear of missing out. None of this behaviour is who you really are, none of this is the authentic you. It is time to become a rebel.

Turning your back on booze is an act of rebellion; we are going against everything that has been pushed on us by society, marketing machines, our parents, our friends and acquaintances. It is probably the biggest act of rebellion I have ever carried out in my life, and I absolutely love the feeling that gives me.

I made sobriety my new obsession. I knew I would need to work on building my knowledge, and I accepted that there would be times when things would feel hard. But I was determined to move into an alcohol-free life no matter what obstacles stood in my way. Feeling happy that I had identified a problem, knowing I was working on improving myself, and being excited about the journey ahead set me up for success. If I had adopted a mentality of feeling miserable and down because I was no longer allowed to drink, then I am pretty sure it would have become an awful experience and it wouldn't have been long before I was reaching for the wine again.

It can be all too easy to tell ourselves that we can't do it, that we always fail, so why should we bother even trying? I want you to let that go now and adopt a mindset that reflects your truth. That truth is that, with determination, you can achieve anything you want.

When I entered my first ever marathon I felt excited yet scared at the same time. I knew it was a huge commitment both in terms of the training and taking part in the event itself. But I was determined, and once the decision was made I knew that nothing would stand in my way. Even if I had to get over the finish line on my hands and knees, I was going to do it.

I faced challenges with my training. I picked up injuries that held me back and frustrated me. I struggled to fit in the time to train, and I recall three-hour solo training runs in the howling wind and driving rain. I would feel broken and beaten, but I kept going. I continued to put one foot in front of the other because I knew that is what I had to do if I wanted to make it. I was determined that nothing would get in my way.

We have all been determined to achieve something at some point in our lives. We have made a decision to do it and we have made it happen, no matter what obstacles got in our way. Maybe it was moving home, having a baby, or changing career.

Use the space provided to write down times in your life when you have made a decision to do something and you were absolutely determined to reach your goal, no matter what got in your way. Think of examples where you achieved exactly what you set out to accomplish.

_____

_____

_____

_____

_____

_____

Reflect on this for a moment, now that you know you have the ability to do almost anything if you are motivated enough and you feel hungry and excited for the outcome. You have that strength already; you don't need to go and look for it, because it already exists inside you.

Think about the mindset you had in the example(s) you wrote down. What was the difference? Why did you become so determined? Use the space provided to describe your mindset and frame of mind at a time when you felt like nothing was going to stop you achieving your goal.

_____

_____

_____

_____

_____

_____

_____

_____

So now you know your own personal mindset map for success, you can clearly see what your frame of mind needs to look like in order for you to commit to something and see it through. You also know that you have this mindset within you because you have used it before.

If your mindset about alcohol isn't yet aligned with the examples you have described, make sure you keep working on it. Continue learning and moving to a place where you feel the same way as you did in the past when you were so committed and determined that nothing could stop you achieving your goal.

Mindset is the key. Work on wanting an alcohol-free life – make it your new passion, get excited about the journey ahead and embrace sitting in a space where you may not know all the answers right away. Enjoy knowing that you will learn about yourself and you will grow as a person, rather like a caterpillar transitioning into a beautiful butterfly. You have nothing to fear, and quitting drinking will change your life for the better.

There is nothing holding you back but yourself. Facing fear takes courage, and you know you already have that inside of you, too. It is a leap of faith to an extent, which is why I want you to embrace the joy of not knowing exactly what will happen instead of telling yourself stories about what may or may not change as you go forward. I have never heard anyone complain about being sober; I only ever hear people complain about how drinking alcohol has a negative impact on them them.

Become comfortable not knowing. You don't know all the answers at the start. Trust in the people who have helped you expand your knowledge, put yourself first in this and remind yourself about the reasons why you made the decision to take a break from drinking. Above all, know that you will be OK and that it is fine not to have all the answers in the first couple of months; allow yourself to go through the process of change.

Give yourself permission to get excited about sobriety because, if you stick with it and remain alcohol-free, you will understand exactly why it was worth getting so incredibly excited about.

Day 10 | The worry trap

Have you ever found yourself worrying about things? Maybe you have played through catastrophic scenarios in your mind of how everything will end in disaster and how your life is going to be completely ruined because of one bad decision or one unreasonable person who won't stop causing disruption in your life.

I even used to worry about how much I worried! It was draining and it overwhelmed me. My solution was to drink. It felt like it gave me a break from the emotional turmoil and the constant sense of dread that something awful was going to happen.

Of course, alcohol didn't help. When I awoke the morning after drinking, the worries were always back in my mind, the danger felt closer than before and I had lost any ability to rationalize or fight due to the alcohol-induced brain fog.

Worry is a negative type of overthinking. Many of the people I coach are highly intelligent and articulate people who have a tendency to overthink and therefore worry. When we worry, we have an internal conversation with ourselves where we enter a loop of negative thoughts that can gain momentum rather like a snowball growing in size as it rolls down a snow-covered mountain side. We rehash the same thoughts over and over, we look for solutions and get caught up in different scenarios as we play it through again and again, and all the while the snowball gets bigger and bigger.

Disengaging from worry can feel extremely challenging – once the thought has entered our head we feel a strong urge to try to find a rational solution. But the more we search, the more we worry. We start looking for evidence that nothing bad will happen. We might even search online to ease the worry, or we might try to avoid thinking about it altogether, but none of it works. The worry always wins.

People who have generalized anxiety often find themselves struggling with worries and having an internal dialogue about what they fear might happen in the future. These kinds of worries often start with two words: 'what if?'. Can you recall the last time you asked yourself a question starting with those two words?

Use the space provided to write down any 'what if?' worries you have at the moment, or have experienced recently.

_____

_____

When we ask ourselves 'what if' questions we usually end up going round in circles, listening to the same conversation over and over, and as we do this we end up creating even more 'what ifs' than we started with in the first place.

I used to have a repetitive worry that I couldn't shake off about the fear of someone leaving a negative review when I worked in my old marketing business. At the time we had over 300 positive online reviews and we had never received a bad one. When a client who hadn't had the experience he had expected threatened to leave a negative review, it felt as though my whole world had been knocked off centre. To you this might seem totally irrational, but that is exactly what worries are: irrational, negative thinking. My internal dialogue would go something like this:

- 'What if he leaves a bad review?'
- 'My reputation will be ruined.'
- 'Nobody will want to use our services.'
- 'The business will collapse and I will be a failure.'
- 'I will have no money and no job.'
- 'My staff and my family will be disappointed in me.'
- 'I will have nobody.'
- 'I can't allow this to happen.'
- 'But I can't control someone else's actions.'
- 'What if he posts a review on more than one website?'
- 'It will destroy me.'
- 'Maybe I can handle one bad review, but not two?'
- 'No, I can't even handle one, I need to give him a refund – this is so unfair.'
- 'But we didn't do anything wrong, the client misunderstood.'
- 'What if he doesn't understand and becomes more angry.'

Did you notice how I started with one 'what if' and ended up creating even more worries for myself? Of course, at the time I was also drinking heavily each day and it was like fuel to the fire of my anxiety and worries. Since I quit alcohol my worrying has significantly faded, but it took time and I am keen to address this right now if you have found yourself falling victim to the worry-witch.

Worrying can feel a bit like a craving for alcohol: it is overwhelming and you can't seem to shake it off. In the end, it seems easier to give in and submit rather than stand in the storm of discomfort until it passes.

Just like a craving, there can be triggers for worries – sometimes they appear out of the blue and blindside us, rather like the client at my old business who threatened to leave a negative review, and on other occasions the trigger is less obvious.

You might see an image on social media, in the news or on TV that triggers a worry, or you could hear information in a conversation or in the media that starts the worry chain, or maybe you find yourself in a certain situation that starts the worrying. I have had worries triggered by all of these examples, and I have equally had worries appear from thoughts that just popped into my head out of the blue.

I have tried to suppress worries, and it just made them come back stronger. I also attempted to distract myself, and that didn't work either. I have even worked on thinking positively (which I am pretty good at) but it was a useless antidote to worrying. I have categorized my experience of worrying into four different types:

- **Overgeneralizing:** one bad moment means the whole day will be awful.
- **Fortune-telling:** convincing myself that, by worrying, I can predict the future.
- **Maximizing:** convincing myself that I have minimal ability to adapt to a challenging situation and magnifying the likelihood of something bad happening.
- **Black-and-white worrying:** worrying about extreme, catastrophic outcomes with no middle ground.

I have tried to avoid situations that caused worries and seek reassurance from other people that things would be OK. I have made lists and gathered information, and none of it really helped.

Since I quit drinking my worrying has subsided and I have learned that:

- Having negative thoughts is normal and I accept that from time to time they will come to mind. Real problems do happen in our lives and it is perfectly normal to think about them. Life isn't great all the time, and I have learned to accept this.
- We never stop thinking. We have thousands of thoughts every day. It makes complete sense that some of them are going to be negative and some will cause us to worry.
- Almost all my worries and 'what if' thoughts have never come true, despite my conviction that the worst-case scenario is bound to happen. By recognizing that our worries very rarely turn into reality, we can start to see them for what they are: a trick of the mind.

Use the space provided to write down a worry that you have had in the past that no longer bothers you. Can you identify some of the 'what if' messages you asked yourself? Did your 'what ifs' come true?

_____

_____

_____

_____

_____

_____

_____

When I was a chronic worrier I found some powerful tactics that helped me manage the worries in a far more rational way. I wouldn't say they totally wiped out my worries but they certainly helped. The game-changer, obviously, was stopping drinking – it ended my chronic worrying for good.

Make worry time

This strategy worked really well. Instead of worrying all the time about a specific issue that wouldn't leave my mind, I would create a specific time to worry instead. I set half an hour aside in my diary each day, and that became my worry time. During the day I would tell my worries that I wasn't prepared to engage with them now, and that I had set time aside to talk to them in the morning during our scheduled 'worry time'.

When the time came I would sit in front of a mirror and have a conversation with myself about the worries on my mind. Throughout the day I would remind myself that I was not available to engage with worry at the moment and I would push the worries towards their next allotted time.

After a few days I had a breakthrough. I was worrying less during the day and was able to stop my worries in their tracks by reminding them that now wasn't the right time. Then, as I sat in front of the mirror for my morning worry meeting, I discovered that the strength of the worries had started to significantly weaken, as though I was becoming less bothered by them.

Of all the worry-busting tactics, this one worked best for me by far.

Stop procrastinating

We are often able to take proactive action to deal with a worry. It can feel challenging, and we might have fear about taking ownership and stepping up when we need to do it, but if we do nothing and remain stuck in a worry loop procrastinating, nothing is going to change.

If you know there is a way that you can end your worry by taking action, consider what you need to do in order to get back on track and end the worry. You might want to write a list of worries that can be dealt with by taking specific steps and use it as a 'to do' list by setting intentions to destroy them.

Journal it

Talking to a close friend or family member is a great way of easing your worries, but if you find it a challenge to talk to other people then your journal is your best friend. It allows you to work through your feelings, thoughts and, of course, your worries. Writing can be incredibly powerful, and it will help you uncover solutions to problems that might be causing you to worry.

Practise relaxation

Practising meditation, relaxation, yoga, breathing exercises or visualization can calm your mind even in the most challenging situations. By practising regularly you will find that you become more present and more mindful. This will give you a sense of being grounded and develop your mental resilience when it comes to worrying.

You will also find that relaxation-based activities will allow you to release much of the tension that you might be carrying and feel more at peace.

If you are a chronic worrier, as I once was, then I would recommend you read the book *The Worry Trick* by David Carbonell.

Day 11 | Accountability is responsibility

You may have heard people using the term 'accountability' in relation to quitting drinking. If you aren't sure what it is and how to use it to your advantage, then I would like you to take some time over this chapter.

Accountability is more than just staying true to the commitments you have made. It is about taking complete personal responsibility for your own actions and choices and understanding how they impact on both yourself and other people.

It is commonly accepted that accountability is one of the big keys to successfully quitting drinking. Alcohol can cause us to deny our problems, fail to communicate, believe we are trapped, become sad and depressed, and convince ourselves that nobody can help us. By taking personal responsibility we feel empowered in our own choices and we can make a game-changing decision that puts us in the driving seat of our own future.

Start to see the process of being accountable as a necessary step on the path to freedom. It may seem challenging, but you won't regret the benefits it will bring you and the support you will experience as your confidence in becoming accountable grows.

It is common to see people who want to quit drinking embark on the journey without the proper support or accountability required. They find themselves with nobody to turn to during the tougher times and have only themselves as the voice of reason. This can quickly turn into inner conflict, rather like the worry trap we discussed yesterday, and before long the internal turmoil can become overwhelming. We can talk ourselves into more worries, more fears and more problems, and feel that drinking is the only solution to stop the discomfort.

I have seen people actively avoid becoming accountable because they know that their behaviour will be placed under a spotlight and they will have to take responsibility for their own actions. This is exactly why accountability works. If we run away from it, we are sending a clear message that we aren't ready to commit, and we aren't willing to be open and honest with ourselves or others.

It can feel hard to reach out to someone about something so personal, especially if you don't know them well. But just like many other aspects of this experience, we need to use our courage to defeat our fears and take a leap of faith, safe in the knowledge that we believe in the process and we have a true desire to do whatever it takes to make a permanent change.

When you commit to working with a mentor or accountability partner you make a commitment with yourself to be completely honest and open. There is no point in lying; even if you have a setback you, are far better off talking it through and working together to ensure you learn from the experience and become stronger. There are a number of steps you can take to becoming more accountable, and today I would like you to decide which accountability solution feels best for you.

An accountability partner

Start by searching for a mentor or accountability partner. If you can share your journey with someone who has experienced the same struggles and challenges that you have faced, then you will give yourself a safe place to openly discuss what you are going through. A good accountability partner will be understanding, provide advice and give guidance without any judgement or pressure.

A mentor or accountability partner is not just about having someone to turn to when the going gets tough. It is about making a commitment to yourself and to them and keeping to your word while they work with you to reach your goals.

There are no strict rules around choosing a partner: sometimes people team up with someone who quit drinking around the same time that they did; on other occasions they might align themselves with someone who has been sober for a longer period of time. An accountability partner may even be someone close to you who may well drink themselves, but has your best interests at heart and dedicates their time to helping keep you on track so you can reach your goals.

You should also learn to lean on your accountability partner when you feel triggered or face a challenging situation. Ensure you understand the boundaries and set clear expectations in terms of how and when it is acceptable to communicate. Have boundaries clearly in place from the outset so there is no confusion on either side.

At the time I quit drinking I made myself accountable to the people closest to me; this included my wife and my daughter. They became a key part of my support team, and I knew that they were there for me to talk openly and honestly about how I was feeling and that they would help me through any difficulties I faced.

Many sober-communities and Facebook groups have the ability to allow people to connect with a mentor or accountability partner. Take your time choosing and ensure you find someone who feels like a good fit. Remember that, as well as you becoming accountable to your partner, they will often want to become accountable to you. In essence, you become a team and support each other on your respective journeys.

My own Be Sober Facebook group has a mentorship programme, and many members will simply post in the group if they are looking to connect with someone for support. Due to the size of the group it is often possible to find people who live in the same town, city, county or state as you. Think about whether connecting with someone locally feels right or whether you would prefer someone further away.

An accountability statement

As well as connecting with someone on a personal level, it also makes sense to write out an accountability statement. It doesn't need to be a huge amount of words; it simply needs to state exactly why you have made the decision to be accountable, and outline what the risks will be if you don't stick to the promises you have made. You can keep your statement somewhere close to you so you can revisit it at any time, for example on your phone or in your purse or wallet.

Only you can choose to be accountable, and it is a very important and personal part of the process of making a lasting change.

A sobriety coach or programme

You could also look to work with a sobriety coach or join a programme, either online or face to face. This will give you accountability and provide you with the structure and support you need while allowing you to partake in one-to-one or group sessions that will ensure you feel fully accountable. It is important to research any programmes you are considering joining, or any sobriety coaches you are thinking of working with, to ensure that they feel like a good fit. You can look at my own programme online at <www.joinbesober.com>.

I openly shared my decision to quit drinking online and felt as though I had made myself publicly accountable in doing so. I wouldn't recommend doing this at an early stage in sobriety, and we will talk more about 'coming out' as sober later in the book. Through sharing this very personal information, I felt as though I had no choice but to keep going. It was as though I had applied a positive kind of pressure to myself, but this doesn't work for everyone, and please wait until we look at this in more depth before you make a decision to tell the world that you no longer drink.

It is very important not to become accountable to someone who might want you to drink. I have seen cases in the past where a partner doesn't want their significant other to quit because they prefer having someone drinking alongside them. This can lead to a conflict of interests, and they might make attempts to derail you for their own selfish means. You need to be completely honest, and if you feel someone you are considering becoming accountable to might disrupt your progress, please find an alternative option.

Celebrate success

As well as sharing any challenges with an accountability partner, coach or mentor it is also important to celebrate your successes. No matter how big or small they might feel to you. It might be a milestone in terms of how many days you have been alcohol-free or maybe you have just experienced your first social night out without drinking.

Bask in the joy of growth and share your wins with your accountability partner. You are accomplishing some incredible achievements and you deserve to feel proud of the progress you make and the milestones you conquer.

Equally, you need to make sure you do the same for them. Take an interest, make a note of their own milestones and celebrate their victories together as a team. Check in with them regularly and show that you care by asking questions and paying attention to their progress. Chances are you will end up making a friend for life that you share a powerful and unbreakable bond with.

Use the space provided to write down what you feel you would gain personally from having an accountability partner.

_____

_____

_____

_____

_____

_____

Write a profile of your ideal accountability partner in the space provided. Consider whether they have already quit drinking or are at a similar stage in the process to you, as well as their location, gender and any other attributes that might be important in making your choice.

_____

_____

_____

_____

_____

_____

Now consider where you might find someone who would be a good fit for you. Write your thoughts in the space provided.

———————————————————————————————

———————————————————————————————

———————————————————————————————

———————————————————————————————

———————————————————————————————

———————————————————————————————

———————————————————————————————

Now you have identified what the profile of your accountability partner or mentor looks like, how about you take some action right now to find someone?

Are you willing to do that? Know that you are helping yourself by doing this. If you need to put a post in a group online, what is stopping you from writing it and posting it right now? If you need to send a message to someone or have a face-to-face conversation, take that step today.

Believe me, once you have this additional support on your side you are going to feel stronger and better equipped for anything that arises as you continue on your journey.

You don't have to limit yourself to just one accountability partner; some people have several and add more as they go forward. I have found that, even by making new friends in the sober-community, once I tell them my story of drinking and quitting and they have shared their own with me, we are in effect accountable to each other.

You deserve to have support and to be accountable. Be open-minded and never allow your success to be contingent on someone else staying sober. If you connect with someone who stopped drinking around the same time as you, if they were to have a setback and drink, it doesn't mean you need to do the same.

Finally, review your progress with any partner you choose and be honest. If you don't feel it is working out, simply thank them for everything they have done to help you and explain that you are trying something different. Don't people-please and hang on to relationships you have formed because you are afraid of letting people down.

Day 12 | Counting the days

Most people who quit alcohol count the days since their last drink. It is rare that I meet someone sober who doesn't know how many days, months or years it has been since they stopped. If they don't know it off of the top of their head, they almost always have an app on their phone that gives them the data very quickly.

Every day sober is another day you put further distance between you and alcohol, yet another milestone to celebrate. Before long that distance becomes so great that drinking starts to become something from your past. That was the old version of you, and now you are someone new. Counting the days can be a great way to notice your own growth, a springboard to success that helps you create momentum in sobriety.

Before you rush into counting the days, consider both sides of this. There is an argument that counting days can be counterproductive to the point of increasing stress and anxiety. A number of high-profile sobriety coaches urge their clients not to count the days and to embrace simply being free.

This thought process makes sense – the last thing we want to do is dwell on counting days and feel as though time is standing still. Using an app or manually counting days could induce a sense of feeling stuck, a little like counting the days of a prison sentence. However, my own experience, and that of many others who have quit drinking, is the opposite, and if we manage it correctly, I believe that some form of day counting can be incredibly motivating.

Surely you want to celebrate when you reach a big milestone such as 100 days alcohol-free and would want to know when your sober anniversary is? Many people forget that when we quit drinking we have two birthdays, rather like the Queen of the UK. Make sure you let all your friends and family know, so they are well prepared with cake, cards and gifts for you!

I did get a little fixated with my day counting app in the first month after I stopped drinking. I would look at it multiple times during the day, wishing time away. In hindsight I realize that this was neither productive nor healthy.

After a while I stopped obsessing over the days. The novelty wore off, and as time went by I was simply enjoying life too much to be overly bothered about how many minutes, hours, days and months it was since my last drink.

Every week that passed I found myself opening my day counter app less and less, and after a few months I was hardly ever looking. These days I might check it once in a while and it is usually when someone asks me how long I have been sober.

One other factor to consider is that if, like me, you have found yourself returning to day one over and over you might find that a particular point in time becomes a mental block for you. For example, if you have never gone beyond ten days without drinking you might feel increased stress and heightened anxiety as the tenth day approaches and start to convince yourself there is no way you can do it. If you think that might happen, I suggest not counting the days until you are beyond any obstacles like this.

Try to identify any such challenges ahead of time and write them down in the space provided. How might counting the days hold you back?

_____

_____

_____

_____

_____

_____

If you prefer not to use an app to track your days, you could consider adding your sobriety date onto your phone. You could do this using your calendar or write it down in your journal so you can find it if you need it.

If I was pushed to give a straight yes or no answer as to whether someone should count the days since they quit drinking, then I would say yes, but I would add that it should be done in a way that feels right. In some cases that will be through the use of an app, and in others it will simply be keeping a note of the date that they quit.

Day counting can be a great way to reflect on how far you have come, but for some the prospect of a lifetime of never drinking can feel daunting at the start. So you might use day counting to reflect on the past rather than to look towards the future. But, do remember, even in the hardest days during sobriety, you have to remind yourself that your worst days alcohol-free will always be better than your best days as a drinker.

Some people have a fear of returning to day one if they were to have a setback. There's no need to undo all your hard work if you have a slip. I recently had a client who drank a glass of wine after 30 days alcohol-free. She couldn't clearly explain why she did it; she simply reached for a half-finished bottle that had been in her fridge for weeks, poured it and drank. She described it as though she was on autopilot. She felt devastated that she was now facing the prospect of returning to day one.

In this instance my first recommendation was for her to count the days as 30 minus 1 to reflect the one setback she had experienced. Or she could instead use a percentage score system, which in her case equated to a 97 per cent success rate.

She loved both of these options as they gave a true reflection of her achievement while acknowledging the setback without wiping out how far she had come. She decided to go with the 30 minus 1 suggestion, and I am happy to report that she is now several months alcohol-free and still only has a single 'minus 1' on her sober statistics.

Use the space provided to write down what benefits you see in counting the days.

_____

_____

_____

_____

_____

_____

I have listed some of the best apps for counting the days in the resources section at the end of this book. Take some time to explore them all and discover which one might be a good fit for you.

Day 13 | When does it start to feel easier?

This was a question I asked myself over and over in the first couple of weeks after I stopped drinking. I had educated myself with books, podcasts, videos and blog posts about all the benefits and joys of an alcohol-free life, and I knew that in order to reach this 'promised land' I had to first endure some rough seas and storms, but I was willing to make this trade-off and ride out any rough seas in return for what I believed was on the other side. You should be willing, too, because it really is worth it. Alcohol had come close to ruining my life and, if it needed me to go through some hard times before things got easier, I was prepared to do it.

I felt like I was prepared for the voyage. My sober toolbox was full to the brim, and I had all the tactics and support I believed I needed in place. But now I had to face my fears and get through whatever was thrown at me. Probably like you, I am always telling myself stories and predicting the future. The outcomes in my mental predictions are rarely positive; instead, I will convince myself that something will go wrong until I end up relying on using the worst-case scenario as my guide when it comes to deciding on the best course of action. In this situation the worst case was that the boat would sink: there was no life raft in my toolbox.

Of course, this kind of fortune-telling behaviour is counterproductive and usually leads to increased stress and worry. I discovered that it was far better to approach the journey with an open mind and a sense of curiosity where I would simply try to observe whatever came up. Initially, this seemed far easier said than done, but I tried to watch my journey from above as an observer, rather like a spectator watching a boat in the ocean from high above in a hot-air balloon.

We looked earlier at how I learned to manage my emotions. I also made a conscious effort to 'feel' any feelings that came up, instead of 'thinking' about them. This is something that has served me well in many areas of my life since I stopped drinking, and I developed a specific set of strategies that allowed me to 'feel' instead of 'think'. For each feeling I had a go-to method of 'feeling' them and I became aware when I caught myself dwelling on a feeling or overthinking it. As soon as I caught myself in the act, I knew it was time to switch from 'thinking' to 'feeling'.

In my case, this mostly applies to how I handled negative feelings. I had no problem feeling the happy feelings – I just wished that I could experience them more often – but that was one of the reasons I was embarking on this journey.

Below are the main types of negative feelings I experienced at different points on the journey to being alcohol-free:

- Sadness
- Fear
- Vulnerability
- Being self-critical
- Anxiety

- Shame
- Withdrawnness
- Hostility
- Guilt
- Anger.

Once I had learned how to feel each of the feelings, it enabled me to experience a level of comfort and acceptance in knowing that they had arrived. When I truly felt it, rather than dwelled on it, the feeling would pass and eventually it would 'release'. I would then find myself back to my baseline of happiness again. I have detailed the strategies I used to release and feel some of these feelings in the hope that you can test them for yourself.

- **Sadness:** This would usually send me into a low mood, and I would feel generally down and withdrawn. Often I would be self-critical and look within myself for a comfort that didn't exist. Methods I found to release sadness were shouting out loud, 'I feel really bloody sad right now', or crying. I know that sounds self-defeating, but a good cry would usually release any sadness from within me. I also discovered that listening to music, speaking to close friends and dealing with the source of the sadness were all incredibly helpful strategies.

- **Fear:** After years of anxiety I often felt fearful, and this was my darkest demon. I felt like I was constantly battling with anxiety for control of my happiness. I found that writing in my journal to gain a rational perspective and meditating were the best ways to release the feeling. Over time I learned that when fear cropped up, it was a sign that I needed to reach inside of myself and draw on my courage to overcome it.

- **Guilt:** While I wasn't wracked with guilt I did occasionally experience it. There were occasions where I felt it was appropriate to take responsibility for some of my past actions and make amends by way of an apology. However, some things were best left in the past and I would release the emotion instead with physical exercise such as running or swimming.

- **Anger:** This is possibly my favourite feeling to release, and it is also one that came up on a fairly regular basis. Shouting it out loud worked very well for me, often with swear words included that I won't repeat here. Physical acts such as ripping up weeds in the garden also served as the perfect way for me to release anger. Another great tactic that works for anger is taking 'timeout' for 15 minutes before returning to calmly express why I feel angry. This allows me to give some thought to how I want to express myself, consider solutions and plan what I might want to say in advance.

Use the space provided to write down those feelings you experience the strongest. If you have had a break from drinking in the past, you might have a good idea what might arise. If not, think of other times where your feelings have challenged you and describe how it felt.

You can also take this process one step further and write alongside each feeling or emotion what you believe is causing you to experience it and then describe what action you might take in order to release it. Gaining this kind of clarity on your feelings and emotions will make you much more mindful and in tune with how you feel. With practice you will notice that you are much more capable of managing uncomfortable feelings and quickly able to take positive steps instead of trying to suppress them.

_____

_____

_____

_____

_____

_____

_____

It also makes sense to note down how much time you spend dwelling on negativity. For example, let's say that someone made a spiteful comment that caused you to feel upset and angry and it resulted in you experiencing a low mood. You might find that the mood lasts for a few hours or, in extreme situations, possibly days or even weeks. This can be hugely detrimental to your wellbeing and overall enjoyment of life.

Next time you find yourself with an uncomfortable feeling or emotion, note down how long you spent with it before you moved into a more positive place. This will be your 'personal best' record. Going forward your goal is to reduce the time and set a new PB during each spell of discomfort by being mindful of how long you spend stuck in negativity. If you spent three hours feeling down after a conflict last time, then aim for no more than two hours next time. Each time you set a new PB make a note of the new time and continue to try to get it down to a level that you feel is acceptable.

If you have ever released your feelings and been able to 'feel' them instead of dwelling and thinking about them, describe how you did this in the space provided in order that you are aware of what works for you. If you have never done this, write down a plan for letting go of each type of feeling you previously described.

_____

_____

_____

_____

_____

_____

_____

I experienced these negative feelings most intensely in the first week without alcohol. After seven to ten days I could feel myself growing stronger and noticed how something that might have made me angry or sad a week earlier wasn't having quite the same impact any longer.

As each week went by, my wall of mental resilience grew bigger and stronger, every passing day felt like another brick in my defences. The stronger I became the more I grew in my ability to handle different emotions and feelings. Even when something caught me off guard or out of the blue.

However, just because I had quit drinking, it didn't mean my life was suddenly perfect. Challenging situations and problems still came up, and I continued to experience difficult emotions on occasion. We are human and we are designed to experience emotions and feelings – they are mostly triggered to protect us from danger – but alcohol sends the entire system off balance and we can find ourselves with danger alerts triggering from even the slightest disruption in our life.

Like so many things in life, with quitting alcohol it often has to get worse before it gets better. I recall as a youngster that I suffered from a tendency to pick the skin on the same spot on my hand; I would do it over and over and ignore my mother's pleas for me to leave it alone. Before long it started to bleed, then a scab formed, yet I continued to pick – it was like a comfort blanket to me. Over time, with ongoing scab picking, it became infected and painful. I knew I had to go to the doctor, and when he informed me that I would need an injection in my butt cheek I knew that this was going to get a whole lot worse before it got better. This was the early 1980s and I was only young, so that syringe looked like a huge metal knitting needle and this draconian medic was planning on ramming it into my tender cheek!

The injection was incredibly painful. I was around ten years old at the time and remember crying in my mum's arms after the doctor had done his work. She took me for a milkshake afterwards to try to soothe me – it was banana flavour and has been my firm favourite choice of milkshake ever since.

But worse was to come before it started to get better. My hand had to heal and I had to resist the huge temptation of picking at the scab. I had to sit with urges to touch it and tell myself that I needed to be self-disciplined or it wouldn't heal and I would make it even worse than it already was. This could mean another trip back to Dr Butt Stabber and I really didn't want that.

Reading back the episode of my compulsive scab picking, it makes me realize how many hallmarks it has of my experience with alcohol and quitting. Just like the scab, when I drank I was harming myself and I started to realize it, then it required some pain and discomfort in order to start the path to recovery. This was followed by a period of uncertainty and challenges while I healed.

Thankfully, within a couple of weeks my hand was almost back to normal, and looking back I can see exactly how we often need to have an acceptance that things will get worse before they get better. It can feel hard when we don't know when the discomfort will end; we are left with uncertainty and a limited number of answers, and this can be extremely challenging.

The good news is that the discomfot does end. I can't tell you exactly when this will happen for you, and this is why you should adopt an approach of being open-minded and curious about whatever comes up on your own personal journey.

In my case I experienced a significant shift in the way I felt and noticed the bad feelings fading after a couple of weeks without alcohol. The cravings significantly diminished, and I was starting to feel much happier. But, equally, I have seen some people have tough times that last for a month or two while others may feel incredibly happy – known as the 'pink cloud effect' – almost straight after they quit, only to experience a crash and a flood of negative feelings and emotions several weeks later.

It is rare for anyone to have no negative emotions, discomfort or cravings. They usually come up at some point; only in rare cases do people experience none at all. Learning to accept that these negative emotions are likely to occur will set you up for success, and ensuring that you have go-to tactics in place for dealing with any bad feelings is critical so you can navigate the waters should they become turbulent.

There is something powerful in being able to sit in a state of not knowing. Uncertainty can be painful, and wondering when discomfort will end is extremely challenging, but if you can learn to embrace and accept that this is part of the process and a sign of your mind and body recovering, it can liberate you from the risk of falling into the trap of thinking alcohol might be a solution.

I make no apology for repeating myself here, but the biggest breakthrough in my case was moving to a mindset where I truly believed that I wanted to be alcohol-free more than I wanted to stay stuck in the same place I had been for over two decades. This change in mindset came about from educating myself, understanding exactly how destructive alcohol was and noticing how it had impacted my life, at the same time as learning about all the benefits of an alcohol-free lifestyle and becoming super-motivated to get to that place.

Try to see the first couple of weeks as an adventure into unknown seas. I can almost guarantee that you will run into some choppy waters, and there might even be times when it feels like your boat might capsize. You might even find a few hefty waves smash into the side of your vessel when you are least expecting it. But, if you want this new life, nothing will get in your way. You will keep following your internal compass and your ship will weather even the most ferocious of batterings.

It won't be too long before you see land on the horizon. This is the place you have dreamed of, the land where you will be free, at peace and happy. That watery crossing is one that you have to take – do it in the knowledge that you don't know what might come up and be OK with that. You are on a voyage of discovery, and I am certain that you have a taste for adventure.

Day 14 | When the racing mind takes over

Overthinking, worrying, storytelling, and constantly thinking about problems and feelings seem to be traits common among people who develop addictions. These behaviours often stem from our childhood or past experiences, and addiction can become a method of soothing the pain that has been dumped on us. The root to healing these issues will very likely be in dealing with the past. Earlier in the book we looked at your inner child. Begin to notice what triggers you, and draw parallels with the way you were treated by your mother or father (or siblings). If you find a link, take a closer look at this and work on letting go of it for good as the second phase of your journey to freedom and peace.

An exercise that really helped me was to identify my own negative traits and then to look at the other people in my life and examine their behaviours. I made direct comparisons with my mother. I didn't include my father, as he was never in my life and I knew very little about him.

I have provided some examples from my own journal; you can do the same sort of exercise if you feel it will be beneficial. It is important to be really honest and list as many of your own traits alongside triggering behaviour of others as you can.

I made a negative traits chart, which looked like this:

Rejection/abandonment issues

Simon: Even the slightest hint of being rejected or abandoned triggers me. I have cut people out of my life when they have betrayed my trust in a 'strike first' defence move in the past. Anything that makes me sense rejection is a trigger, as are most types of disappointments. I also become fixated and obsess over things that will make me feel wanted (the opposite of rejected). When people show an interest in my business or offer me publicity opportunities, talks and interviews, it brings me joy as I feel wanted and appreciated.

Mum: lived on her own for a long time after breaking up with my stepdad. She was self-sufficient during this period before she had a flurry of boyfriends. Her mum and dad stayed together right up until they died, but her father was violent and incredibly strict. I believe that her mother aligned with her father, and this probably made my mum feel alone, afraid, unsupported, sad and unable to feel heard.

People I like: don't give me rejection and abandonment signals. I don't let people in who are critical of me as I see this as a sign of rejection. I realize that I have surrounded myself with amenable people who won't abandon me. I often play the 'rescuer' in order for people to feel they need me in their lives. This strengthens the feeling of being wanted. Many of my friends fit this criteria.

People I dislike: have given me signs they might abandon me, often through being critical or judgemental. When this happens I become triggered and will usually fall out with them. I have lost a number of friends where conflict has erupted when I felt like they were rejecting me.

Unable to take criticism

Simon: Because of my abandonment issues, criticism has come to equal a threat of rejection.

Mum: I believe she also struggles with this. When I have made any constructive criticism in the past she has become upset. Yet she often criticizes me and rarely acknowledges my achievements in life.

People I like: do not criticize me – if they do, they know how to say it without upsetting me. Most of my friends fit this criteria.

People I dislike: have criticized me at some point – this includes friends, people in authority, work colleagues and family members, and it almost always leads to conflict.

Obsessive nature

Simon: I have faced addiction issues with work, alcohol, exercise or anything else that allows me to detach and soothe myself without facing up to my own insecurities. I also obsess over minor things that cause me uncertainty and my mind will race until they are settled.

Mum: obsesses and worries over uncertainty. She will project her worries onto me in the quest for reassurance. She has not suffered from addiction, but my father was a gambling addict.

People I like: tend to be addiction free, stable and don't obsess over things. I have aligned myself with people who are the opposite to both myself and my mother. When I encounter people who obsess, I tend to play the role of a 'rescuer' and try to help them.

People I dislike: Some of the people I dislike are obsessive, but this has never been the reason for falling out with them; this tends to happen when my rejection and abandonment issues are triggered.

Oversharing (super-honest/I can't lie/trust is critical)

Simon: I have always done this. My life is an open book (like one you are reading right now). Although I share so much information about myself, I struggle with emotional connection with some of the people in my life, especially my mother. I expect honesty from others and struggle being around people who hold back or keep secrets. If I believe I can't trust someone, I see no point in that person being in my life any longer.

Mum: is very open in terms of sharing information, but disconnects on an emotional level. I don't believe she lies to me, and I am unsure how she feels about people who lie to her.

People I like: Some of the people I am close to tend to be quite guarded and don't overshare, yet some of my friends tell me everything that goes on in their lives. Regardless, trust is critical for me, and I only remain connected to people I trust.

People I dislike: People who lie and can't be trusted. I see this as a sign of rejection and actively avoid having these people in my life.

I ended up with around 15 different sections covering the various negative traits I see in myself. I found the exercise to be incredibly revealing, and it made me realize that I have subconsciously avoided certain types of people and situations. It also enabled me to see how my mother's traits had been reproduced in me and my own behaviour patterns by adding to my issues around abandonment and rejection.

If you feel that working through this exercise for yourself will be beneficial, set some time aside and begin to explore. Be open-minded about whatever comes up, notice patterns and think about what you feel should change. Just because you have a negative trait, it doesn't mean it is wrong. Usually, it is a defence mechanism to protect yourself from your own insecurities.

This exercise will enable you to work on the areas that you feel you need to improve. It makes sense to start with those that cause you the most discomfort. You will find books, podcasts and articles online about each specific trait and can work through the traits as part of your own personal journey of self-growth. You might even want to add any areas that require work into your personal freedom plan.

Over the long term this will ensure you reach a place of true peace, where you become your authentic self and have a mindful approach around your own behaviours. However, this can be challenging, and I only recommend doing it if you feel strong enough to do so. You can come back to this exercise at a later date if you prefer.

A racing mind

As with sobriety, much of this journey is about becoming aware. Your mind will be racing for a reason. If you can discover what it is, you can start to piece together the puzzle and take steps to solve it – if you believe that gaining more clarity will be beneficial.

I would describe my racing mind as a busy train station. Each train is a 'thought' and they seem to come every few seconds. There is noise and chaos all around; the station is never silent as long as I am awake. Sometimes I will jump on one of the thought trains, and often the decision about which train to board is related to my own specific insecurities. When I step back and join up the dots becomes much easier to recognize my behaviour, pause and think rationally about whether I should act on a thought or not.

Some of the most common causes of a racing mind are:

- bipolar disorders
- depression
- anxiety
- PTSD (post-traumatic stress disorder often from childhood emotional neglect)
- OCD (obsessive compulsive disorder)
- ADHD (attention deficit hyperactivity disorder)
- addiction, particularly to substances like alcohol and drugs.

A racing mind can also be triggered by stress, especially if it leads to feelings of panic or worry. Regardless of the cause, a mind that won't settle is an unpleasant experience, and it is important to learn tactics to soothe it.

Eighteen months after I quit drinking I was diagnosed with ADHD. My wife had noticed many different traits that had become much more apparent since I stopped masking everything with booze. I was impulsive, hyperactive, obsessive, forgetful, lost personal possessions, couldn't relax or sit still for long periods and had regular mood swings. I was prescribed medication, and since then, I have found that many of the symptoms greatly improved. I credit sobriety for enabling me to get clarity on the fact that I have ADHD, as it was another problem that I was masking with alcohol.

To calm a racing mind, take the time to discover which of the following tactics work best for you, and know that you have them on call whenever you might need them.

Meditation/yoga/breathing exercises

When our mind is racing, it can begin to create a sense of panic, which can lead to an elevated heart rate and faster breathing. Using meditation, mindfulness, yoga or breathing exercises can allow us to quickly get back in control.

Breathing exercises and meditation worked incredibly well for me, and I learned that I could turn to them whenever I began to feel my thoughts were overwhelming me. With practice I was able to quickly calm my mind and return to a state of peace.

Even the simple process of bringing your attention to your breath and focusing on nothing else as you slowly breathe in and out through your nose is often enough to start to make you feel more relaxed and calmer.

As well as the apps I have suggested previously, YouTube also has a wealth of exercises. You can search for specific topics if you are experiencing a particular worry that you wish to address.

Physical exercise

It is well documented that exercise improves mental wellbeing, and I have found it helps significantly when it comes to managing my mind. However, when you are in a spiral of discomfort it can be difficult to move from a place of self-pity to physical exercise. When I felt at my worst, I knew that I needed to get moving and put one foot in front of the other to get back in control, but I simply couldn't do it. My wife would shout at me to get moving as I sat at the bottom of the stairs in my running kit with just one trainer on, while tears streamed down my face and I complained that I couldn't do it. She never realized how much motivational talk helped me.

Another excellent physical exercise tactic is to do something that elevates your heart rate and quickly release endorphins. Short bursts of high-intensity exercise are often perfect for this, and I found that launching into 25 jumping jacks would often calm my racing mind.

If you don't want to do anything too physical, a light jog, cycle, swim or a brisk walk will help move you to a much better place.

The worst thing you can do is nothing. Take that first step even when it feels challenging.

Distract yourself

If you have a hobby or activities that you enjoy and become engrossed in when you do them, you can use these as a tool for calming down your racing mind. If the hobby is calming, it can help quiet your mind at the same time as focusing you away from the thoughts.

If you don't have any hobbies, take some time to think about what brings you joy. The easiest way to do this is to think about the activities that cause you to lose track of the hours when you are immersed in them. This is a strong sign that you are doing something you love.

Think back to when you were younger. Which hobbies lit you up? Painting, sports, crafts, cooking, gardening, writing, reading, puzzles and music are all excellent options

Call a friend or talk to someone

The process of airing our problems and having someone ready to listen to our worries and concerns can significantly help reduce the intensity of racing thoughts. If you have a close friend or family member who can provide a friendly ear, make sure you lean on them.

Sometimes people hold back because they don't want to project their worries and stress on to someone close. Imagine if the situation were the other way around, would you want your friend to reach out to you so you could reassure and help them calm down?

Pick up the phone and dial.

Write it down

Your journal can often be your best friend – learn how to use it to your advantage. The process of writing out your feelings, thoughts and emotions can be incredibly calming and bring about a sense of more rationality and calm.

Many people continue to use their journal long into sobriety, and I often hear this credited with being one of the most helpful tools to quit drinking.

MOVE

Sometimes the thought of taking even a single step to start using a tactic felt like a momentous journey and I would struggle to move, rooted to the floor in misery.

I previously shared a tactic for moving from a place of feeling stuck that helps launch into using a tactic. The process is a simple case of counting down from ten to one and then saying out loud or in your head 'MOVE' before you take that all-important step and jump into whatever tactic you need to use to help yourself.

Once I discovered this tactic, when I found myself frozen on the floor awash with self-pity I would count down, then 'MOVE'. It worked, the process launched me into action, and before long I would be meditating or out running in nature and the racing mind would be fading away as my focus shifted towards a positive place.

The most important point is to start trying to notice your mind when it begins racing or when thoughts start to become overwhelming. This is your internal warning system and a sign that you need to act before it sends you into a downward tailspin.

Use the space provided to write down examples of when your racing mind has taken control. Try to be as specific as possible: can you identify what might have triggered this?

_____

_____

_____

_____

_____

_____

_____

Next, write down in the space provided what has worked for you previously. If you haven't tried to calm your mind before, note down which tactics you might use in the future.

_____

_____

_____

_____

_____

_____

It might be worthwhile using a mood-tracking app on your smartphone. This allows you to monitor your mood and any episodes of negativity. As you gather the data, you will notice patterns and work on taking positive steps to make improvements and changes. You will find apps that I recommend in the Resources section at the back of the book.

Day 15 | Coming out and social life

You are now over two weeks into your break from alcohol. Congratulations! My hope is that you are now starting to feel yourself emerging from the other side, and that your life is starting to become easier.

Maybe you have even found yourself smiling more, or noticing that you feel calmer. You might have spotted that you don't react in the same way you used to in certain situations, or that your anxiety and stress levels have reduced. Use the space provided to write down the changes you have already noticed after 15 days without alcohol.

_____

_____

_____

_____

_____

_____

Don't lose heart if you haven't seen many changes at this point; it is still early days and it can take a bit of time to start noticing big positive improvements in some cases. Continue to pay attention to what is happening, keep journaling and stay curious about anything that arises for you.

I also hope that you are feeling extremely proud of yourself, not only for getting through the most challenging part of the journey, but for taking such a big step and embarking on something that could be potentially life changing if your final decision is to cut alcohol out long-term.

Today I want you to begin thinking about the prospect of 'coming out' if you have decided to totally quit drinking after your break. This is the term used when somebody who has become alcohol-free announces it to their friends, family and acquaintances. Personally, I believe that I took this step too early in the process. I was so excited about my new alcohol-free life that I wanted the entire world to know. I believed that I had found the secret formula to happiness and assumed everyone else would be just as enthusiastic as me.

I previously mentioned the 20/60/20 rule. It was the experience of 'coming out' that first made me realize that it was a pretty accurate measure of how people react when you announce you are sober.

Right now you don't need to tell anyone you aren't drinking if you don't want to do so. There are no rules, and it is very much up to you who you tell and how you tell them. My recommendation is that you should communicate to the people closest to you as early as possible, in order that you have their support and make yourself accountable to them. Other than this, I suggest cutting yourself some slack and simply considering how you might talk to your wider circle as you go forward.

As you approach the end of your break from drinking I will ask you to decide how you want alcohol to feature in your life in the future and whether you want to take a further break or consider stopping drinking for good. It makes sense to be firm on this decision before you make any kind of public announcement about sobriety. You don't need to decide right now, but do begin to give it some thought.

For now, my advice is to use your journal to create three groups of people. You don't need to list each and every person by name within the groups – you will know who fits into each one. Broadly, the groups should be split as follows, but you can describe them as you wish:

- the people closest to you – your support team
- closer friends, family and acquaintances, but not those who you would consider within your 'inner circle' of trust and love.
- your wider circle of friends, acquaintances, social media friends, colleagues and family members.

If you make a decision to quit drinking long-term, then I recommend considering when you might announce it to each group. I strongly suggest having the first group on side as early as possible. You might then decide to inform group two after two months alcohol-free and the third group at some point after three months, for example.

I know some people who have been sober for over 12 months and are yet to make any kind of public announcement, and I am friends with others who 'came out' within the first week or two. There are no rules: do whatever feels right for you and know that you can adjust your plans at any point as you go forward.

Use the space provided to write down each group and at what point you might want to make an announcement to each of them.

_____

_____

_____

_____

_____

_____

_____

Regardless of whether or not you make an announcement, you may well find that people ask you why you aren't drinking – if you are at a social event, for example – and the last thing I would want is for you to feel caught out. Take a moment to consider the following three different approaches if anyone questions your choice not to drink before you have 'come out'.

Tell the truth

I have always favoured this approach. If someone asks you why you don't drink, it is fairly simple to respond with 'I am taking a break from alcohol'. However, this leaves the conversation open for further questions such as 'Do you have a problem with drinking then?' or 'Why are you doing that?'

In this instance it is important to be prepared. You could use one of the following responses, but do ensure you take the time to consider what feels right for you.

- 'I am taking a break for the health benefits, and I have already noticed some incredible changes.'
- 'I noticed that the amount I was drinking had crept up and decided to take a break.'
- 'I am on a detox and part of the plan involves not drinking.'

Make an excuse

The last thing I want to do is encourage you to lie, especially after we discussed working on being authentic earlier in the book. However, I would hate for you to find yourself caught in a difficult situation during your break from booze, so making an excuse is something you might want to consider.

If you feel that making an excuse is the right option, then do it: you need to ensure your sobriety comes before everything else, and it is important to protect yourself at all times, especially in the first few weeks.

Some of the (many) excuses you might consider using are:

- 'I can't drink as I am on medication.'
- 'I am driving so I can't drink.'
- 'I have to be up early for work tomorrow, so I can't drink.'
- 'I am training for a marathon/triathlon/other event so I am taking a break.'
- 'Alcohol reacts badly with me, no thanks.'

Keep it short and change the subject

The third option is to keep your response fairly short and then change the subject. William Porter, the author of *Alcohol Explained*, who wrote the foreword for this book, also uses this approach.

Your response might be along the lines of:

'I'm not drinking tonight. You have such a lovely home, when did you move here?'

I have a habit of oversharing, though it isn't always appropriate to tell everyone I meet my entire life story. I learned a brilliant tactic last year that quickly helps me decide who I should tell and what I should tell them. It is called the 'traffic lights' tactic. When you engage with someone, simply assign them a colour: green, amber or red (just like traffic lights):

- **Green light:** This means you trust this person and that you are happy to share personal information and talk openly about your sober story and how alcohol has featured in your life. Choose your 'green light' people carefully.

- **Amber light:** This is someone you can probably trust, but you feel you should proceed with caution. You might share some of your story with them, but don't give them everything unless the light changes to green.

- **Red light:** You can sense that this person may not understand why you don't drink, or that they might judge you or make a spiteful comment. If someone has a 'red light', don't give them anything – keep your response short and change the subject.

Practise this tactic and you will soon find that you are very much in control when it comes to deciding who to be open with about your choice to take a break or quit drinking.

Social events are one of the biggest sources of worry when people quit drinking, and I want you to ensure that you feel fully prepared. However, I also want to make you aware of something that happens almost every time someone stops drinking. It always makes me smile, and I am going to share the story of Jenny so you can see why.

Jenny was mostly a home drinker. She would drink wine from 6pm every day while she was cooking dinner, and once she started, she found it very hard to stop. She would usually drink around two bottles a night, but more recently it had been creeping up to three and it was starting to cause her worry.

She often found herself thinking about drinking during the day. Whenever something came to mind that troubled her or made her feel anxious, she found she could ease the discomfort by telling herself that she would be drinking later, and this helped to weaken the negative feelings, as she had a 'reward' to look forward to.

Each day she would head to the same store and buy two or three bottles of wine. She preferred it when her husband, Harry, drank with her; when she drank alone it made her feel awkward. But lately he had been uninterested in drinking and could take it or leave it. Jenny wondered how anyone could do that. Recently, she had noticed that even the process of picking the bottles off of the shelf in the store was giving her a sense of relief. This made her feel uneasy: how could a substance have this kind of effect without even using it?

Once or twice a month Jenny would head into the city with her girlfriends for food, drinking and dancing. If the weather was bad, they would congregate at one of their homes and drink the night away. These evenings were wild affairs, and Jenny has many 'war stories' that are often discussed in depth with her friends to roars of laughter as they recall embarrassing episodes and scrapes with the law.

These nights out would usually result in Jenny returning home at around 3am, although on some occasions she didn't make it home, despite her best intentions. Harry was often waiting up for her when she got home; he told her that he worried about her on these boozy benders and found it difficult to sleep, especially after she once became involved in an altercation where punches were thrown. Harry had started to worry about her drinking and felt that it was putting a strain on their relationship.

The days after these sessions were a complete write-off. Jenny had become used to having hangovers every day, but the pounding head and sickness after a night out with the girls were on another level. She liked to shut herself away in her bedroom and stay under the quilt for as long as possible. She would often stay in bed all day when the hangovers were especially bad, and call on Harry to bring her a supply of energy drinks, paracetamol and coffee.

Her drinking had been causing friction between her and Harry. He would often be grumpy on the days where the hangovers were at their worst, and Jenny would feel anxiety at the prospect of facing him when he entered the bedroom. But she needed the tablets for her headache, and coffee to give her some energy, and there was no way she was leaving the room.

Over time, arguments started to erupt between the couple as Harry became more concerned about her drinking and he grew frustrated that she wasn't taking responsibility for herself. Jenny was starting to become anxious and stressed when she wasn't drinking and the more the friction built, the more she had found herself turning to alcohol. She had recently started to drink as early as lunchtime while the kids were at school and Harry was at work. This seemed like a good idea, as it eased the uncomfortable feelings she was experiencing – until one day when he returned home early and she was asleep in the living room.

Harry knew she had been drinking; it was obvious. What followed was a huge argument, during which Harry threatened to leave her for good unless she changed her ways. He also called her an 'alcoholic'. This devastated Jenny. Her own father was an alcoholic, and he died of liver disease at the age of 47. She certainly didn't consider herself anywhere near as bad as him, but she was starting to understand why her behaviour was causing concern and the last thing she wanted was for her love of wine to destroy her marriage.

This was the point when Jenny reached out to me for one-to-one coaching. She wasn't particularly keen on the idea of quitting alcohol as she still believed it helped her in so many positive ways. But she could see the devastation it was causing, and she was desperate not to end up divorced because she couldn't get her drinking under control. She knew something needed to change.

Initially, Jenny was dead set on trying to work out how to moderate her drinking by having wine only every other day. This failed after three days; she felt like she was missing out, and it felt like a punishment. Moderation seems to be a rite of passage into sobriety; almost everyone tries it, almost everyone fails at it.

She was also angry that she would miss out on those wonderful nights out with the girls and was preoccupied with the fact that there was no way she could quit alcohol because she would be left without any kind of social life. Why should she have to face being the boring one stood in the corner drinking water, or, worse, missing out altogether?

However, as we worked through Jenny's beliefs around alcohol and explored what an alcohol-free life might look like, she started slowly to change. She was beginning to feel empowered by the knowledge that this was her own choice to make and it was very much a lifestyle decision to become part of the sober-community. She didn't realize how much damage alcohol could cause, even though it had killed her father, and she was totally unaware of the role drinking was playing in her anxiety and moods.

Even as she started to see the benefits in quitting drinking, she kept going back to how much she was going to miss those boozy nights out with her friends. It was a real obstacle for her, and I explained that I needed her to trust in the process, take a break, and keep working with me in order that she could be prepared for anything that came up.

Initially, Jenny agreed to take a 30-day break from drinking. Her husband was very proud and did everything he could to help her. This included removing all the alcohol from the house and setting boundaries in place to ensure she stuck to her goals. Jenny got herself a journal and plenty of zero-alcohol alternative drinks, and made sure she knew what to do when any difficult feelings came up. Although she was apprehensive, I could tell that she was starting to get a little excited about the adventure ahead of her

As the weeks went by, Jenny stuck with it and was noticing how much happier she felt. She observed how she was starting to enjoy a life without alcohol and began to wonder why she hadn't done it sooner.

She had stopped mentioning the boozy nights out with her friends, and instead proudly announced to me that she had joined a new yoga class and started horse-riding again, something she hadn't done since she was a teenager. I recall how she sent me a text along with a photo one evening as she cooked on her outdoor grill with Harry. It read 'Loving life! Haven't done this for years'. They were both smiling, enjoying being in each other's company again.

Towards the end of her 30-day break I asked Jenny how she felt about extending her alcohol-free commitment and she readily agreed to a further 50 days. 'I just feel so good,' she exclaimed, 'and it just seems to keep on getting better. I don't want this to end.' She excitedly told me how she had joined a number of online sober groups, made new friends and felt like she was part of something really special, as though she had joined a secret movement that only a small number of people were ever lucky enough to discover.

Not long after this conversation Jenny excitedly called me and told me how she had just received a message inviting her out with her girlfriends for their latest drinking date. I knew what was coming.

Jenny: 'I just got an invite to go out drinking with the girls.'

Me: 'I wondered when that would come. How do you feel?'

Jenny: 'I feel great! I know I was worried about losing this part of my life, but now it just seems like the most boring thing, and I have no interest in going. I can't believe it but I'm totally disinterested. I think I will have a date night with Harry and go to the movies instead.'

Me (smiling to myself): 'Good for you! That sounds like a great idea.'

The reason it makes me smile is because I experience this happening so often. People become hung up on their current alcohol-based activities and put an obstacle up that holds them back. They can't see what a life will look like without their drinking buddies or spending hours in the pub. They have conditioned themselves to believe that this is all there is to socializing. They have become blinkered to the fact that there is a wonderful world out there and when the blinkers are removed their old life seems rather colourless.

As they cut alcohol out of their lives, everything changes: they discover new hobbies and activities, they start to experience joy from the simple things in life, and before long they find themselves hooked on sobriety. Over time they find that an invite to attend a boozy night out seems like the most awful idea; they don't want to jeopardize their sobriety and, above all, it no longer seems like fun.

One of my sober-friends is Dave. You might want to follow him on Instagram (@ soberdave) – he shares some fantastic posts and inspirations. He once told me how his drinking life felt as though he was looking at the world through a very thin telescope. All he could see was his drinking activities around which his entire life revolved, and nothing else. After he quit, he said it was as though he had put the limiting telescope down and was now viewing life through the Hubble Space Telescope with a wide lens that allowed him to see the entire world in all of its incredible colour and depth.

That said, there are rare cases where people continue to head out on the boozy nights with their friends even after they have quit. I don't recommend doing this until you feel strong enough. One of my sober-friends tells me how she proudly stays until the very end of the night while she is out with her friends; she is always the last one on the dance floor and loves to watch the carnage unfold before driving them all home. The next morning she describes how she feels rather smug when she wakes up hangover free, happy and without any lost memories or regrettable behaviour to worry about.

Personally, I find drunk people annoying. When I have socialized around people who drink it is fine for the first couple of hours, but as they begin to spray me with spit, repeat themselves, talk loudly and not listen to what I am saying, I find myself wanting to leave. It stops being fun, and I know that I could be doing something far more interesting with my time.

In my case, I have learned to embrace 'JOMO' over 'FOMO' (the Joy Of Missing Out over the Fear Of Missing Out) and I encourage you to do the same because JOMO feeds your MOJO! Last New Year's Eve I stayed home with my wife and daughter: we watched movies and snuggled under new fleece blankets I had treated us all to earlier in the day. We ate popcorn during the movies, then laughed, played games and sang after it had ended. Of all the many celebrations, I remember this one with the most fondness, yet not one drop of alcohol passed my lips.

Use the space provided to reflect on a time when you had fun socially without drinking. If you struggle, then you might want to think about events during the daytime or maybe from when you were younger.

_____

_____

_____

_____

_____

_____

_____

A social event is fun because it is fun. Drinking doesn't make it more fun. Remember the two weddings I mentioned earlier in the book? I didn't drink at either of them – one was boring and one was a wonderful day that was filled with fun and friends.

In the early stages of my sobriety I made sure I was prepared for social events and had a toolbox of tactics that helped me deal with them. The first couple of social occasions were challenging, but before long I wasn't even thinking about alcohol; it just felt natural, and I can honestly say that I have more fun socially being sober than I ever had when I was drinking.

Surround yourself with support

Whenever I go to a social event I always make sure I have someone supportive with me, usually my wife and sometimes a good friend. This really helped me in the early stages. Even though I knew I didn't want to drink, it helped me feel strong and safe and gave me someone to talk to if I felt uncomfortable.

When I attend a sit-down event I will try to put myself next to other people who don't drink – if at all possible.

Visualize

Before I attended an event I would always take the time to visualize how it would go. I would use my journal to write it out. I found this to be a great help and enjoyed playing through the entire scene right from what I would be wearing, arriving at the venue, how the event would go, right through to heading home to my comfy bed.

This kind of visualization can be very powerful and allow you to explore different situations that may arise during the event, such as someone asking you why you don't drink.

Exit strategy

Even now, whenever I go to an event I will always have an exit strategy. Because I usually drive, this is fairly easy to do. When people get drunk and annoying I will often slip off unnoticed because the fun has ended. But equally, if people drinking around you begins to feel triggering, then you know it is probably time to leave. Drunk people don't generally notice when you head home early.

Alcohol-free drinks

There are so many incredible zero-alcohol drink options available these days. These drinks have been a huge tool for me in my own sobriety, helping me to fill the void in my evening ritual of opening a bottle and pouring a drink as I watch television. I am a huge fan of the zero-alcohol spirits and botanical drinks and I recommend you look closely at these. I have had many clients tell me they credit these drinks as being a huge part of their success in sobriety.

If I am heading out socially, I will always take the time to ensure the venue has drinks that I will enjoy. If not, I will call ahead and ask if they are happy for me to bring my own – I have even handed my own bottle of Seedlip to a bartender and asked him to keep it behind the bar just for me.

Another great idea is to speak to a friendly bartender and tell them that you don't drink and let them know what you would like to be served ahead of time. If you don't want to draw attention to the fact you aren't drinking by people hearing what you order, this is well worth considering.

I like to try to keep a glass in my hand at social events as it prevents people offering to buy me a drink. That said, when anyone asks me if I would like a drink, I will usually reply with, 'Yes please, I'd love one. Seedlip and tonic water, please'.

Finally, take the time to ensure your experience at an event is not about alcohol – leave that to everyone else. For example, if you are attending a BBQ, instead of thinking about drinking, make your experience about something else. You could put yourself in charge of the music or the party games, for example, or if you enjoy cooking you could get involved in the food.

The fact is that you don't need to worry about socializing, because when you quit drinking your 'life lens' widens, everything changes for the better, and you start to enjoy a wide and diverse mix of activities and hobbies.

And remember JOMO – you don't have to go – experience the joy of saying no and missing out.

Day 16 | If you experience a setback after you quit

We looked at how to handle setbacks earlier in the book, but today I wanted to explore this in more depth and ensure you are set for success no matter what happens during your break from drinking.

You are fast approaching three weeks alcohol-free, you are no doubt feeling proud of yourself and hopefully beginning to consider whether alcohol ever really added to your life or whether it was, in fact, taking away from it.

By now you should be armed with plenty of tools and tactics that you can use if you experience cravings or discomfort in the early weeks without alcohol. The more you use the tactics and realize that you don't have to submit to discomfort, the stronger you will become. There is huge power when you realize that you can sit with a craving and watch it pass. As you feel it weaken, your inner strength grows and you start to feel as though you are in control, not the booze.

I also hope that you have made yourself accountable to a few people who are close to you and that you have support on hand. Remember that support and accountability don't have to be with someone face to face; support groups online can provide the same sort of help. It might also be worth looking at local face-to-face support groups as a source of additional motivation and guidance.

While none of us wants to have a setback and will approach a break from drinking with a view that we will stick to it, there can be occasions where urges to drink might feel overwhelming. This is fairly rare, and most people are able to overcome them if they have the right mindset, but I do encounter situations where people can find cravings unmanageable and this can result in a setback where they drink, even though it isn't what they wanted to do.

You may have already encountered cravings and discomfort and started to learn that, as the minutes pass by, they weaken and subsequent cravings don't feel quite so powerful because your mental toughness has grown. It is so important to have an approach of total determination. I want you to believe you will do this, no matter what gets in your way. When obstacles arise, your job is to smash them down instead of returning to the start.

I want to ensure you are set up for success and feel confident that you know exactly what to do if you start thinking that taking a drink might be a good idea. Maybe you should fold the corner of this page so you know exactly where to turn should that happen. Then you can quickly jump back in if you need it. Hopefully you won't need to read this chapter again, but at least you know it is here for you should you need it.

This chapter is also here to help if you have a setback or a strong craving during your break. Come back to it in the future if you need to do so.

Dealing with strong cravings and discomfort

The simple fact with cravings is that you have to train yourself to resist them and it can take a bit of practice. Cravings are normal, and you should expect to experience them at some point. We create strong neural pathways with the habit of drinking, and it takes time to form new ones and for old habits to fade.

Cravings can be intense, but they will always pass. You have to practise sitting with them and watching them fade, or learn to use tactics to disrupt or weaken them.

It is your responsibility to know how to cope with cravings and to ensure you are prepared to deal with whatever comes up. This book should already have armed you with plenty of tools, but only you can actually notice a craving and pause to allow yourself to take action in the moment. If you allow a craving to sweep you away without taking a moment so you can make a choice, then you will find yourself struggling.

One tactic you can use is called PEATS; try to use this system if you experience strong cravings or uncomfortable thoughts and feelings.

P – Pause: The most important step to halting a craving or uncomfortable feelings is taking a moment to pause and reminding yourself that you have the power of choice in the situation. This moment of pause is critical; practise pausing ahead of time to ensure you feel prepared for anything that comes up. Maybe you could pause right now for a few seconds to prove that you have the ability to do it.

E – Evaluate: Once you have paused and recognized that you hold the power of choice, it is much easier to consider what the best action to take is in order to address the situation and achieve the outcome you want. Start to think about which tactic will work best for you and make a decision to use it.

A – Acknowledge and Act: Don't try to fight the craving or discomfort, acknowledge that it is with you. Then slowly countdown from ten and 'MOVE': the moment you say 'MOVE', you should jump into a tactic without delay.

T – Tactic: Jump into action. Turn to the tactics you have learned that work best for you. This might be leaping into 25 jumping jacks, going for a run, calling a friend, reading a book, walking the dog or meditating. There are many tactics – make sure you take the time to learn what works best for you before you need to use them for real.

S – Shift: your beliefs. In the midst of a craving you might tell yourself that a drink is going to help you relax and eliminate the feelings. While it might deliver this result for an hour or two, in the long term you will feel much worse than when you started. As you feel a craving pass, take the time to identify what your beliefs are and notice how they are false. You may have already explored them earlier in the book, in which case you can read back your notes and get clarity on the truth.

When the craving passes, take the time to write down exactly how it felt in your journal. This data is powerful, and you should draw on it to help you as you go forward. Note down what you felt were the key contributors to weakening the discomfort and refine your plan going forward to ensure you use these skills to your advantage.

Don't wait to have an intense craving or an emotional episode to practise the tactics in this book. You can use them in countless different daily situations. Slow down, pause before making decisions and become more self-aware, use the tactics to dissipate discomfort, and you will be well prepared whenever a craving strikes.

Remember, as the weeks go by, the cravings become weaker and less frequent. It doesn't take too long before they stop altogether and you find yourself rarely thinking about drinking. The more you sit them out and stay strong, the sooner this will happen.

If you have already experienced cravings or discomfort, use the space provided to write down what has worked for you, and what you have noticed about the strength of subsequent cravings after you have allowed them to pass. If you haven't experienced any cravings, use the space to write down a more detailed plan of how you will handle them.

If you experience a setback

Only read this section if you experience a setback. Know that it is here if you need it and adopt a mindset of 'I am never going to read that section'. If you haven't had a setback, don't read any further and continue from tomorrow's chapter onwards.

If you are still reading because you have had a setback, the first thing I want you to do is celebrate, laugh out loud and smile about it. Maybe you could do it right now: a huge deep belly laugh with a broad smile on your face. Go on, do it!

You could choose to get down about it, call yourself a failure and beat yourself up with a tirade of negative self-talk instead. But positivity is power and negativity will drag you down, so don't go there.

'Every cloud has a silver lining' and a setback is no different. I want you to celebrate it, and here's why.

This is as bad as it gets

So you messed up, but you can learn from your mistakes. You will grow stronger from the experience and the improvements you make from what you have learned. It will only get better. Almost everyone has a setback at some point before they feel they have sobriety mastered. Celebrate that you now have this out of the way and you are free to move forward with greater knowledge and power.

This is an opportunity

Smile at the fact you have been given a gift – the gift of an opportunity to learn what else you need to explore in order to break free from alcohol once and for all. The likelihood is that there is more growth that needs to happen. Even though it might feel frustrating and hard to deal with, treat a setback as a gift and look for the signposts directing you towards greater growth.

Look how far you have come

A setback gives you the perfect opportunity to reflect on how far you have come.

Use the space provided to reflect on where you are now compared to when you were drinking. Notice the differences and improvements.

_____

_____

_____

_____

_____

_____

_____

Now surely that is something to smile about!

This is a success

Now you have looked at how far you have come, remind yourself that you are on a journey and it is rarely a straight road; there are often potholes, sharp twists and turns and the occasional bump along the way. You could never have had a setback unless you had success before it happened. Celebrate your success and remind yourself that this is a journey, not an overnight change.

You can stop worrying

You might have been worrying about having a setback and living with anxiety. Now it has, nothing catastrophic happened, and you are still showing up and reading this book, so you are clearly committed to succeeding in sobriety – another reason to celebrate!

You can stop worrying now – let it go right here and now.

Now you can take responsibility

It can be easy to blame people, places, events and external factors for a setback, but now it has happened I want you to take complete ownership without any blame or judgement. Simply own the responsibility for your actions without berating yourself. This means you can take control of the future by ensuring you make healthy choices that are in your own best interests.

You will be stronger now

Almost without exception, every person who has a setback learns from it and makes changes and adjustments to their life to ensure they don't have a repeat. They also develop new levels of mental resilience by going through the experience and emerging stronger than ever before.

You can help others

Going forward you can help other people by sharing what you learned from your own experience of a setback. Take the time to understand what tactics work for you, what you could have done differently and how you will change things in the future, and you will be in a great position to inspire other people who are in the early stages of their own sober journey.

You don't need to reset to day zero

Some people falsely believe that a setback means they have to reset their sobriety day counter back to zero. You may recall how we looked at this previously, but here's a reminder: rather than setting the counter back to zero, you might favour simply adding 'minus 1' alongside the number of days you have been alcohol-free or express the total number of booze-free days as a percentage figure.

Don't spend any more time or waste any further energy dwelling on the negative. Instead, harness that energy to focus on understanding how you can change going forward. Use the space provided to identify what you can do differently and what you might need to adjust in order to avoid any further setbacks.

Think about the people, places and any thoughts or feelings that contributed to your setback. Write down how you will address them and what changes you will make going forward in the space provided.

_____

_____

_____

_____

_____

_____

_____

Now let's draw a line under the setback and move forward with renewed energy and positivity about the incredible future that awaits you.

Day 17 | What to do with the extra time and money

We've looked at whether it is worthwhile counting the days since you quit drinking; the decision is down to your own personal preference, and something you should try for yourself in order to discover what feels right.

While counting the days can be a great way to stay motivated, many people don't realize how much money they save when they stop buying booze, and this can provide an even greater reason to embrace an alcohol-free lifestyle.

The financial cost

Many of the popular day counter apps have built-in functions to allow users to track how much money they save each day when they stop buying alcohol. When I initially stopped drinking, money was not a huge motivator for me – I was more concerned about the damage I was causing to my mental and physical health. However, when I started to notice the savings racking up over time, it reinforced my new-found belief that a sober life is the best choice.

Apps that track how much money is being saved require users to input how much they were spending on alcohol each day. I was drinking between one and three bottles of red wine every day, usually with a bottle of beer before I started on the wine, and occasionally spirits afterwards; it wasn't a cheap habit.

On average, my daily spend was £30, every week I was spending over £200 on a substance that was ruining my life. I multiplied the figure to work out the annual cost, and my jaw dropped as I realized my habit was depriving me of more than £8,000 a year!

A recent report looked at the financial cost of cocaine addiction. A gram of average grade 'street price' cocaine sells for around £120 here in the UK. Users will commonly cut this down into around ten 'lines' or 20 'bumps'. Depending on the severity of the addiction, a gram might only last for a few hours, a couple of days or weeks. Let's assume the average cocaine user gets through between one and two grams per week, which would cost roughly £200 – that's the same as my own alcohol spend.

I was shocked to discover that the average marijuana habit cost less than my drinking outgoings. With an ounce of weed costing around £200 and yielding roughly 40–60 joints, an average user might smoke between three to six joints a day – on this basis an ounce could last up to three weeks before the supply requires replenishing.

The realization that my drinking problem was costing the same as an addiction to a class A drug was another wake-up call. I was addicted to a drug and I was no different from any other type of drug addict. The fact is that addiction is addiction and the substance we choose is simply a means to an end.

Use the space provided to calculate how much you spend on alcohol annually. Work out how much you spend on a weekly basis and multiply the figure by 52 to work out the annual cost. If you have been drinking for several years, you might also want to work out how much you have spent over the last five or ten years.

_____

_____

_____

_____

_____

_____

_____

Don't lose heart over the money you have wasted. Instead, think about how much you will be saving as you go forward.

On Day 9 of Part 1 I asked you to write down some motivating rewards to give yourself at three different points on your alcohol-free journey. Take a moment to reflect on your answers now, and ask yourself whether you want to revise them now you have a clear understanding of exactly how much money alcohol has been draining from your bank account. You may also wish to review the points at which you receive the rewards – these could be points in time or specific milestones or achievements. Use the space provided to do this.

_____

_____

_____

_____

_____

_____

_____

As you go forward, you may well make a decision to live alcohol-free and, if so you will be making one of the best choices of your life. I recommend always having a nice treat to look forward to and keeping a note of when you have earned it. Given how much money you are saving, you are completely justified in enjoying a lovely reward every so often.

If you feel confident enough to do so, I would love to see you enjoying one of your rewards. If you use Instagram, please tag me using @besoberandquit in your 'reward' photos and share your success!

What a waste of time

Money doesn't buy happiness or fulfilment. I had a successful business, a lovely house and a sports car, my family and I took several holidays a year and I haven't had money worries for many years. But I was emotionally disconnected and my life was controlled by an addiction to a poisonous substance.

Since the day I took my first job I believed that money was the only path to success; the more I had, the happier I believed I would become. When I was 30, I sold my first business for almost a million pounds. I felt thrilled and thought that this would mean a life of complete bliss and fulfilment. But the reality was that nothing really changed. It simply meant that, instead of buying cheap wine, I could now move on to more expensive bottles. I had more time to drink, and when I attended sporting events I could sit in the expensive seats where free alcohol was included.

Just like when you buy a new car and have that 'new object' feeling for a while afterwards before it becomes the 'new normal', this felt much the same. After a few weeks, I was back to my baseline of feeling pretty miserable and began questioning why all that money hadn't made me happy.

Life coach Tony Robbins sums up this happiness illusion perfectly: 'Success without fulfilment', he says, 'is the ultimate failure.' He states that many people believe that when they reach a certain point in their careers they will become instantly fulfilled, but often they are left feeling depressed with a sense of 'Is this all there is?'

People reach their goals having assumed that doing so will change the way they feel when they get there. Many people fail to pause for a moment to celebrate what they have achieved and instead set themselves bigger targets to aim for and shift their own expectations further.

Robbins goes on to explain how these high earners and achievers fail to ever be satisfied with who they are and what they have accomplished because they don't take the time to look inwards and instead only focus on the next big goal, leaving themselves feeling unsatisfied and unfulfilled.

He also says that achieving fulfilment is fairly easy, and suggests using the simple formula of practising gratitude, celebrating our achievements and giving to others as a way of changing our overall sense of happiness and finding peace in our lives. The good news is that you don't need to be a millionaire to feel fulfilled.

Consider what the word 'success' actually means to you. I have realized that success has very little to do with money and everything to do with my state of mind and knowing that I am showing up each day as the best version of myself.

After you cut alcohol out of your life you will notice a huge gift comes your way almost immediately. That is the gift of time.

Have you ever calculated how much time you spent drinking? When I added up all the wasted hours it equated to roughly 35 hours each week. That was almost 2,000 hours a year, which is close to three entire months out of every year thrown away.

That figure didn't include the time lost to hangovers, or the time wasted thinking about drinking. If I factor this in, too, then I imagine it would be more like six months out of every year that I lost.

I can never get that time back, but now I am free from my addiction and have a new passion for life, I have found that I make the most of my time. I appreciate how precious it is and ensure I value each and every moment. The same thing will happen to you if you decide to turn your back on alcohol.

Use the space provided to calculate how much time you have lost to drinking. Don't see this as a negative. Instead, reframe it as the amount of time you will be gaining without alcohol in your life.

_____

_____

_____

_____

_____

_____

_____

Use the gift of time wisely. The worst thing you can do is sit around feeling bored because you no longer have alcohol. Boredom leads people back to drinking, and you should be feeling more motivated by now and noticing the extra time you have available. Use that motivation as a springboard to discover the colourful and vibrant new world that is waiting for you.

We looked at your passions, hobbies and interests earlier in the book. I want you to ensure you are using your time to enrich your life and do what you love – whether that is spending more time with family and friends or taking part in sports, relaxation, outdoor pursuits or education. If you need to spend some time researching the best way to pursue the activities you want to partake in, get online and search for the right clubs, groups or places that will enable you to do exactly what it is you are looking for.

Time waits for nobody and we can never claim it back. This is your time and this is your story – you deserve to make it amazing.

Day 18 | Nutrition and diet

I often speak to people who find themselves eating more sugar after they have stopped drinking. It is a fairly common occurrence, and I want you to ensure that you don't give yourself a hard time if you have been reaching for more doughnuts and ice cream than usual, it's OK!

Not everyone experiences cravings for sugar, but it is important for you to be mindful if you suddenly notice that you are digging into tubs of ice cream, eating chocolate bars and devouring more than usual, especially if you rarely ate them in the past.

In order to become aware of what you are eating, it is sensible to keep a food diary, perhaps using apps such My Fitness Pal. But don't get down about it: you definitely aren't the only one who has developed a sweet tooth after quitting alcohol.

View any newly developed eating habits as a transition phase in your alcohol-free journey. The phase does not last for ever – it passes – and if you feel that you need a sugary snack in the early stages of sobriety to give yourself a boost, then go ahead and do it.

I occasionally encounter people who want to begin a diet or quit another addiction at the same time as stopping drinking. I always encourage them to cut out alcohol first. It can be overwhelming to attempt more than one big change at once. After two or three months alcohol-free your resilience and mental strength will have significantly improved, you will be well past any cravings or discomfort, and will find yourself in a great place to begin making other improvements. Please don't bite off more than you can chew at the beginning.

There are a number of theories behind the reasons why we might experience sugar cravings when we quit drinking. My view is that it is mainly linked to the effect that alcohol has on the reward centre of our brain.

When we drink alcohol it produces a chemical called dopamine which makes us feel pleasure; the chemical acts like a reward and is designed to help us survive. When we receive a hit of dopamine our brain will encourage us to repeat the action that caused it. The brain does this because it believes that whatever caused the dopamine hit is good for us, but in the case of alcohol this is a cruel trick that keeps us coming back for more.

Alcohol and sugar both stimulate the reward centre and cause a rush of dopamine – but we don't need booze, chocolate or ice cream to survive. After a dopamine hit our brain will create a craving for us to repeat the action, a feeling we find it hard to resist.

Many people view alcohol as a treat or reward, and once they have cut it out of their life there is a void. The reward centre is still calling for stimulation, so we seek out sugary snacks, which provide a similar dopamine hit and eases the craving.

Some alcoholic drinks are also high in sugar content, which can increase the intensity of sugar cravings. Sugar is thought to be addictive: in essence, the more we have, the more we want it.

If you have found yourself having lots of sugary treats, start to consider what healthy swaps you could make. There are many low-calorie healthier ice creams and chocolates available, or you could swap the treats for fruits, nuts or other alternatives. Experiment with your choices so that you can find a happy medium.

Over time you should find the desire to eat sugary foods diminishes; by becoming aware and paying attention to what you are eating, you will naturally start to make small changes that will lead to a more healthy diet.

As well as being aware of overindulging in unhealthy treats, it also important to pay attention to your overall nutrition plan.

Most people lose weight after they quit drinking, but it can take a bit of time. Having a sensible nutrition plan combined with taking regular exercise is the best way to ensure you see results in the shortest amount of time.

Better still, a healthy diet in sobriety can help reduce the intensity of cravings at the same time as restoring our brain health and cognitive functioning, leading to improved moods and a more positive outlook.

It makes sense to create meal plans ahead of time. I like to write mine out for the week ahead as it allows me to ensure I am getting a balanced mix of proteins, fresh vegetables, grains and fruit, and I won't find myself rushing to prepare meals at the last minute. Protein is one of the most important nutrients in the early stages of sobriety as it contains amino acids that help rebuild neurotransmitters in our brains.

Eat three meals each day – breakfast, lunch and dinner – along with a mid-morning and mid-afternoon snack. Even if you don't have time to cook every day, you can prepare meals for the coming days in advance or stick to quick and easy recipes instead.

It is crucial to drink plenty of water each day – create a foolproof routine that ensures you stay hydrated. I keep my water bottle next to the kettle in my kitchen; when I make my morning cup of tea this reminds me to fill it up and keep it with me throughout the day.

Water makes up around 60 per cent of our body weight; we depend on it to survive. Every single cell and organ in our body requires water in order to function fully. If we don't take enough water, we can experience a variety of side effects including:

- reduced energy
- headaches
- reduced brain function
- dry, wrinkly and flaky skin
- weight gain
- reduced metabolism.

Not drinking enough water has also been shown to increase our appetite and cravings for sugar, so you will likely find that taking the right amount of hydration each day will reduce the urges for sugar. Give it a try and monitor the changes in your journal.

There are conflicting studies around the right amount of water to drink each day, but the commonly recommended guidance is known as the 8 × 8 rule: eight 8oz glasses (roughly 2 litres) of water a day.

As you go forward, start paying attention to your overall nutrition and hydration. Try to keep a log of what you eat and how much water you drink, and slowly start to make small improvements when you feel ready.

Don't feel any pressure to change too much in the early stages of being alcohol-free. If you need treats or comfort food, then go ahead and do it. But if you decide to quit alcohol for good it is time to start paying attention and noticing where you could make positive changes.

Just like sobriety, your mindset is important. There is no point changing your diet if you are left with a sense of deprivation. Look at everything you will gain, not at what you are losing. You might need to educate yourself in order to get clarity on what you believe, so that you can form new and healthy belief statements that will serve you long-term.

Use the space provided to make notes or create a nutrition plan if it is helpful. If you don't feel ready to explore this area right now, you can come back to it later.

_____

_____

_____

_____

_____

_____

As well as looking at your diet, focus on the amount of exercise you take. It is recommended that we spend around two to three hours a week doing moderate aerobic activity, such as running, cycling, swimming or brisk walking. It is also suggested that we engage in two strength training sessions each week with one or two sets of ten repetitions with weights that are heavy enough to tire out our muscles.

If you prefer more vigorous aerobic exercise, the recommendation is to spend one or two hours a week split over two or three sessions. Greater amounts of exercise will provide more health benefits, but take care to train sensibly and work on your form in order that you avoid picking up injuries.

Day 19 | What you can expect

I recently conducted a survey where I asked members of the Be Sober Facebook group to share their experiences of quitting alcohol. I wanted to find out more about how they managed to cut booze out of their lives and what the benefits have been in terms of their health, wellbeing and outlook on life.

Over 500 people completed the survey, and participants came from all over the world, with the greatest majority living in the USA, UK, Australia and Canada.

My hope is that by sharing the results of the survey with you it will give you a good idea of what you can expect to improve in your life if you make a decision to cut out alcohol for good.

Participants were asked to answer specific questions and provide any comments they felt might be relevant. There were literally hundreds of comments, so I have shared the most relevant, interesting and inspirational later in the book.

Question 1 – What is the longest period you have quit drinking for?

553 people responded to this question. The responses were:
- Up to one week – 31
- Up to one month – 62
- One to three months – 147
- Three to six months – 87
- Six to twelve months – 89
- Over twelve months – 137

It was great to see so many people had succeeded with extended periods of time without drinking, with 56 per cent of participants answering that they have had over three months alcohol-free.

Question 2 – Are you sober now?

553 people responded to this question. The responses were:
- Yes – 438
- No – 41
- Trying my best – 74

I have often wondered what percentage of my group (which currently has over 13,000 members) are actually sober. Is all the hard work and support actually working, and helping people a lasting change? Clearly the answer is a resounding 'yes'.

I was overwhelmed when I saw that almost 80 per cent of people who responded to this question were currently living an alcohol-free life.

Question 3   During your longest period alcohol-free did you notice improvement to your sleep?

Participants were asked to provide a score from 0 to 10 – a score of zero meaning they had seen no improvement whatsoever (in other words, things had stayed exactly the same as they were when drinking) and a score of 10 being the biggest possible improvement.

The average improvement to sleep was 72 per cent out of 553 people who answered this question. This is an incredible improvement and provides concrete evidence that quitting alcohol has an enormous difference on the quality of our sleep.

Improved sleep leads to us feeling more motivated, energized and productive during the day. Good-quality sleep also impacts our mood and all-round sense of wellbeing.

Question 4 – During the longest period alcohol-free did you see an improvement to your productivity, in particular with work, energy and motivation levels?

553 people responded to this question and the average improvement was 77 per cent.

An increase in motivation and productivity was one of the biggest changes people who completed the survey had noticed.

I had the same experience when I quit. Without alcohol in my life I found a new level of energy, and felt a real hunger to do things with all the extra time, money and drive I had.

So the simple fact is, if you want to increase motivation and productivity by 77 per cent – quit drinking.

Question 5 – During your longest period alcohol-free did you notice improvements to your skin?

552 people responded to this question and the average improvement was 66 per cent.

People tell me all the time how they have noticed a change to their skin. They often receive comments or compliments about how their skin looks 'glowing' or how they suddenly look ten years younger. How good does that feel!

So instead of spending money on miracle cure skin products, the answer is to cut alcohol out of your life.

Question 6 – During your longest time alcohol-free did you experience any weight loss?

553 people responded to this question and the average improvement was 43 per cent.

We know that alcohol contains a lot of sugar and is also loaded with empty calories. Some alcoholic drinks are worse than others, with beer, lager and alcopops among the most likely to cause weight gain in drinkers.

However, when it comes to weight loss, quitting drinking is only one part of the picture. We also need to ensure we have a sensible diet alongside a regular exercise routine.

It didn't surprise me that weight loss was one of the lower scoring areas of change. However, the survey still showed a big improvement across the people who answered this question.

Question 7 – During your longest period alcohol-free did you notice positive changes to your mental health (such as anxiety, stress, happiness levels and depression)?

552 people responded to this question and it was the biggest improvement of all with an average improvement of over 77 per cent.

As well as seeing my own anxiety fade away to almost nothing and discovering a new sense of peace and happiness in my life, I have also spoken to countless people who have managed to eliminate stress, depression, unhappiness and worry all through quitting alcohol.

So here is the proof. If you want to see an improvement of over 77 per cent in your mental health, stop searching for the key to happiness and quit drinking – you will be amazed at what happens.

Question 8 – What tools did you use to help you quit drinking?

534 people responded to this question and were able to select multiple answers to share what helped them most on the journey to quitting alcohol.

- 'Sober' books – 443
- 'Quit drinking' websites – 307
- Online sobriety groups – 418
- 'Quit drinking' videos – 218
- Paid programmes – 183
- Face-to-face meetings – 95

Having the right tools around when you quit drinking can make the whole experience so much easier. They can make it fun and allow you to connect with new people, make friends and feel part of the sober revolution.

Many people also mentioned how much of a help podcasts were, too.

There are many incredible tools available to people who want to change their relationship with alcohol. At the end of the book you will find resources to help you discover some of the most powerful tools available.

Question 9 – During your longest period alcohol-free have you experienced an improvement in relationships with the people closest to you (close friends, work colleagues, family and loved ones)?

The survey asked people to measure how much their relationships with the people closest to them had improved, for example family, friends and work colleagues.

The results showed an average improvement in relationships of 68 per cent from the 560 people who answered.

I hear stories about improved relationships all the time. I have seen parents who have reconnected with their children after years of feeling distant and couples who have found a new love after drifting apart. There's my own personal story of reconnecting with my dad after six years of not having contact following a petty argument.

So many of the areas in this survey where huge improvements have been seen, for example in mental health, are problems that some people spend a lifetime trying to resolve, often without success.

I hope that by sharing the results of the survey it will help you understand that quitting drinking is all about what you gain, not what you give up. This is backed up by the data and the incredibly powerful comments from participants. For more inspiration, insight and motivation, turn to the back of the book to read some success stories from participants in the survey.

Day 20 | Are there any downsides?

I have a positive outlook on life and try to avoid negative thinking. My glass is always half full (though not with wine) and rarely half empty.

What kind of outlook do you have? Do you feel more positive and empowered about the choices you have been making?

Whenever I speak about sobriety, I share all the positive and powerful changes that have happened in my life, and this often inspires people to make changes to better themselves. But it would be wrong not to consider whether there are any downsides when you quit drinking.

My initial answer to this question was simply 'NO, of course there aren't any downsides!', but is this actually the case? Let's consider this question more closely. Playing devil's advocate and digging deeply into everything that changed in my life, I have spoken to members of the Be Sober Facebook group to ask for their experiences of anything they might consider a downside of sobriety.

I was surprised to find that there actually were some downsides on the path to being totally alcohol-free. However, even experiences that may have seemed negative were often part of a journey of growth and personal development that is ultimately leading us to a far better place.

The main downsides that presented themselves were.

Cravings

I know it sounds obvious, but this was the biggest downside that people identified. Cravings can cause significant discomfort and feel incredibly hard to get through. However, they pass, and over time totally subside.

Learning to get through cravings and learning that we can overcome them makes us stronger people. This skill enables us to deal with all manner of situations in other areas of life that can feel too uncomfortable for others to handle.

This inner strength is part of your sober-superpower.

Switching addictions

After quitting drinking, I found myself becoming addicted to work and exercise without even realizing I was doing it. Thankfully, I became much more mindful through my experience of stopping drinking and eventually I recognized my new behaviour patterns and took steps to adjust them to suit the lifestyle I wanted.

Dating

Sober dating can feel awkward at first. Do you choose to only date other people who don't drink and exclude yourself from 95 per cent of the population? Or do you date anyone who meets your 'swipe-right' criteria, whether they drink or not?

Only you will know what feels right, and there can be a bit of trial and error before you work out exactly what you want. Try to see it as part of your own personal journey of getting to know yourself and understanding your needs and desires.

I usually recommend that people are upfront with any potential dates, and tell them that they don't drink as a lifestyle choice. This avoids any uncomfortable conversations when meeting face to face and will usually rule out anyone unsuitable without needing to sit through a three-course meal while they sink two bottles of expensive wine as you look on from the opposite side of the table feeling bored and wondering why you didn't go to that yoga class instead.

Fear of failure

When we quit drinking so many areas of our life improve, but that doesn't mean that we won't continue to have ups and downs from challenges that might come our way. This is part of life and we should develop an acceptance that it happens.

At some point on the sober journey it is very likely you will have to face up to some fears. It might be a fear that you will return to drinking even though you feel confident, or it could be the fear of the unknown, or worries about having to deal with a difficult situation without having alcohol as a coping mechanism to lean on.

The good news is that when we stop drinking we usually also become 'emotionally sober'. This enables us to handle difficult situations with more clarity and logic. We are also far less likely to react in an emotional manner and will find ourselves with a calmer outlook and the courage to face up to any fears and overcome them.

Sober-fatigue

After four or five months sober I found that the initial honeymoon period had faded and I wasn't quite as elated as I had been in the early stages of sobriety. I felt slightly flat and a little less motivated than previously. There was no way that I was returning to drinking, but the sober-high wasn't quite so intense.

I spent some time journaling to explore why I might be feeling this way and eventually realized that the feeling was a signal from my mind that it was time to grow further. My 'quit drinking' journey was incredible and I felt absolute resolve in my decision. The flatness was pointing me in a new direction, pushing me to begin looking at healing issues from my past that impacted my present-day behaviour.

The feeling gave me a nudge to get outside of my comfort zone, explore new hobbies and make more friends. It was also the catalyst for a new project, which produced my first book, *The Sober Survival Guide*.

Our feelings and emotions are there to serve us, so instead of running away from them and becoming down when they appear, I have learned to ask myself, 'What is this trying to tell me?' and then I set about finding the answer.

The mask comes off

There is no escaping the fact that when we quit alcohol we remove the mask that we have usually worn for many years to hide away from any hurt, pain or stress in our lives. Without this mask we are effectively facing the world 'naked', as Annie Grace, author of *This Naked Mind*, describes it.

This can be an uncomfortable but incredibly powerful experience which often leads to us wanting to deal with any unhealed emotional issues or life challenges that have been unaddressed. Quitting alcohol forces us to look at the raw and real version of ourselves in the mirror. Sometimes we will see things that we don't like, but without booze there is no hiding from them, and we feel compelled to continue our growth and deal with whatever we discover.

Becoming a taxi driver

During my drinking days I would rarely drive anywhere after dark as I would be over the limit. After becoming alcohol-free I quickly discovered that many of my friends were overjoyed that I was almost always available to pick them up after they had been out for a night on the town. When they realized they no longer needed to get a taxi I found that I was being asked to give them lifts more and more often.

Personally, I quite enjoy these late-night driving trips and don't mind helping out. But it is important to set clear boundaries and to ensure that nobody takes advantage of you.

Sex

There is no getting away from it, the first time you experience sober sex it feels rather strange. Bearing in mind I had drunk daily for over 20 years, it was like losing my virginity all over again.

The only downside was the fear I had built up and the stories I had been telling myself before the experience. The truth is that sex is infinitely better when we are fully present, able to remember and in tune with all of our senses.

We have to step outside our comfort zone on the first couple of occasions, but after this it becomes a natural process.

Lack of energy and tiredness

During the first week after I quit drinking my sleep was disrupted and I found myself tossing and turning as I attempted to settle. When the morning came I was tired, irritable and snappy. Combined with cravings to drink and internal discomfort, it felt like a real challenge.

Many people experience sleep disruption and a lack of energy; it can impact us in different ways. I experienced a few nights of rough sleep before things started to settle down. After this my energy improved to levels that I had never before experienced.

However, some people have issues with energy and tiredness that can last much longer. In these instances it is vital to ensure we are paying attention to our diet, hydration and exercise. If things don't improve, it is worth taking professional medical advice, even if it is just to put your mind at ease.

Dealing with weird reactions

We have already looked at how people might react when they realize that you don't drink. No matter how prepared you believe you are, I am almost certain that you will find yourself feeling confused by some of the reactions you experience.

Some people seem to delight in mentioning your sobriety at every available opportunity and others might even try to encourage you to drink. Remember to reinforce your own personal boundaries and protect yourself from any potential risks.

One of the reactions that amuses me the most is when I am out with drinkers, usually at a restaurant and they say, 'You don't mind if I have a beer, do you?'

My standard response is, 'If I were vegan, you would still eat a hamburger, wouldn't you? So drinking is no different; it really doesn't bother me'.

Rather than reacting emotionally to any strange comments or reactions, try to view them with curiosity and ask yourself why people might choose to react in a particular way and what their reasoning might be for doing so.

FOMO and social challenges

Attending your first social events after quitting drinking can be challenging. It certainly was for me and I had to ensure I drew on everything I had learned to ensure I was set for success. I would be lying if I said I felt relaxed and had an amazing time on the first few social occasions; however, I did still enjoy them. I had reached another milestone and could drive myself home feeling proud, and wake up in the morning hangover free, sober and happy.

The early social events are a learning curve. We are discovering what we truly enjoy and at the same time finding out what we don't like. We can feel exposed, and if we haven't planned an exit strategy it can seem as though we are trapped. Make sure you plan in advance and before long you will enjoy social events more than ever before.

You will also find that some events no longer appeal to you. This may cause you to experience FOMO (fear of missing out). It is important to let this go, as it does not serve you in a positive way. Work on enhancing your JOMO (joy of missing out) by learning to say no when you feel it is the right decision.

It is better to be authentic and politely decline an invite than to please people and show up when you know you won't have a good time.

Use the space provided to write down any downsides you have noticed during your break from drinking. Then dig deeper and explain why they might serve you in a positive way over the longer term.

_____

_____

_____

_____

_____

_____

If you find yourself dwelling on anything negative that has come up since you stopped drinking, take a moment to consider whether you are looking at the bigger picture. It is usually a case of experiencing short-term pain for a longer-term gain. Take the time to get complete clarity and understanding, to avoid falsely convincing yourself that you are worse off than when you were drinking.

Day 21 | Review your freedom plan

Hopefully, today you find yourself celebrating three weeks alcohol-free. Take the time to recognize what a fantastic achievement this is; treat yourself to something nice as a reward for doing so well. How about a movie, a nice meal, or a trip out with friends or family? You have probably saved money already, and you deserve to enjoy something nice to honour your progress.

It has been a couple of weeks since you last reviewed your freedom plan, and today I would like you to reflect on what is working well and what you might need to adapt in your plan as you continue your journey of growth.

Over the past few weeks you may have identified areas of your life that you hadn't previously considered that you might now want to work on. You may wish to incorporate these areas into your plan as you go forward. There is no rush to bring about change, especially if you have bigger goals to work towards. Instead, break down your targets into smaller milestones and tick them off one by one as you get closer to reaching your objectives.

You may have also noticed that some of the points on your original freedom plan don't seem as important now. The likelihood is that you will be feeling much more grounded and calmer and will be able to handle problems that previously felt like a huge challenge with much more ease. It makes sense to review your plan regularly to check on your progress and assess whether it continues to reflect what you want to achieve.

Imagine if you had six months left to live, what would you change in your life? What would you do with the time you had left? I often ask myself this question when I consider what I could adapt to live a happier life as it helps me easily identify what I love to do and pushes me in the right direction.

Another great question to ask yourself is what job would you be happy to do without being paid for it? I work with a client who loves to be around dogs. She simply can't spend enough time in their company and enjoys walking and playing with them. She told me that she would happily walk and play with dogs all day as it brings her so much happiness, yet she was working in a grocery store in a job she hated and earning close to minimum wage at the time we had this discussion. We quickly identified a need to change, and she now works as a dog groomer and walker and has experienced a huge lift in her levels of contentment and happiness.

Take a moment to reflect on what you wrote in your freedom plan. You may also want to refresh yourself by reading Day 24 of Part 1 again. Then use the space provided to reflect on your progress and note down any changes you would like to make.

This is the final opportunity in this book to review your freedom plan. I encourage you to carry out your own review at least once a month to ensure you are heading in the right direction and remaining on track in terms of what you are working towards.

Pay attention to the following steps to ensure you remain focused and aware of the best steps to making long-lasting change, not only with regard to quitting alcohol, but to all areas of your life that you would like to adjust as you go forward.

- **Nothing is set in stone:** Be open to adapting and adjusting your goals. Don't assume that because you have made a plan you can't change it. Be flexible and open-minded and allow yourself to change your goals to ensure they match with your values and personal needs.

- **Break it down:** Make sure you break down any bigger goals into smaller milestones to ensure you know what you need to do and to allow yourself to feel that you are making constant progress.

- **Stop making excuses:** Making excuses can hold you back; be totally honest with yourself when you catch yourself making an excuse. Take the time to write it down and work out where it is coming from. Then create a plan to overcome your excuses and a strategy to force yourself in the right direction.

- **Track your progress:** It is essential that you review your progress on a regular basis to ensure you are staying on track and moving towards making the changes you desire. You will also no doubt want to make adjustments and changes to your plan over time, so by reviewing it regularly you can ensure you stay up to date and keep moving towards your objectives.

- **Identify and remove obstacles:** Watch out for negative self-talk and an 'I can't do this' attitude. Both of these are a warning sign that you have identified an obstacle that you need to overcome. Take a practical approach, use your journal and create a plan to remove any obstacles in order that they don't get in your way for too long.

- **Take responsibility:** You are in control of your own journey; nobody else is going to do this for you. You will no doubt have support and help along the way, but ultimately your life choices are in your own hands. Take personal responsibility for seeing through the plans you make and know that you hold the power to achieve your goals.

- **Setbacks are part of the journey to success:** We have already looked at setbacks when it comes to quitting drinking, and my hope is that you now recognize that setbacks in most areas of life help to set us up for longer-term success. Treat any setbacks as an opportunity to come back stronger; they are often a sign that we might need to make changes or try a different approach.

- **Get out of your comfort zone:** If you are planning on working towards some big goals, there will likely be occasions where you have to get outside your comfort zone. It might mean you need to have conversations that make you feel uncomfortable, or face up to a fear which you have previously avoided. Leaving your comfort zone gives you the courage you need to overcome these challenges and will allow you to continue moving in the right direction. You might want to practise getting used to being outside your comfort zone by writing a 'bucket list' of things you would like to do but have always been afraid to try. Then get out there and do them!

- **Focus on the positives:** Remain focused on the positive aspects and work on maintaining a mindset that radiates confidence and excitement about your personal goals. Remind yourself why you are making changes, and the benefits you will gain from doing so. During any challenging moments refer to your journal and reflect on the reasons why you have made a decision to improve these aspects of your life.

- **Live by your values:** Regardless of your freedom plan and any changes you might be making, start to become aware of what your personal values are, and pay attention when you find yourself doing something that goes against them. You will recognize this fairly quickly because it feels comfortable. Align your life with your values: the more you do this, the more happiness you will experience.

- **Focus on the future you:** Big changes can take time to achieve; don't lose heart if it feels like it is taking too long to get to where you want to be. Instead, take the time to remind yourself of how far you have come and consider who you are doing this for.

Day 22 | Continuing to grow and goal setting

If you are now beyond three weeks without alcohol – what an awesome achievement! You should be feeling very proud of yourself; take a moment to reflect on how you feel and what your experience has been up to this point.

If you haven't completed three weeks alcohol-free, please don't worry or put yourself under too much pressure. Take the time to understand what needs to change in order to succeed with a break from drinking going forward. Remember that quitting alcohol is similar to learning a new skill – it takes practice. Instead of becoming disheartened, I urge you to continue learning and keep going. I am certain you will get stronger and reach a point where you feel a powerful change that will enable you to find complete freedom from drinking.

We are now nearing the end of Part 2 which is structured around your 25-day break from drinking. You may have committed to a different length of time, and in a couple of days we will be considering what your next commitment will be. You might decide that you would like to extend the break, or you may choose to cut alcohol out of your life altogether. Start to give some thought to what feels like the right choice.

Most people think that being sober is simply a case of no longer drinking, which in essence it is. However there is so much more that happens when we remove alcohol from our lives. I am sure you have continued to notice positive changes happening as the days have gone by. Use the space provided to note down the top five changes you have experienced.

_____

_____

_____

_____

_____

Bear in mind that you are only three weeks into the journey, and I imagine you have already found it fairly easy to identify positive changes. Just imagine what will happen as you continue down the alcohol-free path.

In my case it was as though I had removed a heavy suit of armour that I had worn for over two decades, and which I believed had protected me from emotions, feelings and true connection. Once the suit of armour was removed, I felt vulnerable and naked, but I knew that I had to feel my true emotions in their raw and real form, without the ability to escape from them or suppress them by drinking.

Most people absolutely love the journey of growth and enjoy discovering and connecting with the authentic version of themselves. Of course, there can be times when you have to face up to a fear or deal with discomfort, but we find ourselves far more grounded and calmer in sobriety, and problems that might have caused a huge meltdown in the past no longer have the same impact.

The experience of becoming sober sets us up for success in many other areas of life. Most people realize that if they have the strength to quit alcohol then they have the ability to overcome almost any challenge. Everything else starts to feel pretty easy by comparison, and they start to feel less limited in their own abilities and develop a new level of confidence in themselves.

Combine this new level of confidence with reduced stress and anxiety and it can feel rather like we have developed some kind of sober-superpower. After three weeks alcohol-free you may well be starting to feel the energy pulsing through your body. The great news is that this is just the start; it generally gets better and better.

Many people who quit drinking use their new-found sober-superpower to improve themselves in many different ways. They begin to pay attention to aspects of their lives that might not be fulfilling them and they face up to it, make a considered decision, and do something about it.

I have seen people improve their relationships, change careers, become better parents, launch into new hobbies and commit to taking on challenges that they would never have considered when they were drinking.

It is important to feel stimulated, and we should ensure that we continue to grow as we move down the path of self-discovery. Consider setting goals that align with the freedom plan you created to ensure you are focused and have a clear direction on what you are aiming to achieve.

You may also want to consider setting yourself a longer-term goal in the form of a challenge, to give you an objective to work towards. After I quit drinking I entered the Valencia Marathon, which was due to take place six months later.

Having this big event on the horizon gave me something incredibly positive to focus on and definitely assisted in me not thinking about drinking so much. This would be my 15th marathon, and I decided I would set myself a target of running it in my quickest ever time. I figured that without my daily drinking I would be likely to run faster and have more stamina. I discovered that I became so much more immersed in my training without the constant distraction of alcohol.

I dedicated myself to training and it felt wonderful having something positive to focus on alongside my sobriety. Six months after I quit drinking I found myself at the start line of the marathon in the beautiful city of Valencia. I already knew that I was stronger and faster from the combination of training and not drinking, but whether that power and energy would last for the entire 26 miles was another matter.

Usually during a marathon I would slow down as my mental and physical strength faded when I entered the last five or six miles; instead, I sped up and drew on new reserves of power and energy. I had never experienced a run as strong as this; I was overtaking other competitors the entire way and had complete mental focus and control over my pace with the ability to accelerate and push harder whenever I needed to do so.

I ended up smashing my previous personal best record, completing the race in three hours and 34 minutes. I appreciate this won't get me a place in the Great Britain Olympic squad, but it was quick for me and I credit my sobriety for giving me a huge boost and improving my overall level of focus, mental stamina, fitness and performance.

As you go forward you might want to consider whether setting yourself a new challenge would be worthwhile. You don't have to enter a marathon (although if you do, please tag me in a photo on Instagram using @besoberandquit so I can celebrate your success with you). It doesn't need to be a running event, of course; this is simply what worked for me due to my own personal preference.

There are numerous challenges that you can take part in, no matter what your interests or hobbies. Use the space provided to describe what challenges might appeal to you and what you would need to do in order to achieve them. If you feel ready, maybe you could also make a commitment to go for it!

_____

_____

_____

_____

_____

_____

If you found yourself committing to a new challenge, good for you. If you don't feel ready to commit to a new challenge or you struggled to think of something appealing don't worry too much – you can come back to this at any point. Continue to give it some thought over the coming days and weeks and write down anything that catches your interest.

Pay close attention to the changes you experience as the days and weeks go by and embrace the joy of personal growth. I have referred to this experience as a 'journey' many times throughout this book. Stop thinking about a destination; the journey never ends and there may not even be a specific destination. We constantly grow, develop and improve ourselves; the joy exists in the journey, not the destination.

Many people describe the experience as being rather like falling in love with themselves for the first time after spending years in a place of self-hatred, shame or guilt. Remain curious and open-minded about what happens during your own personal experience. There is no right or wrong. Don't try to force anything, but do ensure you continue to notice everything without judgement.

I also encounter people who discover things about themselves that have been covered by the mask of alcohol for many years. In my own case it became apparent that I was displaying certain behaviour traits which were much more obvious after I became sober – for example hyperactivity, attention issues, impulsivity and mood swings.

Eventually, as I've previously mentioned, I had a formal assessment for adult ADHD and was positively diagnosed. If I hadn't stopped drinking, I would never have pulled back the curtains on my life and discovered this about myself. Now I am aware, I can do something about it.

My journey hasn't ended; I don't think it ever will, and neither will yours. The realization that happiness is with me right now as I travel on my journey was a huge breakthrough. This isn't a case of enduring pain to get somewhere, like a long-haul flight in cramped economy seats; this is about enjoying every moment, learning to live in the now and making positive changes to our lives as we continue to move forward.

So smile. You are sober – enjoy it!

Day 23 | Taking back control

Have you ever been on a long drive with children in the backseat of the car while you are at the wheel? If so, you will have no doubt set off on your journey with them laughing and chattering away to you, or amusing themselves as they remain strapped into their safety seat in the back of the car.

Everything feels good: your child is safe and content while you are very much in the driving seat; right now you are in control. However, as the journey progresses, the child becomes agitated and frustrated because they don't have your full attention. Talking to the back of your head has become boring and they begin to shout and throw toys in your direction in an effort to engage more deeply with you.

You feel your mood shift as your anxiety increases. Your concentration is no longer fully on the road as you try in vain to calm the ever increasing rage from the backseat. You are suddenly torn between the need to drive safely and the desire to soothe your child, and you are failing miserably at both tasks.

You decide that the best option is to ignore the cries for attention – safety is your priority – so you turn up the music on the radio to suppress the screams and refuse to engage. This fuels the rage further, and now your child is attempting to wriggle free from their safety seat so they can interact with you. The cries continue and before long a full-blown tantrum erupts. Eventually, you decide that the only option is to give up and pull the car over in order to calm your upset child.

You hug and reassure them as you wipe away the tears. The cries slowly subside, and you feel relieved and happy that they are finally content. But you still feel anxious because you know that as soon as you begin driving again the tantrums will likely recommence with even more fury.

You are no longer in control of the car and your child has now learned that you will give in if they cause enough commotion.

Now let's switch the frustrated child for an alcohol craving, which can feel very similar. It often begins like a nagging voice in the backseat of the car before growing louder and more angry. It attempts to grab your attention by using almost any means possible. If throwing toys doesn't work, the craving will break free from the seat restraints and clamber into the passenger seat beside you. From there, it can shout directly into your ear and play all manner of mind games with you.

You grit your teeth and use willpower to remain in control of the wheel; you know that letting go could result in a serious accident. But the craving persists and is now playing with the controls of the car in an attempt to cause you to give it the attention it so desperately desires.

You continue to ignore the craving, hoping that it will get bored and retire to the backseat, but it doesn't happen. Before long it is fighting for control of the steering wheel and pushing you out of the way. You are grappling for control, and before long you have completely lost it and you decide it will be easier to give in and allow the craving to take the driving seat.

It can sometimes seem easier to take a drink rather than put up with the discomfort that a craving is causing. This is an illusion. The pain of giving in and drinking will be worse than the discomfort of sticking it out.

This analogy is designed to emphasize how a craving creeps up slowly and then builds stronger in our minds. When we try to ignore a craving, it doesn't cause it to vanish; it makes it get louder and work harder to get our attention. The more we try to ignore or fight it with willpower, the more it will continue to wrestle for control and this can feel extremely uncomfortable.

We have looked at tactics for dealing with cravings previously in the book and my hope is that you have learned how to handle them effectively. There is nothing to be gained by attempting to suppress them; instead, you need to pause, then acknowledge them and accept that they are with you, before calmly telling them that you won't be joining in with their games today, and using a suitable tactic to weaken their power.

Right now you are into your fourth week of your break from alcohol and you may have experienced some uncomfortable cravings for alcohol. Hopefully, you were able to acknowledge them and have found tactics that have helped dispel cravings.

It is important to continue educating yourself and ensuring that you know what to do when discomfort appears. Cravings can catch you off guard, and you need to ensure you are prepared and fully equipped for whatever might arise.

By now I would hope that you feel in control and that episodes of the backseat craving attempting to take hold of the steering wheel have long since passed. However, the journey is by no means over, and it is vital that you keep moving forward and growing stronger by looking inward and making new discoveries about yourself.

Right now I would like you to consider whether you are in the driving seat or whether alcohol is in control. Take a few minutes to answer the following questions and you will soon have an understanding as to whether you feel liberated and free from alcohol or whether it still has some kind of hold over you.

If alcohol still has a level of control in your life, don't panic. Instead, try to view it as an opportunity for further growth, spend some time understanding what you need to work on and set about making the necessary improvements.

Answer the following questions:

1 You are attending a party. As you walk towards the front door you can hear the noise from inside. Are you:

a. Thinking about the people you will be meeting, wondering what the food will be like and looking forward to how much fun you will have when you get inside?

b. Thinking about how quickly you can have a drink and then worrying where the next one will be coming from?

2 You have had a stressful day at work and return home to a house that needs cleaning and a pile of overdue bills on the doormat. You feel anxious and overwhelmed and start to think about whether alcohol would help ease your feelings in this situation. Do you:

a. Recognize this for what it is – simply a thought – and allow it to pass before deciding on what tasks you will complete in order to achieve a sense of accomplishment?

b. Grab hold of the thought about drinking and start to convince yourself that alcohol would help the situation, as you believe it enables you to successfully relax?

3 You are invited to a social event and feel anxious about attending. You know that guests will be drinking heavily and that some of them will likely encourage you to drink. Do you:

a. Give the event a miss? You are starting to feel that these kind of social gatherings aren't much fun any longer and you can think of plenty of other activities you would enjoy far more.

b. Attend the event either because you didn't want to say no or because it would provide a perfect excuse to blame someone else if you were to drink?

4 You have been overwhelmed with cravings to drink and used several different tactics in an attempt to weaken them, but nothing seems to be working and the discomfort doesn't appear to be passing. Do you:

a. Recognize that alcohol will not provide any benefit and that you can never return to the place of 'ignorant bliss' so there is no point drinking anyway? Instead, you remind yourself that these feelings always pass and decide to have a nice bath with low lighting and candles followed by an early night in bed.

b. Decide that drinking is the only solution and that it will solve the problem instantly? After all, you are grown up enough to make your own decisions.

5 After several weeks alcohol-free you are feeling pretty good and finding sobriety fairly easy. You start to wonder if you really had a problem in the

first place. Suddenly the thought of drinking just occasionally enters your mind and you dwell for a moment on the possibility. Do you:

a. Acknowledge that this thought has come to mind and then allow it to pass? If it fails to weaken, you turn to a suitable tactic in order to move it on quickly so you can go about your day in peace and happiness.

b. Grab hold of this thought and invest time and energy considering how you could make moderate drinking work for you? You might also use confirmation bias to convince yourself that you are capable of occasional drinking, especially as you have successfully taken a break from booze.

Finally, answer the following question:

Which of the following describes you best:

a. It's as if my mindset has shifted. I no longer have a desire to drink and don't feel as though I have lost anything; in fact, I feel as though I am gaining so much. I am enjoying this journey and excited to continue on the path. I have learned to deal with discomfort, and I am able to face up to fears and overcome challenges much more easily than when I was drinking.

b. I feel as though I am using willpower to stay sober. I am missing drinking. I think about it all the time and believe my life is much worse without alcohol as it helps me cope with challenging situations.

If you have answered mostly 'a', well done, this means you are feeling liberated and free from the grip of alcohol. You will probably not want to return to drinking and might now see alcohol as a substance that has taken away far more than it ever gave you.

On Day 25 we will discuss what the next step is as you approach the end of your break from alcohol. You might have already given some thought to how long an extended break might be or whether you feel ready to turn your back on drinking for ever. There is no pressure to make a decision now.

If you answered mostly 'b', don't despair; this exercise has allowed you to recognize that you have further room for growth in order to reach a place where you feel truly free from alcohol. Later in the book you will find a section entitled 'If you still have a desire to drink' which provides additional options for you to consider to ensure you get to where you want to be.

Under no circumstances should you be calling yourself a failure or berating yourself if you don't yet feel as though you have had a big mindset shift. It takes time and it takes work. I have no doubt that you have applied yourself to this process and I am confident that you have noticed changes and begun to believe that you hold the power of choice and the ability to change. We only fail when we stop showing up and choose not to keep trying any longer. The fact you are reading this page tells me that you are not someone who gives up. Keep reading, continue learning and notice as you grow stronger.

Day 24 | Common questions and concerns

Hopefully this book has helped to set you up for success. You can't unlearn what you now know and, as we discussed previously, there is no possibility of you ever returning to a state of 'ignorant bliss'. The only way you can end the internal conflict is to ensure that your subconscious and conscious minds are in harmony and both fighting for the same side. Until you do this, you will find that the internal battle between the two sides will rage in your mind.

If you still have a desire to drink, then you haven't yet managed to get both sides working together. Don't panic: this is simply a sign that you have room for further growth and that you need to continue working on your subconscious in order that it falls in line and holds a firm belief that living alcohol-free is the lifestyle choice that is right for you.

You might want to consider using a paid programme such as my own at <www.joinbesober.com>, or look at working with a one-to-one quit drinking coach to give you a more intense path to sobriety. At the end of the book you will find a list of additional resources and options that will provide extra support, accountability and education.

Today I wanted to address some common questions and concerns that often come up when we quit drinking.

I am experiencing strong withdrawal symptoms. What should I do?

It is common to experience some kind of withdrawal symptoms and cravings to drink in the early stages of sobriety. Only around 10 per cent of people with an alcohol problem are physically addicted to drinking; for the remaining 90 per cent it is a psychological addiction.

Most people with a psychological addiction experience short-term mild symptoms such as:

- increased irritability
- tiredness
- headaches
- sweating
- mood changes
- mild shaking
- sleeping problems
- loss of appetite.

These symptoms will usually occur within the first week of you stopping drinking and pass after a few days. Accept that these feelings are due to the process of your mind and body healing, and know that they will fade as you continue to remain alcohol-free.

Track any symptoms of withdrawal in your journal and pay attention to how much easier they get as the days pass by. If you have any specific symptoms, you might want to consider scoring them out of ten on a daily basis to allow you to closely track the changes.

A small number of people can experience more severe withdrawal symptoms. These usually only affect those who are physically addicted to alcohol as opposed to people who are psychologically addicted. If you have any concerns, please seek medical advice.

A small percentage of those who are most severely physically addicted to alcohol can suffer from a symptom known as delirium tremens (DTs). DTs can be fatal if left untreated. While it is highly unlikely this is something you will experience, it is important that you are aware of the warning signs in order to seek medical treatment if necessary.

Out of all the people I have worked with, I have never encountered anyone who has suffered from DTs. By sharing this information with you I hope it will serve to help you further understand the damage that alcohol can cause.

Symptoms of DTs include:

- heightened irritation
- light sensitivity
- rapid heart rate
- vomiting
- tremors
- breathing difficulties
- seizures
- high blood pressure
- hallucinations
- delirium
- confusion.

This hasn't been included to scare you; I simply want you to have a level of awareness. DTs usually only affect a very small percentage of the very heaviest drinkers who have become physically dependent on alcohol.

Once again, if you experience any of the symptoms listed or have any concerns about withdrawal symptoms, please seek medical help immediately.

I have stopped drinking but I am in constant fear of slipping up.

Worrying about having a setback and falling back into your past patterns can overwhelm your mind and drain your energy. Focus your strength on moving forward and remind yourself that you are sober in this moment and there is no reason for that to change.

If a lifetime without alcohol feels too much to think about, work towards smaller goals. When you start to worry that you might have a setback, make a commitment to yourself that you won't drink today, no matter what happens. Make that same commitment each day, and then focus on taking each day as it comes and put the work in to growing stronger.

You will soon find these uncomfortable feelings subside. Don't push them away; instead acknowledge that they are with you. Write them down in your journal and explore where they are coming from. Perhaps you have had an experience in the past where you felt like you always failed, for example. Try to discover what is at the root of your feelings and emotions.

This time things are different; there is no logical reason for you to fail if you are putting in the work and you have a clear understanding of what you need to do to find freedom. Start to feel confident in yourself, and each time you slip into a state of self-doubt use a tactic to quickly move out of it.

I always drink at home. How do I stop?

I was also a home drinker and realized that I had to create an environment for success. This meant removing all the alcohol from my house, including bottles I had kept for guests and the dusty bottles of booze I had kept for a 'special occasion'.

You need to be totally honest with yourself and work out exactly what you need to do in order to create an environment that will keep you safe in your sobriety. If you leave any loopholes, there is a chance you will take advantage of them and drink if you encounter a difficult period.

If you share your home with others, make sure you get them on board so they can help you remain alcohol-free and have an environment that supports your sobriety rather than risks derailing you.

How can I get through Christmas and holiday periods without alcohol?

If you can get through today sober, you can get through Christmas Day and holidays without drinking.

Instead of approaching special days with a sense of fear and worry, you should reframe your thinking and get excited about how good these occasions will be without alcohol involved.

Use your journal to write down everything you will gain from not drinking on these occasions. A few examples might be:

- feeling fully present with my kids
- not falling asleep mid-afternoon after drinking too much
- being able to remember the entire day
- no risk of an argument after drinking too much
- another milestone reached on the sober journey.

Approach anything that makes you nervous rather like a college assignment. Your task is to experience it alcohol-free and write down everything you discover. Get excited at the prospect of gathering the data and discovering how it feels.

Once you have done this, you will soon learn that the special days are infinitely better without booze and you will have all the information to back this up and tell you exactly why.

I have quit drinking several times in the past and started drinking again. What should I do?

This usually happens when you are relying on too much willpower and haven't experienced a mindset shift. This is often down to us hanging on to limiting beliefs that alcohol will benefit us in some kind of positive way.

Be honest with yourself, write down exactly what you believe and get to work on discovering the truth and educating yourself on these specific areas.

If you are struggling to change your beliefs, consider working with an alcohol coach or joining a quit drinking programme such as <www.joinbesober.com> for extra help.

Is it safe to have 'alcohol-free' drinks that have up to 0.5% alcohol content?

This is down to personal choice. When I first quit I would only drink 'non-alcoholic' drinks that were 0.0% alcohol content. However, when I saw the huge range of drinks that were designed for us sober-rebels I spent some time researching whether it was acceptable to have them when you are sober.

I discovered the following:

- There are many foods that contain a similar amount of alcohol.
- It is impossible to get drunk on 0.5% drinks.
- Most people who are sober enjoy drinks up to 0.5% ABV.
- Most countries class 0.5% ABV or below as 'alcohol-free'.

This was all positive. However, it is also worth considering that:

- There is still some alcohol in drinks up to 0.5% ABV.
- Some drinks can be a trigger and cause cravings for the 'real' thing.
- There is no safe level of alcohol consumption.

I occasionally have a drink with up to 0.5% alcohol content, but will generally stick to those with zero content. My advice is to explore the range of drinks and find something you enjoy that can become your new 'go-to' drink. If it contains up to 0.5% alcohol, it really isn't an issue as long as it isn't causing you any cravings or other problems.

I can't stop thinking about drinking.

It is common to spend a lot of time thinking about drinking after you have quit. If you have drunk regularly for many years, it will take time for the thoughts to fade, but rest assured that they will.

In the first few weeks I was thinking about wine every few minutes, but as time went by the thoughts became less and less frequent. These days I rarely ever think about drinking, and even if I do I recognize that it is simply a thought. I acknowledge it, I don't act on it and I allow it to pass.

By learning that your thoughts always pass you can find incredible strength and remain in control of what you choose to act upon.

I still think alcohol would add something positive my life.

It can be common for us to hang on to limiting beliefs and to think that alcohol might still help us if we encounter a stressful situation, need to relax or want to have fun. The fact is that this is a complete illusion.

Whenever you find yourself thinking like this, take some time to look back at what you have written throughout this book. Remind yourself of the reasons why you quit, the damage that alcohol caused to your life and how it held you back from being your best self. Was any of that adding something positive to your life?

If you are unable to shift this false belief, then you may want to consider a more intense approach by working with a coach or joining a quit drinking programme.

Should I 'pay it forward'?

As you move forward into an alcohol-free life you should consider helping others. This will enable you to become accountable to people in the early stages of their own journeys and allow you to experience a sense of joy from selflessly helping those who need guidance.

When you pay it forward it helps you grow stronger in your own sobriety. There are numerous ways you can do this. I have seen people who have quit drinking who have gone on to become sobriety coaches, bloggers and podcast presenters and who even written books.

The most common way of paying it forward is by connecting with people one-to-one and providing direct support, accountability and advice. It is easy to find people who would benefit from help in Facebook sober groups and online programmes.

I keep having dreams about drinking. Will they stop?

Having dreams about drinking is fairly common. I recall waking up one morning not long after I quit and I was convinced that I had been drinking wine. In fact, I had experienced an incredibly vivid dream, and when I realized what had happened I felt a huge sense of relief as I was certain I had experienced a setback in my sobriety.

My sleep is disrupted. When will it get better?

In my case I had disrupted sleep for the first week or so after I quit, and most people I work with experience the same level of disruption.

Be gentle with yourself and recognize that is part of the process of your mind and body healing and recalibrating. Use your journal to track the quality of your sleep, and as the days go by you will notice that it gets better and before long you will be experiencing the best sleep of your life.

If you quit drinking and find that your sleep hasn't improved after a month, I recommend seeking the opinion of a medical specialist.

I feel tired all the time.

If your sleep has been disrupted, it is likely you will feel tired. Don't overexert yourself. Treat yourself with kindness while your mind and body heal and know that it will get better.

However, some people do experience tiredness and exhaustion further into sobriety and this is often down to other factors. If you feel tired all the time more than one month after you have quit drinking, make sure you:

- drink plenty of water each day
- take regular exercise
- have a healthy and balanced diet
- maintain a regular routine for waking up and going to bed.

If problems persist after a couple of months without drinking, I recommend seeking medical advice.

I feel down or depressed now I have quit alcohol.

This is rare, most people experience a sense of joy and happiness when they cut alcohol out of their life. This is known as the 'pink cloud' phase.

However, some people can feel down and depressed later on, and if this happens you need to pay attention to it. I recommend continuing to use your journal for at least the first 12 months as it will ensure you notice any low moods or uncomfortable emotions that might arise.

If you are experiencing low moods after quitting I recommend:

- looking at your self-care routine (exercise, hydration, diet, sleeping routines)
- ensuring you are engaging in hobbies and activities you enjoy
- knowing what tactics to use to weaken negative feelings
- reaching out to a supportive friend to talk about your problems
- focusing on the future and getting excited about it.

It is important to understand that, just because we quit drinking, it doesn't mean that life won't throw us the odd curveball. Bad things can still happen, but without alcohol we are better equipped to deal with them.

Very few people are happy all the time, and part of being human is having to experience a wide range of feelings and emotions. Learn to acknowledge your feelings and sit with discomfort; it will make you stronger. Then use your journal to make a plan to make positive life changes.

If you are experiencing longer-term depression or low moods, I strongly suggest speaking to a specialist in this area.

Day 25 | Making the next commitment to yourself

Today is the last day out of the 25 alcohol-free days I wanted you to achieve as you worked through the book. If you have completed the full period without drinking – congratulations on your huge success! I am sure you have experienced tough times and felt as though it was a real challenge on occasion. But you have done it and proven to yourself that you have the inner strength and determination to be sober if you wish.

If you have had setbacks along the way, don't worry. You are reading this page right now and continuing to move forward. You haven't failed, and you are still putting the work in. We only fail when we stop trying, and you haven't stopped trying. Celebrate how far you have come and take a moment to reflect on what you have achieved over the last few weeks.

You may recall that I asked you to take a selfie earlier in the book. Today I would like you to take another and compare the two pictures side by side. Use the space provided to note down the differences you can see in the two images.

You might notice improved skin, less darkness under your eyes and less facial bloating. Many people describe themselves as 'glowing' after a few weeks without alcohol. What can you see?

_____

_____

_____

_____

_____

_____

Today could be a pivotal moment. You have now started to experience the benefits of taking a break from drinking, and you should be past the initial discomfort, and starting to experience some of the wonderful benefits of an alcohol-free life.

Hopefully, you are beginning to notice how much better your life is without alcohol, and you have a sense of excitement about what would be ahead if you cut alcohol out long-term.

Spend some time reflecting on what you have written in your journal and in this book to remind yourself of the reasons why you quit and the breakthroughs and improvements you have experienced along the way. You have worked hard to get this far, and I would like you to begin reaping the rewards that are sure to follow as you go forward.

So today, on Day 25 – the last – I would like you to make a further commitment to yourself. I would like you to decide if you need alcohol in your life any longer and whether you would like to make the decision to move into an alcohol-free lifestyle and become sober.

If deciding to become alcohol-free for life feels a little overwhelming at this stage, then I would like you to consider making a commitment to having an extended break from drinking. How about 60 or 90 days this time?

If you don't feel that you can make a commitment and that you want to continue drinking, please read the final section 'Final thoughts as you move forward' before making a decision about what to do next.

Use the space provided to make a fresh new commitment to yourself. Make sure it is a promise that you know you will see through, and be totally honest with yourself in terms of what you will need to do in order to make it happen.

_____

_____

_____

_____

_____

_____

If you have made the decision to quit alcohol for good, I can assure you that you won't regret it, and will soon be living your very best life.

If you have chosen to extend your break from booze, then you will continue to experience some incredibly powerful changes and will likely soon decide that there is no benefit in ever drinking again. You may want to continue the strategy of extending your booze breaks until such time as you feel ready to make a firm and final commitment to yourself.

No matter what you decide, please make sure you continue to educate yourself and become an active member of the sober-community. Stay accountable and ensure that you have support close at hand and that you know which tools and tactics you need to overcome any challenges that arise. Use the resources section at the end of this book to discover programmes, books, websites and podcasts that will be suitable for the next stage of your journey.

Finally, if you have chosen to quit drinking for good, how about writing a break-up letter? My own break-up with alcohol felt like a relationship that had turned toxic, and when I found the power to bring it to an end, I wanted to get complete closure. I found that writing a break-up letter helped me release the feelings and get a sense that it was truly over. I shared my letter on my blog, and if you feel comfortable doing so, you could share yours publicly, too.

This is one relationship that you will be pleased you ended, even if, just like a break-up, you feel pain and sadness at the beginning and there might even be a few tears. You have to know that you can move forward now: you are free and there is no going back.

You hold all of the power now: you have found freedom and can begin to experience the life you deserve packed with joy and happiness.

Remember to enjoy the journey. This isn't about a specific destination. We keep growing as we travel down our life-path with heightened awareness and strength. We know how to overcome difficulties and discomfort, and we embrace the lifestyle that we have chosen for ourselves by becoming a 'sober-rebel'.

Own your new lifestyle, be proud, stay passionate and continue to be hungry to learn.

Tomorrow's version of you will thank you for the actions you are taking today.

Final thoughts as you move forward

Hopefully by now you feel confident in your decision to extend your break from alcohol, or maybe you have made the choice to quit drinking completely. However, there may be a chance that you still have a desire to drink – if so, please don't worry.

If you still feel as though alcohol would bring some kind of positive benefit, don't despair. I am sure you have experienced some positive changes while you have been reading and will have learned the truth about alcohol which will have helped to change the way you think about drinking. At a minimum, this book should have given you the firm foundations you need to move forward.

You should be proud of yourself that you have recognized there is a problem and you have taken positive action to deal with it. The vast majority of people do nothing more than suppress their worries about how much they are drinking by drinking even more. You are different: you have faced up to the challenge and taken a powerful and courageous step in the right direction.

You have to remember that this is a journey: this book should become your springboard to further success as you continue down the path to freedom. If you still believe that alcohol will add something positive to your life, or if you have a desire to drink, it simply means that you are holding on to limiting beliefs that have not yet changed in your subconscious mind.

Do you recall how we looked at the internal conflict called 'cognitive dissonance' that rages in your mind? If you still have an urge to drink, it likely means that your subconscious and conscious minds are not yet fully in harmony with each other.

In order to achieve this, you need to continue soaking up as much information as possible about the benefits of living alcohol-free. Learn as much as you can about the dangers of drinking and how alcohol ruins lives. The more you digest, the more your subconscious will listen and over time it will fall in line and the two sides will unite as one in your mind.

The worst thing you can do is give up on the idea of quitting; you will simply return to a place of ongoing conflict and this is a painful place. Keep working on becoming alcohol-free and immerse yourself in the world of sobriety.

You may also want to consider finding a more intensive level of support. Here are some options:

Work one-to-one with a quit drinking coach

A one-to-one coach can provide invaluable support, accountability and tactics for helping you overcome whatever is currently holding you back. Many coaches offer a free initial introductory call so you can ensure that they feel like a good fit and understand what you are aiming to achieve.

Take your time when it comes to choosing a coach, and do your research before you enter into a relationship. You might want to ask for references or speak to other people they have worked with. My website has profiles of recommended coaches. Visit <www/besober.co.uk/alcohol-coaching> to find out more.

When you work one-to-one with a coach you will have access to a wealth of support and will find that you quickly become accountable to them and feel incredibly motivated to show your coach and yourself that you can reach your goals.

Join a paid programme

The downside of working with a coach on a one-to-one basis is that it can be expensive. An alternative, lower-cost option is to join a paid programme. You are welcome to join my own programme which provides group coaching and includes an audio course alongside a wonderful community of supportive and caring members.

You can find out more about my programme at <www.joinbesober.com>.

Find a mentor

If you are a member of a Facebook sober group, you could consider finding a mentor or accountability partner. Many people are keen to partner up with someone else who is on the same journey so they can support each other.

While this doesn't give you access to professional help, the extra accountability along with having someone you can share your experience with can be very powerful.

Before agreeing to partner up with a mentor or an accountability partner, make sure you take the time to ensure they are a good fit for you and that you will be a suitable match for each other.

I recommend having an initial chat without making any commitment and ensuring that both parties understand what each person will expect of the other.

Join a face-to-face group

There are many face-to-face groups that you can attend locally. A quick search on the Internet will show you what is available in your area.

These can be a perfect option for extra support and accountability. Most are low cost and also give you the opportunity to meet new people and make new friends.

You can usually attend a trial meeting to ensure it is what you are looking for without an obligation to continue if you decide it isn't suitable.

Immerse yourself in further learning

Regardless of which option you feel would be right for you, it is essential that you continue your learning. Approach sobriety as though you are studying for the biggest exam of your life, set aside time each day to further your knowledge and immerse yourself in the sober-world.

One of my clients told me recently how she watches two videos from my YouTube channel each day. She says it is her equivalent of taking two 'sober pills' each day as they enable her to stay focused and motivated at the same time as furthering her knowledge.

The Resources section provides some excellent ways to further your learning.

Success stories: how it feels to be sober

The following comments were shared by participants in the survey presented in Day 19 in Part 2. There were far too many to include them all so I have selected the best ones; otherwise they would have taken up a book all of their own. I hope you find inspiration, insight and motivation from what you read.

'I love the feeling of EMPOWERMENT. I think if I hadn't read/heard that you could literally flip the script on alcohol – that you have the power to say no to something that is hurting you, that is not giving you the benefits that have been made up by the marketing industry, that YOU can be the one leading the way against something harmful to society ... that it is not your fault because alcohol is an addictive, toxic substance and you do not need to feel SHAME – it feels good, it feels exciting, it gives my life even more purpose. This change in mindset is what is helping me not crave booze. And living without craving booze is pretty damn great. So many more hours in the day!!! So many possibilities! I would say that one of the biggest benefits to an alcohol-free lifestyle is FREEDOM and EMPOWERMENT. Yay!! Thank you!!'

'I am shocked at how clear-headed, positive and energetic I am. Alcohol had overtaken my life and stolen my personality – all the things that I loved doing. I lost 14 kilos, I am fit, focused and motivated. I am simply the best possible version of me right now – I know, I can feel it – from within. People look at me as if I've swallowed a magic pill that they want to race out and buy. They comment on how happy I am and how much better I look. I glow – from within. I am so proud of the new me. My self-love, care and esteem had never even existed and now they are skyrocketing – I know I will get even stronger. I am a new me – and I love me! Wow!! I have also given up sugar which has taken me even further down the life long journey of self-actualization – I can now see and smell it ... powerful, heady stuff. I could never go back – ever. It's just not worth it.'

'It has been awakening to realize that all of the problems I was experiencing with anxiety and depression were as a result of the drink I was consuming to ease the symptoms. I never thought I could ever be a non-drinker but since completing the 30 days alcohol-free and experiencing how good life is without alcohol, I now love my new AF lifestyle where I am totally in control of all my decisions and have not regretted one moment of it. I look better, feel better and most importantly, I'm enjoying living again.'

'Thank you, Thank you. Thank you! I never could've imagined I would feel so amazing from abstaining from alcohol. I've been a heavy drinker for over 20 years. I fell into a routine of drinking daily to the point of not remembering the night before. I joined the group in November and I'm grateful every single day for the opportunity to actually feel life. I feel amazing and I will be forever grateful to Simon and the entire community.'

'Alcohol is so tied to anxiety for me. Everything about alcohol – its allure, its promises, its initial endorphin boost – were really anxiety prompts in disguise. Society underestimates how frighteningly addictive it is on emotional, psychological, spiritual, physiological levels because of its own deeply embedded anxieties and associated profiteering. What is extraordinary is that we don't consider "not drinking at all" the norm. Those of us who choose to avoid the substance are "rebels", which is exactly the opposite of what it should be. The daring, the risk taking, the going out on a limb that we feel simply facing the present moment sober is what people who pick up a drink should feel – that they're taking risks, they're going out on a limb, they're rebelling against their health and well-being and reducing the chance to really do what it is they're here to do in this life.'

'Quitting drinking has been the best thing for me. I feel so much better and I am sleeping properly for the first time in many years. My skin is so much better and my body doesn't feel that it is on fire anymore. I am less anxious and definitely more calm. I am 240 days sober, and a year is my next goal. I love going to bed sober and waking with a clear head and great sleep. I have learned so much about how alcohol works in your body and it is pure poison. You will never regret giving an alcohol-free lifestyle a go!!!!'

'Being alcohol free is a gift I've given myself and my family. It erased my anxiety and has improved my overall outlook. I couldn't have done it without quit lit, online resources and podcasts. These powerful tools reinforce everything in my learning about sobriety. It's been wonderful and will only get better.'

'I feel like I was just totally sucked into the marketing campaigns that drinking was fun, safe, earned, and a great part of life. I have learned that it's absolutely none of those. Sober life is fun, safe, earned, and has brought joy back into my days. I hope everyone alive figures this out. It's like having keys to a secret I wish I could share.'

'FACT: I am much better off without alcohol in my life! Thank you, Simon, for all you do to help this movement.'

'I've lost 11 pounds since 1 January after a two-year struggle. I joined to start the road to being alcohol-free. The combination of the videos, journaling, quit lit books and the Facebook group have helped the most. I have the energy now to work out and cook healthy meals. I no longer wake up at 3:30am in a panic or at 5am dreading the day ahead. Now I purposely get up an hour earlier to read, work out or watch videos. My mood and mental health have improved drastically since stopping alcohol. My goal is to reach one year alcohol-free. I am excited and happy about the changes I've made so far. I feel incredible after two months. I can't wait to see how I feel after a year free from the poison!'

'One hundred and fifty days sober. Down over ten pounds, cholesterol down 50 points, triglycerides down 50 points, blood pressure back in normal range. Feeling happy.'

'Quitting drinking has been the most surprising experience of my life. I was absolutely dreading it. I thought I would only be sad about it for ever. I did not realize what I would be gaining instead. It's truly been the shock of my life.'

'In my opinion, education was the number-one factor. Learning about alcohol, what it contains, how it impacts our bodies, minds, emotions, etc. was the thing that changed my life. Understanding how alcohol rewires the brain, and how to get my life back, was the key to living a sober life. Along with that were the other tools, other experiences and stories, Facebook groups and supports. The number-one resource for me was Annie Grace's *This Naked Mind*. I love being sober. Today I am 307 days AF. Almost one year. I am never looking back.'

'Quitting alcohol has been one of the greatest gifts I've ever given to myself and my family. Some things that helped me quit are: my strong faith in God, believing I could quit, and finally making a very firm decision to quit. Thank you for all you do, Simon!'

'Quitting drinking four years ago transformed my life from depressed to unlimited hope. But quitting drinking hasn't actually been the differentiating factor. It was the factor that has made all the subsequent changes in my life possible. I have been highly active in multiple AF forums over the past couple of years. And a belief that I see frequently which puts people at risk of failing to remain AF is the idea that quitting drinking will, by itself, change your life. Quitting drinking provides enormous physical benefit. And opens up the mental, emotional and spiritual bandwidth to make the choices that lead to a fulfilled existence. For me, those choices weren't even apparent when I was still drinking every day. I was just stuck and couldn't figure out why. I didn't understand that alcohol was my limiting factor until I eliminated it out of sheer exhaustion. Life is good. (Now.)'

'I have been sober for almost two months now, I am an active mum of three very busy children/teenagers and I work as well as run a family farm. I have been getting amazing results from not drinking when it comes to my exercise programme at the gym and actually getting out of bed to do it. My eating has improved 100 per cent. I am not as cranky with my children, and I am actually taking a lot more care of my skin and body. I lost weight within three weeks of not drinking but am now concentrating on muscle gain. My digestion has improved dramatically. I honestly thought I had IBS but not anymore; I actually had red wine IBS. I have started reading books again which I used to love and, most importantly, I feel that I am making a positive change in my children's lives as they are not seeing me drink every night . . . How boring and gross!!! Hoping it will provide them with a lifestyle choice that is beneficial to them, not negative and unhealthy. I love them too much.'

'There is no doubt that giving up alcohol and living an AF lifestyle will improve just about everything you do, everything you feel. Your mental health will improve 95 per cent – leaving the 5 per cent to typical life challenges. Nothing compares in my life personally to what I experience now on a daily basis. I used to live in a hole, hung-over and tired every day until I had that drink at 4pm. It sucked the life out of me . . . I was functioning. Hiding behind my functioning life while raising my children, fooling my friends and family. But, I was living a miserable existence. So unhappy, tired and depressed everyday. Without alcohol now in my life, I'm strong, calm, energetic, in great shape, and look 20 years younger. Happy. So happy. I appreciate life so much more.'

'I've not had a drink for 88 days. My skin (face) is less bloated and has more colour/brightness to it. I sleep soundly for long periods (to the point where my feet ache from being in the same sleeping position for a length of time!). Mentally I feel amazing, like I'm out of a haze. My personality has changed, I'm less impatient, have time to listen to people and I'm remembering more. I don't find people irritating like I used to and I'm far more positive. I wish I'd stopped ages ago. I was concerned I'd find it hard, and that I'd be boring without having a drink but I've found it to be the opposite. The only downside currently is I feel exhausted but hopefully once the evenings get lighter I'll get out and try some jogging to boost my energy levels. Just so grateful to have heard Simon's radio interview, it started me thinking.'

'Quitting drink doesn't solve ALL the life issues (which is a bit of a rude awakening), but it does mean that I'm now totally available to do that work whereas when I was drinking, the post-excessive-drinking next day was just about recovering. That's all I could manage. My drinking life was settling for small, just getting through the day. Alcohol-free life is whatever I choose to make it.'

'Having now been sober for almost two years, l cannot overemphasize the huge benefits on EVERY area of your life once you give up drinking. It has been so life changing for me that l have applied to be accepted for a second degree, this time in addiction counselling. Wish me luck!'

'I stopped drinking alcohol almost two years ago. I now have a new life. I have not felt so good, empowered, strong, capable and most of all happy since I was a child. I will never drink alcohol again. What I have learned in the past two years of how alcohol damages both mind and body makes me shocked that anyone drinks the stuff.'

'Just to say thank you for bringing me to a sober way of thinking. Have felt so much more calm. Things I've been putting off for ages I've got them done and more to go!'

'Many of my relationships have changed, but the ones that really mattered became even closer. I am much more in touch with my feelings, and I fully feel them now rather than drowning them. A big benefit too, I put all the money I used to spend on alcohol into savings and I have a nice nest egg that I plan to spend on a long-awaited trip.'

'There are many varied tools I have used to stop drinking alcohol. Making myself accountable to a trusted friend was really important for me initially then as time went on finding like-minded friends in social media Facebook groups was paramount to my sobriety as was reading and listening to quit literature on audio, watching videos, hearing success stories, etc. My family, especially my older children, were very supportive, too. I kept away from public bars, the alcohol aisle in shops – out of sight out of mind. After 17 months and heading to my first year and a half I feel very proud, happy and calm about my alcohol-free future. Best decision I have made in a very long time. Every aspect of my life has improved and more.'

'My life is 1,000 per cent times better sober.'

'I have lost weight and feel far happier than I have in years. I'm two and a half years sober.'

'Feel 100 per cent better, no shaking, no feeling sick and dizzy, I don't have a horrible taste in my mouth in the mornings, I am able to stay awake longer and be more present in the evenings. Taking up more hobbies such as knitting, reading, etc.'

'I can truly say it has been the best decision I have ever made. After 50 years of destroying my body with alcohol, I now have a good night's sleep and my anxiety has completely improved, the best decision ever made. Sober 17 months.'

'Understanding the neuro-physiology was the key to my success. I found your Facebook group, and then found *This Naked Mind* book plus your book *The Sober Survival Guide* invaluable. I then did the Alcohol Experiment in January. The daily videos and journaling made me really think about the part alcohol played in my life. For me, after several failed attempts ... I don't want to risk trying a glass of wine ... even as an experiment. I have great alcohol-free alternatives. I use my wine glass and pour fake bubbles in it. I drink that as much as I used to drink regular wine. I think it is in the ritual .. that feeling of downtime. I am spreading the word and I genuinely feel that people feel trapped ... not knowing where to get help and support with no stigma. I actually feel so much more confident. If I can chuck alcohol ... I can do anything!! Go me!! And thank you, because if I hadn't found you ... I would not be here xx'

'I love not waking up with that fuzzy head and pounding heart!'

'I went from a very heavy drinker, to stopping. It has now been two-and-a-half years, and I am loving life. I am working on building up parts of my life that fell apart during my drinking days, and that will come with time. My overall life, work, and general wellbeing have never been better.'

'People kept asking what I was doing because there were so many changes in my face. One person said – my goodness, you look ten years younger.'

'I truly believe my depression was because of alcohol, as was my high blood pressure. Both are no longer there. I'm also finding out who I really am. I have dreams again.'

'The most surprising benefit I have noticed is time. Now that I'm not in a rush for my next drink or hung-over, I feel each day has opened up for me.'

'Hope is such a helpful tool – to hope and imagine a better life alcohol free.'

'I never realized that my high levels of anxiety, depression and ongoing battles with insomnia were as a result of alcohol consumption. Cutting alcohol out of my life makes a massive difference to the quality of my life. Anxiety and depression are virtually nonexistent and my relationships have improved, although the social aspect of my life has decreased.'

Resources

Quit alcohol programmes

- Be Sober – Stay Sober: www.joinbesober.com
- The Alcohol Experiment: www.alcoholexperiment.com

Sobriety podcasts

- Love Sober: www.lovesober.com
- Sober Experiment: www.soberexperiment.co.uk
- The Bubble Hour: www.thebubblehour.blogspot.com
- That Sober Guy: www.thatsoberguy.com
- A Sober Girls Guide: www.asobergirlsguide.com
- Alcohol Free Life: www.imperfectlynatural.com
- This Naked Mind: www.thisnakedmind.com

Smartphone apps

- I am sober: Day counter and sobriety motivation
- Sober Grid: Social network for people who don't drink
- Nomo: Sobriety clock and day counter
- Calm: Meditation and relaxation
- Headspace: Meditation and relaxation
- Moody: Track your mood and monitor how you feel.

Mindfulness retreat

Etsuko Ito: www.etsukoito.com/en/mindfulness.html

Sober books (also known as 'quit lit')

- *The Sober Survival Guide* by Simon Chapple (Elevator Digital Ltd, 2019): This is my first book and is designed to serve as the perfect companion in sobriety, rather like a guidebook to sober living. The book is split into two parts: the first gives the reader real-world tactics to help them address their relationship with alcohol and change how it features in their lives; the second part deals with specific challenges that will arise in the months and years of sobriety ahead. The book shows readers how to approach just about anything that might come up: going on holiday sober, the work Christmas party and what to do if you quit drinking but your partner won't make a change.

- *Alcohol Explained* and *Alcohol Explained 2* by William Porter (independently published 2015/2019): William Porter has a wonderful writing style and focuses on the science behind the booze. His books helped me understand alcohol and make decisions about how I wanted it to feature in my life. Both books are highly recommended and approach the issue of alcoholism from a scientific and practical viewpoint.

- *This Naked Mind* by Annie Grace (HQ, 2018): This book was a game-changer for me. It was the first book I have ever read twice in a row and helped me totally change my relationship with alcohol. Annie takes readers on a journey of self-discovery and enables them to bring their beliefs about drinking out into the light to discover what is really true for them. By exploring their beliefs, readers are able to make a real and lasting change to enable themselves to find freedom from alcohol for ever. It worked for me, and I am confident it will do the same for you.

- *The Sober Diaries* by Clare Pooley (Coronet, 2018): *The Sober Diaries* is a great read. It is more of a 'memoir' than a quit drinking book and I wouldn't recommend it as a specific tool to learn how to quit alcohol. But I would recommend having it on your quit alcohol book list as it gives you a wonderful insight into Clare's life as an alcoholic and enables you to see how she dealt with the challenges of quitting drinking and coped with everything that came up in her new-found sober-world.

- *The Unexpected Joy of Being Sober* by Catherine Gray (Aster, 2017): This is a must-read if you are curious about quitting drinking and what an alcohol-free life might look like. The book explores the science behind drinking and the sheer joy we find in sobriety.

- *Kick the Drink . . . Easily!* by Jason Vale (Crown House Publishing, 2011): Another recommended title for your sober bookshelf – it is informative and provides plenty of insights, tips and tactics to help readers work towards a life free from alcohol.

- *Sober Positive* by Julia Carson (independently published 2019): A great book and Julia Carson is a wonderful human being. I was honoured when she joined me on a recent live Q&A session where I discovered how humble she was and how much she truly cared about helping others with alcohol problems through sharing her own story. I love that her book has such a 'positive' outlook and works with the reader to quit drinking and be happy about it – this aligns with my own experience and philosophy that we lose nothing when we quit and gain so much.

- *Quit Like a Woman* by Holly Whitaker (Bloomsbury Publishing, 2020): This is another great book which explores the reasons why alcohol makes us sick and keeps us stuck. Many readers have expressed how much this book helped them and changed their outlook on their relationship with alcohol – I would recommend picking up a copy so you can find out for yourself.

Other books cited in text

- David Carbonell, *The Worry Trick: How Your Brain Tricks You into Expecting the Worst and What You Can Do about It* (New Harbinger, 2016)

- John H. Lee, *Growing Yourself Back UP: Understanding Emotional Regression* (Random House USA, 2001)
- Gabor Maté, *In the Realm of Hungry Ghosts* (Vermilion, 2018)
- Stuart Wallace, *The Self-Talk Solution: The Proven Concept of Breaking Free from Intense Negative Thoughts To Never Feel Weak Again* (Kindle Edition)
- Jonice Webb, *Running on Empty: Overcome Your Childhood Emotional Neglect* (Morgan James Publishing, 2012)

YouTube channels

- Simon Chapple: The Quit Alcohol Coach
- Leon Sylvester: Sober Leon
- Chris Scott: Fit Recovery
- Alcohol Mastery TV
- Allen Carr's Easy Way to Control Alcohol
- Talk Sober
- Craig Beck – Stop Drinking Expert

Websites and blogs

- Simon Chapple – Be Sober: www.besober.co.uk
- Love Sober: www.lovesober.com
- This Naked Mind: www.thisnakedmind.com
- Alcohol Explained: www.alcoholexplained.com
- Mummy Was a Secret Drinker: www.mummywasasecretdrinker.blogspot.com
- Sober Dave: www.soberdave.co.uk
- Hip Sobriety: www.hipsobriety.com
- Soberistas: www.soberistas.com
- Sober Fish: www.soberfish.co.uk
- Club Soda: www.joinclubsoda.com
- Rok Soba: www.roksoba.rocks
- Carly Benson: www.miraclesarebrewing.com
- The Sober Senorita: www.sobersenorita.com
- Sober Experiment: www.soberexperiment.co.uk
- Adult Children of Alcoholics: www.adultchildren.org
- Tony Robbins: www.tonyrobbins.com/

Zero-alcohol alternative drinks

- Atopia: https://www.atopia.co.uk/
- Lyres Non-Alcoholic Spirits: www.lyres.com

- Seedlip Non-Alcoholic Drinks: www.seedlipdrinks.com
- Caleno Drinks: www.calenodrinks.com
- Monday Zero Alcohol Gin: www.drinkmonday.co
- Everleaf Non-Alcoholic Aperitif: www.everleafdrinks.com

I also recommend searching online for alcohol-free drink stockists who deliver to your location as well as searching on Amazon where you will find many of the popular brands.